Managing and Operating A Closely Held Corporation

Michael Diamond

JOHN WILEY & SONS, INC.

New York • Chichester • Brisbane • Toronto • Singapore

This book is dedicated to Rebecca Caleff—no dedication could ever
sufficiently express how much I care; and to Jacki Bruce-Yamin, my
friend.

MRD

Diamond, Michael R.
    Managing and operating a closely held corporation / by
  Michael Diamond.
      p.   cm.
    Includes bibliographical references.
    ISBN 0-471-52107-8 (cloth)
    1. Close corporations—Management.   2. Close
  corporations—Taxation.   3. Close corporations—
  Finance.   I. Title.
HD62.25.D53   1991
658'.045—dc20   90-24802
                                              CIP

Printed in the United States of America

91 92 10 9 8 7 6 5 4 3 2 1

Preface

In 1987 I wrote a book with Julie Williams on the process of incorporation. It was written to offer entrepreneurs and other nonspecialists guidance in *how* to incorporate. The book included discussions and recommendations about some of the less obvious issues with which incorporators could be confronted. While that book addressed some of the needs of small business start-ups (particularly corporate start-ups), a gap remained in the information available to entrepreneurs and their associates about some of the more complex problems affecting the existence of corporations. This book is an attempt to fill that gap; in it I discuss problems relating to

- capital structure of the corporation
- compensation of executives
- taxation of the corporation and its shareholders
- protection of the rights of minority shareholders
- buying and selling of a corporation's stock or assets
- public and private offering of stock and other corporate securities.

In addressing these issues, I provide sample documents that can be adapted to individual situations and local jurisdictions. Nevertheless, you should not rely on a book for definitive solutions to your own complex problems. Be aware that many of the problems I discuss *are* quite complex and do require the advice of a professional. If you believe that one of these issues confronts your business, be sure to obtain such assistance.

With that limitation in mind, I will proceed to describe the nature and lay out the parameters of some of those problems. As before, I have attempted to keep the writing straightforward and clear. The text includes explanations and examples to help you follow the discussion in a practical context. I hope this will assist you in becoming a more informed participant when you are planning responses to various corporate issues.

At this point, a quick review of the nature of the corporation itself is in order. First, corporations are creatures of state law. Each state has a statute that makes it possible for a person to create a corporation by filing a document known as an Articles of Incorporation (or a Certificate of Incorporation or a Charter) with a state official. Once that document has been filed and approved by the official, the *corporation* comes into existence.

The two most fundamental aspects of that existence are 1) that a corporation is recognized by the law as a separate individual, and 2) that a corporation offers "limited liability" to its principals. A corporation is distinct from its owners, officers, and directors. This means that the corporation is liable for its own acts; its principals (the stockholders, officers, and directors) are shielded from that liability. If the corporation does not have enough assets or insurance to pay the claim of an injured party, for example, that party cannot (in any but the most extreme cases) claim compensation from the personal assets of the principals.

The "separate identity" element has several additional implications for the corporation, most, but not all, of which are beneficial. For instance, because of its individual and separate identity, a corporation can exist perpetually. This is true even though its original owners give or sell their stock to others or leave it to their heirs through their wills. While the ownership of the corporation would change by virtue of any of these acts, the corporation, itself, would continue in existence as before, regardless of the reconstituted ownership.

On the other hand, the fact that the corporation is viewed as a separate entity by the law generally subjects it to taxation on its income just as any income-earning person would be taxed. This often creates the situation of "double taxation," which arises when corporate profits, which have been taxed at the corporate level, are then distributed as dividends to stockholders. These stockholders must then pay tax on the dividends distributed to them. One of the major concerns of shareholders, therefore, is how to receive corporate income that has not been diluted by the corporate income tax. There are several approaches to resolving this problem that will be discussed in this book.

Another issue that often confronts the small business corporation is the need for additional capital for growth or to meet increased expenses. Such corporations generally rely on the resources of their owners, which may not be adequate to meet the needs of the company. Gaining access to additional capital from non-shareholder sources is a common problem for small businesses, and the availability of such capital is often quite limited. Choices must be made, such as whether to borrow the necessary funds or find additional investors who will contribute equity through the purchase of corporate stock. The practical and legal considerations involved in these choices will be discussed in Chapter 1, Capital Structure, and Chapter 6, Securities Regulation.

Once the corporation becomes successful, its owner(s) may ask how they can benefit from the corporation's increased value. In a publicly held and traded corporation this is accomplished merely by selling the shares over a stock exchange. The value of the corporation and its stock is set by the market, and, at least for the typical shareholder, there is no price negotiation. The sale of a privately, or "closely held" corporation as they are often called, is quite different. The seller must find a person willing to buy stock in the corporation and then negotiate terms for its sale, including agreement on a mutually acceptable price. A *closely held corporation* is one in which the shares of stock are held by a small number of persons. The shares are not traded over any stock exchange and are often subject to self imposed transfer restrictions.

A corporation can also be "sold" through the sale of all, or substantially all, of its assets. Technically, when the assets of a corporation are sold, the corporation itself does not go out of business. Instead, its assets are transformed from equipment, inventory, accounts receivable, and other tangible goods into cash or the stock of a purchasing corporation. In reality, however, when a corporation sells all of its assets, it is generally preparing for *liquidation*. This term often connotes insolvency or failing business, but sales of assets are a common method for owners of very successful businesses to obtain large amounts of cash for retirement, for other investments, or for personal use. Whether the owner of a corporation sells the stock or the assets of a corporation is determined by a variety of factors—such as tax laws, the needs of the buyer, and those of the seller. Moreover, conditions that may suggest the sale of a company's assets at one point might call for the sale of its stock at some other time. These issues will be addressed in Chapter 5, Buying and Selling the Corporation.

In addition, a small, closely held company that has grown over the years may reach the point where its owner(s) wish to sell its shares to outsiders in the general public. This might be done by the corporation in order to raise more capital for the business or by the shareholders in order to cash in personally on the company's success. The process of going public involves both federal securities laws and state "blue sky" laws and is often time-consuming, expensive, and confusing. The assistance of an experienced professional is of utmost importance in these situations. An overview of the system of security regulation and registration, particularly in regard to the exemptions from the federal registration requirements, will also be presented in Chapter 6.

Occasionally, the owners of a closely held corporation cannot agree on corporate policy or even get along personally. If one of the owners has a controlling interest in the corporation, he or she may dictate to the others, perhaps in a way that serves the controlling owner's interests but not those of the dissenting minority. Because the controlling owner's ability to "freeze out" minority owners can have serious consequences for these shareholders, the law has provided them with various protections. Others might be agreed upon by the owners at the outset, before disagreements make compromise unlikely. Chapter 4, Protecting Minority Rights and Dispute Resolution, sets forth some devices that can help avoid disputes and others that can help resolve them if they do arise.

Another problem faced by every corporation is developing a satisfactory compensation package for the shareholder/employees. In addition, the need to offer salary and benefits sufficient to attract and retain needed outside executive personnel will also arise as the business grows. Among the questions involved in determining the appropriate package are the needs of the corporate principals and the needs of the corporation for outside management. These issues involve the tax and pension laws, general contract law, the economics of the business, and the marketplace in general. They will be examined in Chapter 3, Executive Compensation.

In summary, this book will guide entrepreneurs and their advisers in obtaining information that they will need to plan effectively in their own businesses. The discussions used as examples in this book, however, should be merely a starting place for your own discussion about your business. It is hoped they will alert you to issues that you may not have considered and stimulate your creativity in those you already recognize. The forms provided in the book should be used merely as samples, not as definitive models of how documents should be drafted. You will need to adapt them to the unique requirements of your business and your state's laws. Finally, I hope the book will help you determine when you should seek the assistance of an expert. With all that in mind, let us begin.

Table of Contents

Chapter 1

Capital Structure

Among the earliest and most significant choices faced by the promoters and principals of a corporation are those that concern its capital structure. Some important issues that must be addressed include: 1) how much money or property the corporation will need to begin and maintain its operations; 2) in what form this capital will be obtained (*e.g.*, debt, equity); and 3) what the source of the capital will be (*e.g.*, personal finances, a bank, family and friends, outside investors, the public)? Although the decisions made at this early stage may be modified later, they will have a major and continuing impact on the corporation and its business ventures.

Several factors—such as shareholder control, taxation, cash flow, growth, and the requirements of the financial markets—must be considered when selecting a capital structure. These factors, and the significant issues pertaining to each one, will be addressed in this chapter. In our discussion, keep in mind that the factors are interrelated and that they assume varying degrees of importance, depending on the situation of the corporation and its shareholders. Therefore, no significance should be attached to the order in which they are presented.

Before beginning this discussion, however, a short review of basic corporate finance would be useful. Generally, a corporation obtains funds in three ways: *a*) by selling ownership interests in itself (usually called *shares* or *stock*); *b*) by borrowing; and *c*) by reinvesting in itself profits it has earned through its business operations. The money or property a corporation obtains by selling its stock is known as *equity capital*. Funds that are obtained through borrowing are called *debt* or *debt financing*. Finally, profits obtained through business operations are called *earnings*, and when the earnings are kept by the company to finance its growth or ongoing activities, they are known as *retained earnings*. All three methods play an important part in structuring the finances of a corporation, but only the first two, equity and debt, are relevant to start-up situations (since a company that has not yet begun its business cannot have earnings from its business activities). Let us now look briefly at each of these elements of corporate capitalization.

Equity capital, as has been mentioned, is raised through the sale by the corporation of ownership interests in itself. These interests are represented by stock or shares of stock that, in turn, are represented by pieces of paper known as *stock certificates*. Stock can be divided into different classes, with a variety of different rights and responsibilities attached to each class. The nature of these rights and responsibilities will be determined by the organizers of the corporation after considering the elements mentioned at the beginning of this chapter. Their decisions will be set out in the Articles of Incorporation. Once the corporation has become established, the directors and shareholders can add, delete, or amend classes of shares by amending the Articles of Incorporation.

The most basic class of stock is known as *common stock.* The owners of this form of stock usually have the right to elect the board of directors and to make decisions on fundamental questions of corporate existence. They also generally have the right to divide the residue of corporate profits after all prior corporate financial obligations and the corporation's own financial needs have been met. Thus, whereas their right to corporate profits is the most junior in a corporation's financial structure, the holders of common shares also have the potential for obtaining the largest distribution of the corporation's earnings.

A corporation also may have various classes of preferred stock. *Preferred stock* is imbued with one or more preferences in the payment of dividends or the distribution of assets upon the dissolution of the corporation. These preferences are established, if they exist at all, by the corporate charter, and there may be several different classes of preferred stock, each with its own distinct set of preferences, in the same corporation. The advantage of preferred stock over common stock is that the holders of preferred stock usually will be entitled to financial benefits before the holders of common stock receive anything. If there are several classes of preferred stock, the holders of each class will take according to the preference of their class.

Preferred stock also has its disadvantages, the two major ones being that it does not usually confer voting rights and its financial return is usually fixed. The lack of voting rights means that, generally speaking, the holder of preferred shares is relegated to a rather passive role as an investor in the corporation. He or she normally does not have the right to elect the corporation's management or to vote on many basic corporate issues. The fixed nature of the financial return on preferred shares means that although preferred shareholders usually receive their financial distributions first, the amount of the distribution generally is limited. If the corporation does extremely well, the holders of preferred shares will take their defined distribution off the top of the distribution pool, and the holders of common shares will divide the potentially unlimited residue. If the corporation does poorly, however, the dividends paid to the preferred shareholders might deplete the funds available for distribution before the common shareholders receive anything.

Please note here that the nature of the preferences and voting rights are not fixed by law but are the creations of the organizers of the corporation, who must pay due regard to the practical factors of financial need and the marketability of the shares. Therefore, preferred shares might sometimes be given voting rights. These rights might begin by being dormant, for example, only being brought into play by certain corporate events, such as several poor financial periods in succession. On the other hand, voting rights might be granted from the inception of the corporation but limited to particular issues, such as corporate dissolution or reorganization. Finally, preferred shares might be given diluted voting rights on more general issues; for instance, a shareholder might receive one vote for every five preferred shares held.

A similar range of choices exists concerning the financial rights of preferred shares. For example, a class of preferred shares might have a right to a $1-per-share dividend before any other class receives its distribution. This same class could then share as well in the distribution made to common shareholders. The shares can have cumulative dividends, be convertible into another class of shares, or be redeemable by the corporation. The point here is not to exhaust the number of possibilities for variation but merely to show that the organizers can be creative when setting attributes for the preferred stock that best suit the needs of the corporation. Normally, the only limits are honesty (including full disclosure to any buyer of the shares) and the receptivity of the market for such shares.

Organizers can also raise funds through the *creation of debt*. In simple terms, this means that the corporation borrows money. In many small corporations, the loans are obtained from the principals of the corporation or from their close associates. Occasionally, the funds come from a local bank, with or without the guaranty of one or more principals or of a government agency, such as the Small Business Administration (SBA). Less frequently still, the funds come from the general public in a public or private offering of corporate bonds or debentures.

There are several forms of debt for the organizers to consider. The most basic, of course, is a loan from a principal to the corporation evidenced by a simple promissory note. From there, the complexity of the transaction can increase to the level of a full public bond offering with documents usually running into the hundreds of pages and, occasionally, even higher. A public offering is *very* unlikely in a small business start-up. Even in very successful small companies, "going public" is a rare occurrence. Such an offering is extremely complex and costly and requires the participation of highly trained specialists. Some of the issues involved in public and private offerings will be discussed in Chapter 6.

The corporation gains several advantages by offering debt rather than equity as the form of possible investment. The main advantage is income tax related in that the interest paid on debt is deductible on the corporation's income tax returns. A similar distribution on equity investments is not deductible and is, therefore, more expensive to the corporation and its shareholders. Another advantage of debt financing is that the principals do not give up corporate control when they issue debt to outside investors. Conversely, by issuing equity the principals dilute their own interest in the corporation's current management and in its future earnings.

The primary disadvantage of debt financing is the obligation to repay the debt and to pay interest while the debt is outstanding. There is no similar obligation to repay equity, and the payment of dividends on equity investments is left to the discretion of the corporation's board of directors. Moreover, debt holders, that is, lenders, take precedence over equity holders in corporate distributions. Therefore, unless the equity holders are also the lenders, there may be a drain on the corporation's assets away from the owners of the corporation.

The issues raised in the preceding pages will be discussed in detail in the following sections. Before addressing them, however, let us examine the practical context in which capital must be raised. This will give you some insight into establishing an appropriate and workable capital structure.

We will assume that an *entrepreneur* (the organizer or principal) has an idea for a new business. He or she has already determined that there is a need in the marketplace for such a business and that he or she can fill that need. In order to get started, the entrepreneur needs a location for the business as well as staff, materials, inventory, and reserves. For each of these items, there is a commensurate financial obligation. Therefore, the first step after the entrepreneur determines that he or she can fill a market need is for him or her to determine how much money is needed to get started. In this analysis, the entrepreneur must plan for each item of expense and project it out over several months and, sometimes, several years. He or she must account for the *start-up period*, when the business is incurring expenses but is not generating any income, and for the *early operational stage*, when it is unlikely that the income will cover the expenses. Most companies, even those that become quite successful, sustain losses for several years after the start-up. These expected losses must be accommodated by the organizer's capital planning.

Once the amount of money needed to begin the business has been determined, the organizer must decide where to obtain that money. If the organizer does not have the personal resources required to meet the expected financial need, he or she must plan how to raise the necessary capital. This involves both a financial calculation on what structure would be best for the organizer and for the corporation as well as a practical calculation on what it will take to get outsiders to put their money into the venture. Here is where the abstract legal aspects of capitalization meet the realities of the market for investors' funds, and it is here that such things as the proper mix of debt and equity and the stock preferences needed to induce equity funds into the company first get sorted out.

In most cases, the capital for a new closely held corporation comes directly from the organizers and their close associates. Occasionally it comes from more distant investors or from lending institutions. In each of these situations, a would-be investor will have concerns about the safety of and return on his or her investment that must be eliminated before he or she will participate. In general, the investor wants to increase the return on his or her investment and to decrease his or her risk. The organizer, on the other hand, wishes to keep control of the venture and to maintain a significant equity position in the company (usually with a disproportionately small amount of contributed capital). It is often the organizer's position that his or her idea and efforts to get the business off the ground entitle him or her to a substantial position in the company, even in light of the more significant capital contribution of the investors. Balancing these competing concerns is one of the most difficult and critical tasks facing the organizers of start-up corporations as well as those in corporations that are expanding or recapitalizing.

With this in mind, let us examine some of the attributes of debt and equity interests and discuss them in the context of a newly formed corporation and one that is seeking to expand or to raise working capital. This will allow you to evaluate the efficacy of a certain form of capitalization for a particular situation. Included are some samples of appropriate language for you to consider and possibly adapt for use in the Articles of Incorporation or in loan documents.

ISSUANCE OF STOCK

When a new corporation is created and, often, when an existing corporation needs new capital for expansion or to meet its current obligations, it may issue stock to its current shareholders or to new investors. The mechanics of the issuance are governed by state law, the Articles of Incorporation, and the corporate bylaws. The following discussion includes a brief explanation of a typical stock issuance.

Authorized, Issued, and Outstanding Shares

To begin with, the number and description of each class of shares that the corporation will be permitted to distribute will be established by and set out in the Articles of Incorporation. The number of shares permitted in each class is called the *authorization* or the number of *authorized* shares. The number of authorized shares does not necessarily have to correspond with the number of shares in the hands of shareholders. For example, a corporation might be authorized by its Articles to distribute 100,000 shares of common stock. At the inception of the corporation, its two organizers wish to take for themselves 1,000 shares each. Assuming that the board of directors decides to distribute the 2,000 shares to the two organizers (and, of course, it will so decide since the organizers control the board), it will pass a resolution *issuing* the 2,000 shares from the authorized common stock. It will then transfer the shares to the organizers. At that point, the shares will be *outstanding*. Only outstanding shares are counted when distributing dividends or determining the percentage of ownership of any shareholder.

A simple way to understand the concepts of authorized, issued, and outstanding shares is to compare the shares to the inventory of a retail appliance store. The store has its total inventory of air conditioners in a warehouse. This total inventory represents the "authorized" shares. It is the total amount of air conditioners that the store can distribute. As summer approaches, the store owner orders 100 air conditioners to be brought from the warehouse to the selling floor of the showroom. This is like the "issuance" of shares, in which some of the inventory of shares is brought out to be sold. When a customer comes into the store and buys an air conditioner, this corresponds to the shares being "outstanding," as when an investor purchases the shares from the corporation. Unlike the buyer in the retail store analogy, however, the purchaser of the stock may pay for the shares not only with cash but also with property or by performing services for the corporation. This payment for shares is one of the ways a corporation raises its initial capital and obtains or pays for needed materials and services.

As long as there are authorized shares that have not yet been issued, the board of directors generally has the power to issue additional shares from the authorized allotment. The board might decide to issue additional shares for any number of reasons, including, among others, raising new capital, the need to cover the conversion of shares from one class to another (see the discussion of conversion that follows), or to meet stock option requirements (see the discussion of stock options in Chapter 3). The board can issue additional shares by adopting a resolution to that effect. The resolution will designate the class of shares to be issued, the number of shares from that class, and the terms by which one may purchase the newly issued shares. Those terms will take into account the financial needs of the corporation, the prior success of the business, how quickly it needs the influx of capital, and the price at which investors would be willing to invest in the new shares.

If a corporation has issued the full amount of its authorized shares, it may not issue any additional shares unless its Articles of Incorporation are amended to provide for an increased authorization. An amendment of the Articles, which normally requires the consent of the existing shareholders as well as the approval of the board of directors, is usually accomplished by the board adopting a resolution to amend the Articles by increasing the number of authorized shares of a particular class and submitting the resolution to the shareholders for their approval. Normally, the only shareholders who have the power to vote on such a resolution are the holders of common stock. It is possible, however, in cases where the increased authorization would have an effect on preferred shareholders, that the Articles would permit the holders of the affected shares to vote on this issue. If the board resolution carries, the Articles will be amended to increase the authorized number of shares. The board can then issue those shares and sell them or hold them for other corporate purposes.

If the goal of the new issuance is to raise capital, the shares will be offered for sale. In most small corporations, where the investment of new equity capital comes from the existing shareholders, the issuance of additional shares often is nothing more than a formality needed to comply with the literal requirements of the law. However, when the shares are to be sold to outsiders or when there is an internal struggle for control of the corporation, the price of the newly issued shares and the pre-emptive rights of the existing shareholders become significant issues. The internal pricing problems raised by a new issue will be discussed in more detail in Chapter 4. The issue of pre-emptive rights will be addressed here.

Pre-emptive Rights

Essentially, a *pre-emptive right* is nothing more than the right of existing shareholders to have first opportunity to purchase their pro rata share of any new issuance by the corporation of shares of the same class as those they currently hold. It is a means of protecting the percentage ownership interest of existing shareholders. To illustrate, recall the earlier example of 100,000 authorized common shares, of which 2,000 have been issued and are held, 1,000 each, by the corporation's two organizers. Each organizer owns 50 percent of the corporation, and together they own 100 percent of it. Remember that this is true even though there are 98,000 authorized but unissued shares provided for in the Articles. If the board decides to issue 1,000 of those unissued shares and if pre-emptive rights apply, each shareholder would have the first right to purchase 50 percent (or 500 shares) of the new issue. If one or both declined to exercise their pre-emptive right, the shares of the declining shareholder(s) could be sold to anyone.

Whether pre-emptive rights apply is first a function of state statute. Some states require the existence of pre-emptive rights, but most leave the choice to corporate organizers. Even then, there are two different formats for the statutes. Some establish pre-emptive rights *unless* the Articles provide otherwise, whereas others do away with pre-emptive rights *unless* the Articles require them. When it is the corporation who will decide, the question of whether to permit pre-emptive rights must be considered in terms of corporate strategy and the marketability of the shares. Eliminating pre-emptive rights gives the corporation more flexibility in selling its shares and opens the door for new investors. On the other hand, the absence of pre-emptive rights may inhibit the sale of shares to some potential investors who might be concerned about being "frozen out" by further issuances of stock from which they would be excluded. A discussion of freezing out minority shareholders appears in Chapter 4.

A corporation may also affect its capital structure by what are known as *stock dividends* or *stock splits*. These terms involve similar but not identical processes by which existing shareholders increase their holding of corporate shares on a pro rata basis without the contribution of additional capital. The fact that the stock issued pursuant to one of these devices is *not* paid for by the shareholders indicates that the corporation was not seeking an immediate increase of its capital when it decided to pursue one of these two paths. Descriptions of each of these procedures and explanations of why and how they are accomplished are included in the next sections.

Stock Dividends

One of the primary benefits of owning stock in a corporation are the dividends paid on those shares of stock. Generally speaking, a corporation will distribute as dividends to its shareholders some or all of its profits for a year. This will usually be done in cash and on a pro rata basis, whereby each *share* held of a particular class will receive the same distribution as each other share in that class. Of course, as is pointed out in the next section, different classes of shares may receive different amounts per share, but within a class, the dividend per share is equal. A variety of legal rules circumscribe the corporation's ability to declare a dividend, but even if a corporation is legally entitled to declare a dividend, the decision of whether to do so is reserved to the corporation's board of directors. In making its decision, the board will examine various factors, including the corporation's cash position, its prospects for continued success, and its plans for expansion or for new ventures.

For new corporations or for those that are just beginning to become profitable, it is often legally impermissible, or at least unwise, to declare a dividend. If the failure to declare dividends continues for an extended period, those shareholders who are not part of the corporate management may become concerned or dissatisfied with corporate policy. This dissatisfaction could lead to a change in corporate management (if the shareholders can muster enough votes to elect a new board) or, what is more likely, to a much closer scrutiny of corporate affairs by the dissatisfied group. As a partial solution to this problem, the board might declare a *stock dividend* rather than a cash dividend. This means that the corporation will distribute additional shares of its stock as a dividend rather than cash from its treasury.

The advantage to the corporation of this form of distribution is that it allows the corporation to retain cash while still recognizing the contributions of shareholders. The distribution of stock does not, of course, cost the corporation anything. Its finances are not affected by the number of its shares that are outstanding. Similarly, since the distribution is pro rata, each existing shareholder retains his or her percentage ownership of the corporation. For instance, assume that a corporation has 1,000 shares of common stock outstanding and that Shareholder A holds 500 shares, Shareholder B holds 300 shares, and Shareholder C holds 200 shares. If the board declares a stock dividend of 1 share for each 10 shares outstanding, the total dividend will be 100 shares. Shareholder A would receive 50 percent, or 50 shares, of the distribution (which corresponds to A's 50 percent ownership of the corporation), B would receive 30 percent or 30 shares, and C would receive 20 percent, or 20 shares, of the distribution. Shareholder A will then own 550 shares of the 1,100 shares outstanding, B will have 330 shares, and C will have 220. Their ownership percentage remains unchanged after the distribution, and the corporation has not depleted its cash.

The advantage to shareholders of this form of distribution is primarily psychological. They do not receive any greater ownership rights despite their additional shares; their percentage ownership remains unchanged. If the corporation eventually declares a cash dividend, the total amount received by each shareholder will be the same because the amount available for distribution is finite, regardless of the number of shares across which it must be spread. For instance, if there is a dividend of $1,000 to be distributed, a shareholder who owns 50 percent of the shares will receive $500, regardless of whether the number of shares he or she owns is 500, 750, or 10,000. Moreover, the additional shares are not likely to be saleable. If the corporation is closely held, the shares are, by definition, not publicly traded and may even be subject to share transfer restrictions. Therefore, a stock dividend provides limited benefit to shareholders, particularly in a closely held corporation. It may, however, temporarily assuage the feelings of dissatisfaction that arise and might otherwise increase without a distribution.

The mechanics of declaring and distributing a stock dividend are rather simple. Assuming there are authorized but unissued shares available, the board will merely adopt a resolution declaring a stock dividend to be distributed to a particular class of shares and stating the class and proportion of shares to be distributed. The resolution will also provide for the issuing of the appropriate number of shares to meet the needs of the declaration. The secretary of the corporation will then compute the number of shares to be distributed to each eligible shareholder, prepare certificates representing those shares, and mail them to the appropriate shareholders. If sufficient authorized but unissued shares are not available, the declaration process must be preceded by an amendment to the Articles of Incorporation to increase the authorization.

The only complexity involved with a stock dividend pertains to the accounting procedures needed to record the transaction. The increase in shares must be shown in the corporate stock book, and the financial records must also be modified to account for the dividend. Basically, there must be a transfer on the corporate books from an account called *surplus* or *retained earnings* or something similar to the *capital account*. The capital account is nothing more than the aggregate of the par or stated value per share multiplied by the number of shares outstanding. *Par* or *stated value* is an arbitrary figure, established in the Articles of Incorporation, that is the minimum price at which shares of stock may be sold by the corporation to a buyer). The amount traditionally transferred to the capital account is the par or stated value per share, multiplied by the number of shares distributed in the stock dividend. Many accountants today transfer the fair market value (the value a willing buyer would pay a willing seller) of the stock rather than merely the par value to the capital account. They argue that doing so more accurately reflects the financial nature of the transaction. In either case, the changes take place only on the books of the corporation, and no cash is actually transferred. All corporate cash remains available to meet the needs of corporate operations.

The changes on the corporate books will, however, affect the corporation's legal ability to declare a dividend in the future. The general rule concerning the legality of a dividend is that one may not be declared when the capital account is impaired or when the dividend would impair that account. Remember, the capital account (which is only a bookkeeping device—there is no separate bank account called the capital account) is the par or stated value per share, multiplied by the number of outstanding shares. The capital account is impaired when the *net assets* of the corporation (total assets minus total liabilities) are less than the amount of the capital account. Thus, when the capital account is increased by the entry of the value of a stock dividend, the net assets of the corporation must exceed a higher threshold in order for a dividend to be legal.

Stock Splits

A *stock split* or a *stock split-up* is a transaction that is similar to a stock dividend. Although similar, these transactions are not the same, nor are they intended for the same purposes. A stock dividend is designed to benefit, or at least to mollify, the existing shareholders; a stock split is generally used to reduce the price per share of corporate stock. This makes the stock more affordable for investors to purchase and aids the corporation in raising new capital. As such, it is a device utilized by successful concerns where there is some market for their shares. Essentially, when a corporation splits its stock, it increases its stock by some multiple (let us say for this explanation that it is doubled) and decreases the price per share by a corresponding amount.

An example might be helpful here. Let us assume that a corporation has authorized 10,000 shares with a par value of $.10 each. Assume also that 3,000 of those shares are outstanding, with Shareholder A holding 2,000 and Shareholder B holding 1,000. Finally, assume that the corporation has done extremely well over the years and the market value of the outstanding shares is $100 per share (which, of course means that the total value of this corporation is $300,000—derived by multiplying 3,000 shares by $100 each. Remember, the par value of $.10 per share is *arbitrary* and bears no necessary relationship to the market value per share). This corporation wishes to raise additional capital, but for bookkeeping reasons it will only sell shares in blocks of 100 or more. It is concerned, however, that the investors it expects to approach will not wish to invest $10,000 (100 shares at $100 per share). Therefore, the board decides to split the stock, which will increase the amount of stock and lower the price per share.

If the board authorizes a 2-for-1 split, the effect will be that the authorized shares in the Articles will increase from 10,000 to 20,000 and the par value will drop from $.10 to $.05 per share. The 3,000 outstanding shares will be converted into 6,000, with Shareholder A holding 4,000, and Shareholder B, 2,000. Note that the percentage ownership of A and B has not changed at all. Note also that if the value of the corporation is still $300,000 (and it would be since no commercial or financial event has intervened to change the value of the corporation), this value will be spread over 6,000 rather than 3,000 shares and the value of the stock will drop to $50 per share from $100. Now the board can offer blocks of 100 shares to new investors for $5,000 rather than $10,000, which improves the chances of attracting new investors who will buy into the company and, thereby, increase its capital base.

The mechanics of a stock split are somewhat different from those of a stock dividend:

1. For a stock dividend, bookkeeping entries are made to various corporate bookkeeping accounts. That is not the case with a stock split. The capital account remains unchanged in a stock split (unless after the split new shares actually are purchased). The original capital account in our example was $300 comprised of 3,000 outstanding shares with a par value of $.10 each. The account after the split was still $300 comprised of 6,000 shares with a par value of $.05 per share.

2. The Articles of Incorporation do not need to be amended for a stock dividend (unless the authorized number of shares must be increased). They must be amended to accomplish a stock split because the authorization must be increased and the par value must be decreased.

Again, the board of directors must pass a resolution to carry out the split. It must decide that the split would be beneficial to the corporation and then propose to amend the Articles to accomplish it. In order for the Articles to be amended, the board's resolution must be submitted to the shareholders for a vote. If the resolution is ratified by the shareholders, the split becomes effective, and the secretary makes the appropriate adjustments on the stock records of the corporation and issues new certificates to accommodate the increase in shares held by each shareholder.

Finally, if the shares are entitled to a dividend, that, too, will be affected by the split. For instance, if the 3,000 shares in our example received a dividend of $1.00 per share, when the shares are doubled, the dividend would be cut in half. Although this does not affect the total amount that any shareholder will receive, it does affect the amount per share. Therefore, Shareholder A, who held 2,000 shares before the split and got $1.00 per share, received a total of $2,000 in dividends. After the split, A receives only $.50 per share but now has 4,000 shares for a total dividend of $2,000.

PREFERRED STOCK

Earlier in this chapter, the concept of preferred stock was introduced. Preferred stock is another device by which the corporation can raise capital by making some of its shares more attractive to investors. Preferred shares are created and defined by the Articles of Incorporation. The Articles establish the various preferences and attributes of each class, which are designed to induce investors to purchase the stock while at the same time keeping the needs of the organizers in mind. For instance, one class of stock can be created that is paid dividends before another class or classes of stock. Similarly, a class can be created that is paid before other classes if the corporation liquidates. There are other, more sophisticated, characteristics of preferred stock that can be employed to create a desirable capital structure for a corporation and its organizers. Some of the more typical of these attributes will be explained in the following sections.

Dividend Policy

As we have discussed, a corporation often distributes part of its earnings to its shareholders as dividends. It is usually within the discretion of the board of directors to declare a dividend and determine the amount to be paid. If the board of directors determines that the corporation is in a position to make a distribution of some of its earnings, the board would declare a dividend of, let us say, $1 per share. In the simplest situation, where the corporation has only one class of shares, the holders of shares would be paid $1 for each share they hold.

When there is more than one class of shares, the declaration of a dividend by the board may not be so simple. It is possible, if not likely, that one or more of the classes will be entitled to receive a distribution before the others. If this is the case, the board will calculate how much the preferred class(es) are entitled to and decide whether there is enough corporate profit to meet the distribution requirement.

The amount of the distribution for preferred classes of shares will be established in the corporation's Articles of Incorporation or bylaws. The definition of a class of preferred stock would normally set out the amount per share to be paid and the frequency of payment (*e.g.*, paid quarterly or annually). The Articles or bylaws will also state the preference that any class has over any other class. For instance, the definition of a class might say:

Upon the declaration of a dividend by the Board of Directors, Class A preferred shares shall be paid an annual dividend of $1.00 per share to be paid quarterly on the 15th day of January, April, July, and October. Class A preferred shares shall be paid this dividend before a dividend is paid on any other class of shares.

Upon the payment of said dividend on Class A preferred shares, and upon the declaration of a dividend by the Board of Directors, Class B preferred shares shall be paid an annual dividend of $.75 per share to be paid quarterly on the same dates as provided herein for Class A preferred shares. Class B preferred shares shall be paid this dividend after Class A shares but before a dividend is paid on any other class of shares.

After all preferred classes have received their required dividend, the common shares will divide any remaining amounts deemed by the board to be available for distribution as a dividend.

Cumulative Dividends

While this arrangement might suggest that preferred shareholders have the advantage, particularly in comparison to common shareholders, this is not always the case. Common shareholders generally control the board of directors, and it is the board that has the power to declare or not to declare dividends. By using this control, some common shareholders (who often have elected themselves to the board) manipulate the system against the holders of preferred shares. They do this by having the board fail to declare a dividend, even though the corporation is in a financial position to do so. If this continues for several years, the corporate earnings retained by the corporation grow to a sizeable amount, at which point the board finally declares a dividend. The preferred shareholders are then paid their required amount for that year, and the common shareholders divide the rather large residue. The preferred shareholders are thus deprived of much of what they would have been paid if a dividend had been declared in each year.

To illustrate this point, let us suppose there are 1,000 shares of Class A preferred stock that is entitled to a dividend of $1.00 per share and 1,000 shares of Class B preferred stock that is to be paid $.75 per share. Finally, there are 1,000 shares of common stock that will divide the remaining funds, if any, earmarked for distribution. Assume that in the first year the corporation earns enough for the board to set $2,000 aside for distribution. Class A preferred shares take the first $1,000 (1,000 shares at $1.00 per share) and Class B take the next $750 (1,000 shares at $.75 per share). This leaves only $250 to be divided among the 1,000 common shares (a rate of only $.25 per share).

What happens if the board does not declare a dividend? The $2,000 available for distribution sits in the corporate treasury. If the same scenario is re-enacted in the second year, there would be $4,000 in the treasury because no shareholders have received any dividends. Assume that there are another $2,000 of distributable earnings in the third year, but this time the board declares a dividend. Again, the Class A holders take the first $1,000, and the Class B take the next $750. This leaves $4,250 left for distribution to the common shareholders, at a rate of $4.25 per share. Remember, if the dividends had been declared in each year, the total distributable to the common shares would have been only $750 ($250 per year for three years). The Class A holders would have received a total of $3,000, and the Class B holders would have gotten $2,250. The failure to declare dividends in the two prior years gained the common shareholders a $3,500 increase in their total dividend at the expense of the two preferred classes of shares.

To avoid this circumvention of the rights of the preferred shareholders, the concept of *cumulative dividends*, sometimes modified to become *cumulative-if-earned* dividends, was developed. Whether preferred shares will have the benefit of cumulative dividends is usually a decision made by the organizers of the corporation. Permitting this feature certainly enhances the marketability of the preferred shares, but it also limits the flexibility of the corporation's board. If cumulative dividends are permitted, the Articles of Incorporation or bylaws should include provisions creating the right and describing its terms.

In essence, cumulative dividends allow amounts, to which a class of shares would have been entitled had a dividend been declared, to accumulate from year to year. The preferred shareholders must be paid the entire amount of their accumulated dividend *before* the common shareholders (or any lower ranking preferred shares) can receive any distribution. The cumulative-if-earned variation allows the preferred dividend to accumulate only for those years in which the corporation was legally entitled to declare and pay a dividend but did not do so. Most state laws allow a corporation to pay a dividend only if it had net profits in the year for which the dividend is being paid or when the accumulated assets (including retained earnings) of the company provide a cushion (called a *surplus*) over its obligations (including its stated capital). For those years where the financial condition of the corporation would not permit a legally declared dividend, the cumulative-if-earned provision would deny the cumulative effect for that year.

The language in the Articles of Incorporation or bylaws that creates the cumulative dividend is rather simple. For instance, the provision might state that:

> *Dividends on preferred stock (here would be inserted the class or classes of stock to be covered by this provision) shall, to the extent they are unpaid (or "earned but unpaid") in any year, accumulate from year to year. Dividends on common stock shall not be paid if there are any accrued dividends that have not been paid on the preferred stock.*

Participating Shares

Another way to avoid the manipulation of dividend policy and to increase the marketability of the shares is to allow the preferred shares (or some of the classes of preferred shares) to participate with the common shareholders in the pool of distributable funds remaining after the preferred shareholders have been paid their required dividend. The nature of the participation, if any, again is spelled out in the Articles or bylaws. The provision normally sets out the conditions under which such participation is allowed and the formula for the participation. For example, participation may be limited to situations when the dividend on common stock exceeds the dividend on the preferred stock. In such a case the provision establishing the participation might read:

> *In any year in which the Board of Directors declares a dividend on the common stock of the corporation which dividend exceeds the amount provided herein as a dividend for the Class A preferred stock, such preferred stock shall be entitled to participate in the dividend declared for the common shares. Such participation shall be permitted after*

the common shares have been allocated an amount equal to the dividend payable to the Class A preferred stock. Furthermore, such participation in the residue shall be limited to an amount per share that is one half of the amount per share allocable to the common stock.

In this situation, the formula for the participation of the preferred stock is limited in two ways. First, it is instituted only if a predetermined event, the declaration of a dividend on the common shares that is larger than that provided for the Class A preferred shares, occurs. Second, the common stock still receives a larger distribution per share than the preferred.

As an example, let us assume there are 500 preferred shares and 1,500 common shares in the hands of a corporation's shareholders. The Articles call for a dividend on the preferred stock of $1.00 per share, and, after that amount is allocated, there remains a pool of $5,500 for distribution to the common shareholders. It is clear that the dividend payable to the common shares will exceed that payable on the preferred stock. Therefore, the participation provision would come into play, resulting in the allocation of the first $500 from the distributable pool to the common stock, the balance of $5,000 being allocated at the rate of $1.428 per share (approximately $714) to the 500 preferred shares and $2.856 per share (approximately $4,284) to the 1,500 common shares.

Note that each of the previous two techniques enhances the desirability of the preferred shares to potential investors but reduces the financial benefit to the common shareholders. They also limit the financial flexibility of the corporation itself. Whether either device is necessary and, if so, to what extent, is a decision to be made by the organizers in view of the surrounding circumstances.

Liquidation Preferences

In addition to preferences on dividends, preferred stock may be given preferences on the distribution of assets upon the liquidation of the corporation. While liquidations are often associated with the failure of a business, this is not always the case. Sometimes the owners of a successful business decide that they no longer want to keep it going. This could be a function of age, the desire to retire or to take on new challenges, or the vision of harder times ahead. Whatever the reason, when a company liquidates, it is required by law to pay its debts before it may distribute its remaining assets (which are usually sold and converted to cash), if any, pro rata to its shareholders in the order of their preferences. Remember, the creation of a liquidation preference is initially in the hands of the organizers of the corporation and later under the control of the board and shareholders. They can create a class or classes of stock with a wide range of liquidation preferences. For instance, Class A preferred could be given a preference of $5 per share from the corporate assets remaining after the payment of corporate debts. Thereafter, Class A preferred might participate equally with the common shares in dividing the remaining assets. Whatever the structure, creditors are to be paid first, then preferred shareholders in the order of their preferences; common shareholders then divide the residue, with or without the further participation of one or more classes of preferred stock.

The rationale for the use of liquidation preferences is similar to the rationale for the use of dividend preferences; it makes the stock more marketable to investors. Because of the preferences, holders of preferred stock are generally more secure about the return on and the safety of their investment than are the common shareholders. On the other hand, the former usually have limited or no voting rights and, therefore, have little say in the management of the corporation. In addition, the holders of preferred shares generally do not share, at least not on an equal footing, with the common shareholders in the growth of the corporation. Their return is more secure, but it is also more fixed.

Because of the rather limited role of preferred shares in corporate management and growth, two other features have been developed that affect the status and marketability of these shares. The first is the privilege of converting one class of shares into another class, and the second is the ability of the corporation to *redeem*, or call in and retire, a class of preferred shares. The convertibility factor gives the *holder* of the convertible shares the option, under specified conditions, to convert his or her shares into a different class. The redemption feature gives the *corporation* the right, again under prescribed circumstances, to require the holders of a class subject to redemption to turn in those shares to be cancelled and retired.

Convertible Shares

Generally speaking, the classes of shares of a corporation are defined in its Articles of Incorporation or bylaws and are fixed throughout the corporate existence. In some cases, however, the ability to convert one class of stock into another class would enhance the marketability of the shares and, therefore, the ability of the corporation to raise capital. In order for a class of shares to be convertible, this provision must be included in the definition of the class. The definition should also include the terms of the conversion and the circumstances under which the shares may be converted. In addition, the Articles could include "antidilution" provisions to protect the rights of the holders of convertible shares from detrimental manipulation by management of the corporation's financial structure.

The following clause could be included in the Articles or bylaws in order to establish the convertibility privilege for a class of preferred stock:

Between the dates of January 1, 1991, and December 31, 1992, the holders of Class A preferred stock shall, at their option, and upon notice to the corporation as hereinafter provided, be entitled to convert such stock, or any portion thereof, into the common stock of the corporation at the conversion rate of one and one half (1.5) shares of common stock for each share of Class A preferred stock converted.

In the event the corporation shall authorize additional shares of the common stock of the corporation while there are outstanding any shares of the Convertible Class A preferred stock of the corporation, the conversion ratio as provided herein shall be adjusted so as to reflect the same ratio as if no new authorization had occurred.

This provision includes several critical elements concerning the convertibility of corporate stock. First, it indicates which shares may be converted and the class of shares into which they may be converted. In this case Class A preferred shares may be converted into common shares (although it should be noted that a conversion generally may be permitted from any class of shares to any other or from debt instruments into shares). Second, the dates within which the conversion privilege may be exercised are also set out. Here, a holder of the Class A preferred shares may not convert the shares before January 1, 1991, nor after December 31, 1992. Third, if the holder wishes to convert, he or she must properly notify the corporation of his or her wish to do so. Fourth, the conversion ratio is also set out. In this case it is 1.5 shares of common stock for each share of Class A preferred stock. Therefore, if a holder of Class A stock had 100 shares of that class, he or she could convert all of them for 150 shares of common stock. He or she could also convert only part of his or her holdings. For instance, if the shareholder wanted to convert only 40 of the 100 shares, he or she would then have 60 shares of Class A preferred and 60 shares of common (40 x 1.5).

The mechanics of the conversion could also be set out in the Articles or bylaws. This might include, for instance, a requirement that the shareholder send a written notice, return receipt requested, to the corporation, indicating the number of shares to be converted. The corporation might then send to the shareholder an irrevocable stock power, which would authorize the corporation to convert the shares. The shareholder would sign the stock power and return it to the corporation, along with, by separate cover, the stock certificate(s) representing the preferred shares. These certificates would be cancelled, and new certificates representing common stock would be issued pursuant to the established ratio and mailed to the shareholder. A less formal way to carry out the same transaction would be for the shareholder to submit his or her certificates to the corporation for cancellation and receive from the corporation new certificates for common stock.

The main reason that a holder of convertible shares might decide to convert them is financial. The holder thinks that, by converting, he or she would be better off financially. For instance, let us use the example of a holder of a class of convertible preferred stock that is not participating beyond its dividend preference in the profits of the corporation. The dividend on the preferred stock is $1 per share. If the corporation is doing well and has good prospects, the stockholder might be willing to forego his or her preference of $1 in order to participate more fully in the economic growth of the corporation. Obviously, if the common shares are being paid a dividend of $2 per share, there is strong incentive for the stockholder to convert.

If one or more shareholders decide to convert their preferred shares into common stock, the corporation must have sufficient authorized but as yet unissued common shares provided for in its Articles of Incorporation to meet the need. If there are insufficient available shares, the Articles must be amended to accommodate the conversion requirements. This process is simple but might be disruptive if shareholders are already converting their preferred shares and there are not enough common shares available. Therefore, careful planning is necessary at the organizational stage and at each new issuance of shares, whether the issuance is of the convertible shares or the shares into which they may be converted.

The issuance of new shares brings up an additional problem that was addressed in the sample language for creating the convertible stock. That problem is the dilution of the conversion privilege. In our example, the preferred stock could be converted into common stock at the ratio of 1.5 shares of common stock for each share of preferred stock converted. If there are 1,000 authorized shares of common stock, of which 850 shares are outstanding, and 100 shares of convertible preferred stock authorized and outstanding, it is clear that the preferred stock has control of 15 percent of the common stock of the corporation (because the holders of the convertible stock could exchange it for 150 shares of common stock out of the total authorization of 1,000 shares). If, however, the common sharehold- ers (who control the corporation) authorize an additional 1,000 shares, the convertible stock would then amount to only 150 of 2,000 authorized shares, or 7.5 percent. This action dilutes the interests of the holders of convertible stock and could be financially harmful to them.

To prevent such potential harm, the conversion privilege is accompanied by an antidilution provision. In this case the provision is called into play any time new common stock is authorized while any convertible stock is still outstanding. When this occurs, the conversion ratio in the language creating the convertible stock will be modified to maintain the originally planned relationship. In our example, if the additional 1,000 shares were authorized before any preferred shares had been converted, the conversion ratio would change to reflect the doubling of the authorization for common stock. The new conversion ratio would become 3 common shares for each preferred share converted. Thus, if all of the preferred shares were converted, there would be 300 new common shares out of the 2,000 authorized, or 15 percent of the total authorization.

Redemption of Shares

On the other side of share conversion by a shareholder is the *redemption* of shares by the corporation. In essence, the corporation, by a provision in its Articles of Incorporation, can require the shareholders to sell back to the corporation some or all of their preferred stock subject to a redemption provision. The price to be paid upon the redemption will also be found in the Articles and will be either a fixed amount or will be established by a pre-existing formula. A simple redemption provision might read as follows:

The corporation may, upon resolution of the Board of Directors, redeem and cancel all or any part of the outstanding Class B preferred stock of the corporation. Such redemption may take place at any time after January 1, 1994. The price paid by the corporation for redeemed shares of Class B preferred stock shall be equal to the par value per share plus a premium of three percent (3%) per year on such value beginning as of January 1, 1991, together with accrued dividends on such shares.

Notice of redemption shall be mailed, first class, at least thirty (30) days and no more than forty-five (45) days prior to such redemption and shall be addressed to each holder of Class B preferred stock at his or her address as it appears on the books of the corporation. Such notice shall include the procedure for redeeming shares of Class B preferred stock, together with the date of redemption, the price thereof, and the method of payment.

In the event the Board of Directors resolves to redeem less than all of the outstanding shares of Class B preferred stock, each holder of such shares shall have his or her shares redeemed on a pro rata basis.

Although these paragraphs provide a great deal of information and guidance, they also leave quite a bit to the discretion of the board of directors. In this example, and it must be remembered that this is *only* an example, the board is authorized but not required to redeem certain shares of the corporation. It may redeem all or only a part of the redeemable shares, and it may redeem at any time after a particular date. Even the method of conducting the redemption is left up to the board. These elements of discretion raise questions about the policy and mechanics of a redemption.

A corporation typically redeems its preferred stock in an effort to reduce or eliminate mandatory dispersals of funds (dividend preferences) to senior securities. Often, preferred stock was issued initially because it was a necessary element of raising capital. (Remember, preferred stock gives the holders certain rights and preferences over the common shareholder that may make the stock more marketable.) One of the advantages of preferred stock is that it offers a dividend preference and does so at a rate usually higher than that of common stock. Once the corporation is in a better financial position, the preferences and higher dividend rate work to its disadvantage as well as to the disadvantage of the common stockholders. The corporation is harmed because it is paying out a large dividend when the capital on which the dividend is being paid may not be needed any longer. Similarly, it is harder for the corporation to market its common shares (or preferred shares with a lower preference and dividend) because of the prior call on corporate income and assets represented by the preferred shares. A corporation foreseeing such a situation might make its preferred stock subject to redemption.

Redemption helps protect the corporation from the claims of the preferred shareholders, but it also reduces the marketability of those shares. Since it is to enhance the marketability of the shares that the preferred stock is created in the first place, the organizers or directors might want to add in an attractive redemption price in the event that the shares are recalled. In the sample redemption provision, the shares are paid par value (which generally, but not always, is equal to the original purchase price of the preferred shares, although par value bears no necessary relationship to the price of the common shares), plus a premium of 3 percent per year, together with accrued dividends. The premium figure can set at any amount that the organizers feel is required to sell the shares yet still prudent in terms of the corporation's ability to buy them back. The payment of the accrued dividend assures the holders of redeemable preferred stock that their preference is protected: They will receive accrued but unpaid dividends if the shares are ever called for redemption.

If the board wishes to consider redeeming shares, it must examine its current financial position and its prospects. Then it can determine what, if anything, it can afford to pay out without injuring the corporation's business. This will lead to decisions as to the timing and magnitude of a redemption. It will also lead to determinations about how to pay for the redemption. The vehicles that the board can consider for obtaining the funds for the redemption include:

- corporate earnings

- a loan at better terms than those applicable to the preferred stock

- issuance of a new class of shares with a smaller dividend requirement.

Which of these sources of funds will be used depends on the condition of the corporation and its ability to raise funds in the capital marketplace.

If the board chooses to pay for the redeemed shares out of existing corporate resources, those resources will, of course, be reduced by the payments made. Therefore, corporations often establish special accounts (sometimes called *sinking funds*) in which to accumulate money to pay for a redemption. Each year, the corporation places some of its revenue into the fund so that when the board decides to redeem shares, some or all of the money needed for payments will be available.

The board may also decide that market conditions will permit the redemption of a class of preferred stock, to be paid for from the proceeds of the sale of another class of stock with a smaller dividend than that of the shares to be redeemed. The new stock may be either preferred or common, as long as the Articles provide for the new class of preferred stock (or are amended to do so) or for the number of additional common shares. The question to be answered by the board is what the market will demand in order to accept the new stock. As with the planning of the original classes of preferred stock, the board will have to balance corporate needs with market realities and create a new class that will satisfy both ends of this equation.

Finally, the board might decide to borrow the money necessary to pay for the redeemed stock. This strategy will be advantageous to the corporation if the interest rate on the loan is lower than the dividend payment on the redeemable stock. The fact that the interest payments are tax deductible and dividend payments are not will be an important factor in the board's decision-making process. The other benefits of borrowing the necessary money are that the ownership interest of the remaining shareholders is not diluted by the addition of another class of shares nor are the assets of the corporation reduced by a payment of its own funds. On the other hand, the corporation has taken on more debt with an obligation to repay it at interest. The corporation has less flexibility concerning the payment of interest than it does with the payment of dividends (which is typically in the control of the board); therefore, the corporation must be conscious of its cash flow and liquidity.

As an example, suppose the corporation has a Class A preferred stock that is redeemable and that pays a dividend of $2 per share. Assume also that the application of the redemption formula would result in a total payment to repurchase Class A stock of $100,000 (for this example we will assume there are 5,000 shares of Class A stock that will require $20 each for redemption). If the corporation has the funds available from its retained earnings or from a special sinking fund created for the purpose, it can purchase the stock called for redemption without outside assistance and without issuing a new class of shares. After the payment, the corporation will have $100,000 less in its account, but it will no longer have to pay a dividend on the redeemed shares or on any replacement shares.

If the corporation does not have available funds for the repurchase, it might raise the necessary funds by issuing new stock with, for instance, only a $1-per-share dividend. If the Articles already provide for the new class or for additional shares of an existing class, the board need do no more than issue an appropriate number of those shares. If there is no existing class of shares to meet the current need or if there are no authorized but unissued shares of that class, the board will have to amend the Articles to provide for the shares. Since this often requires the approval of existing shareholders, the timing of the amendment, its approval, and the sale of the newly issued shares must be coordinated with the timing of the redemption.

Once the shares have been authorized and issued, the corporation will attempt to sell them for at least $100,000. Assuming market conditions have changed so that preferred stock paying a $1 dividend can be sold for $20, the sale of 5,000 shares of the new Class B preferred stock will raise $100,000. The proceeds from this sale will be used to pay off the Class A stockholders. There will then be a new class of shares outstanding (Class B) that commands only a $1 dividend instead of the $2 for Class A. On the 5,000 shares outstanding, that is a savings of $5,000 per year on dividends with no diminution in control and no reduction of corporate assets.

The example just given is admittedly simple and does not take into account the time and expense involved in issuing the new shares and redeeming the old ones, but it provides a graphic example of a "recapitalization," a subject that will be dealt with in more detail in Chapter 4. The same example can also be used concerning corporate borrowing to pay for the redemption of preferred shares. With the same basic facts in mind, suppose the corporation could borrow $100,000 at 8 percent per year. The proceeds of the loan would be used to pay off the redeemed shares, and the corporation would pay $8,000 interest on the loan each year rather than the $10,000 required to pay the dividend. Moreover, the payment of interest would be tax deductible.

Of course, at some point the loan would come due, and the $100,000 would have to be paid back, which does not occur when the redemption funds come from the corporation's retained earnings or from a sinking fund established for this purpose. This problem is also avoided by the issuance of new shares. However, each of these methods of funding could be used to pay back the loan. Indeed, the corporation could even engage in further borrowing for the purpose of retiring the earlier debt. These methods of refinancing are common (even the U.S. government pays off debt that comes due with new borrowing), but they can lead to difficulty. For example, interest on debt, unlike dividends, generally *must* be paid. Therefore, in a tight year, the corporation will have the added financial burden of interest payments. Another danger is that when the original debt comes due, financial conditions in the market may be such that the required funds are not available to the corporation or are available only at a very high cost. Therefore, choosing the method for funding a redemption requires careful thought and planning.

DEBT FINANCING

Up to now, this chapter has focused on the equity side of capitalizing a corporation. The other major element of a corporation's capital structure is *debt*. Very often the corporation fills its capital needs by borrowing. Generally, this borrowing comes directly from the principals of the corporation. Occasionally, it comes from a lending institution or an outside individual lender. A corporation may also borrow by obtaining *trade credit*—buying equipment or supplies on credit with payment due at a fixed time in the future. Less frequently, the borrowing will be from members of the public who have no other relationship with the corporation and who are not in the business of lending money. This section will focus on corporate borrowing and the various ways in which it is done.

Evidence of Indebtedness

When one party borrows money from another, the borrower usually gives some form of written evidence of the debt and of the promise to repay it. This document may be a simple promissory note made to an individual or an institution, or it may be a formal *indenture* that governs borrowing from several different individuals or institutions. We will examine each of these documents and the borrowings that they represent.

The most basic evidence of indebtedness is the *promissory note*. In this document the debtor promises to pay to the order of the lender within a certain amount of time, or upon the demand of the lender, the amount of the debt. The note will include the terms of repayment—such as the interest rate, the frequency of installments, and whether the principal will be repaid periodically or will be due in total at the end of the loan term. The note will then be signed by the borrower together with any co-signers or guarantors.

If the corporation decides, because of the size of the loan needed or for other reasons, to borrow from the public, it will probably attempt what is known as a *private placement*. This usually involves an offering of debt instruments to various members of the public. Unlike the simple promissory note situation, where there is some negotiation concerning the terms of the loan, a private placement of debt is really a "take-it-or-leave-it" proposition to the potential lenders. The corporation and its advisors will determine in advance what kind of terms are required to raise the amount of money the corporation needs. These terms might include a high interest rate, a convertibility feature that allows the lender to transform the debt into some form of equity, specific rights of the lenders in the event of a default, or any other feature deemed necessary to obtain the funds.

Normally, a private placement is accompanied by a *private placement memorandum*, which is a disclosure document that is given to potential lenders prior to their lending money to the corporation. The memorandum will describe the offering and the nature of the company and its business. It will include information about the principals of the company and its financial history and prospects. It will also divulge all the risks associated with the loan.

The offering described in the memorandum will usually be of *bonds* or *debentures*. These evidences of indebtedness are very similar, except that bonds are usually secured by particular assets of the corporation, whereas debentures are unsecured and backed only by the general credit of the corporation. Bonds and debentures are distinct from promissory notes in that they normally are part of a larger, more public borrowing. The terms that govern the rights of lenders are found, not in the bond or debenture itself, but in a separate document called an *indenture*. The indenture is likely to be quite long and complicated and, when added to the private placement memorandum, comprises a very complex and expensive set of documents. For this reason, it is unusual for small, closely held corporations to go the route of a private placement of debt securities.

Corporate Borrowing

To begin with, let us review some fundamentals of corporate borrowing. The first rule in this field is that any corporate borrowing must be authorized by the board of directors. As basic as that rule is, it is very often disregarded. Nevertheless, the officers of a corporation must have Board approval before they are legally entitled to bind that corporation as a borrower. This does not mean that the board must examine and approve every instance of corporate borrowing but that it must approve, at least, a policy of borrowing for certain purposes and within certain limits. Thus, if a manufacturing company with a seasonal product needs to borrow every spring to purchase raw materials and pay workers to produce its products, the board may give a blanket approval for the president of the corporation to borrow up to $250,000 each March for the purpose of funding production. The authority granted to the officers may be further limited by other criteria, such as the amount of current inventory or capital reserves or the amount of outstanding debt, which would be triggering mechanisms or limitations as to the timing and extent of authorized borrowing.

Similarly, the authority from the board may be implied. For instance, if the board authorizes the purchase of a new and expensive machine while knowing that the corporation does not have the cash to pay for it, the president might be justified in believing that the board has also approved corporate borrowing to pay for the machine. If corporate borrowing takes place without authority, the corporation may be legally bound to repay the debt, but it is also possible that the corporate official(s) who did the borrowing will be liable to the corporation for any damage it suffers as a result of the unauthorized loan.

The source of the borrowed funds must be considered. For most small corporations, the choice will be limited to private borrowing from the corporation's principals or their associates or from professional lenders. To the extent the corporation borrows from outsiders, it is very likely that the principals of the corporation and their spouses will be required to sign a personal guaranty of the corporate debt. Such guaranties are a fact of life for small corporations. This is due to the limited liability otherwise enjoyed by shareholders, officers, and directors concerning corporate obligations. Because the lender would ordinarily have recourse only against corporate assets in the event of a default, which may not be sufficient to cover the debt, he or she will demand that the corporate principals contract away their limited liability by agreeing to pay if the corporation does not. Lenders also require that spouses sign, even if they are not associated with the corporation, because many states exempt jointly held marital property from attachment when only one spouse is liable on an obligation.

If the principals have the funds needed and are willing to invest them in the corporation, the wisest choice might be to invest in the form of a loan. There are several reasons for this. One is that lenders stand in a better position concerning claims on the corporate assets than do shareholders. If the corporation were to run into serious financial difficulty and were forced to close down, the shareholders would receive a share of the corporate assets only after all corporate debts had been paid. If there were not enough to pay all the debts, the shareholders would get nothing. If, however, the shareholders were also lenders, they would, to the extent of their loans, stand in the same position as other lenders and would have first call, along with those lenders, on the corporate assets. After these debts were paid, including those to the shareholders, the shareholders, *as share-holders*, would divide up the remaining assets, if any. If there were none, they still would have received some of their investment back through the repayment of debt.

A second reason for investing further capital in the form of a loan rather than as equity has to do with taxes. Interest payments on debt are deductible; distribution of profits as dividends is not. Therefore, if the corporation is earning money that the principals wish to distribute, the distribution of the funds as interest eliminates one level of taxation. To give a simple illustration, assume a corporation earned $10,000 profit in a particular year. That profit would be taxed at the rate of 15 percent, resulting in a tax of $1,500. The balance could be distributed as a dividend, where it would be subject to a second tax in the hands of the shareholder. If the shareholder paid tax at the rate of 28 percent, the original corporate profit would be reduced by another $2,380, resulting in a total tax liability on the corporate profit of $3,880. If, on the other hand, the $10,000 was paid out as interest on a loan made by the shareholders to the corporation, it would be deductible for the corporation, thereby eliminating its profit and resulting in no corporate tax. The shareholders would receive the entire $10,000, which would be taxed at 28 percent. In this format, the corporate profits are reduced by only $2,800, with the shareholders keeping $7,200 after tax, as opposed to $6,120.

After seeing this arithmetic, entrepreneurs might be tempted to invest totally through the use of debt. Unfortunately, the Internal Revenue Service (IRS) would take a dim view of such a structure. In fact, if the ratio of debt held by shareholders to equity is too high, the IRS will treat the debt as equity and disallow the deduction for interest. It will claim that the interest is really a "constructive dividend" based on a disguised form of equity investment under-taken to avoid taxes. Proving the IRS wrong could become a lengthy and expensive process. Therefore, if you intend to capitalize your corporation with a mixture of equity and debt invested by the principals, be sure to follow all the necessary formalities. First, be sure the board has authorized the borrowing. This should be done at a properly called meeting at which a quorum is present. The board's resolution should appear in the minutes of that meeting. Second, a note or other evidence of indebtedness should be prepared and retained that includes the amount borrowed; the due date of the loan; and the rate of interest, which should realistically reflect current market conditions. Third, the loan should be carried on the books of the corporation and should be paid according to its terms. Fourth, the amount of debt should be reasonable in terms of the equity that has been invested. For instance, it will raise eyebrows if the corporation has $1,000 of equity and $19,000 in loans from the shareholders. What the precise acceptable balance is depends on the type of business involved and the market conditions at the time. However, a loan-to-equity ratio of 4 to 1 or higher is likely to invite scrutiny. A lower ratio might also be questioned, depending on other surrounding factors.

If the principals do not have the funds to lend and they have decided to borrow from sources outside the corporation, they still must decide where they can obtain the best deal. Banks often make small business loans, particularly if the principals have an existing relationship with the institution. They will normally lend on the basis of a floating interest rate tied to the *prime rate*, which is the rate, usually set by the leading money center banks, that a bank will charge its best business clients. The bank will normally charge a small business "prime plus two" or "prime plus one and one-half." This means the bank will take the prime rate and add two (or one and one-half or some other number of) percentage points to it in order to arrive at the interest rate for a particular loan. For instance, if the prime rate is 10 percent, prime plus two would result in an interest rate of 12 percent. As the prime rate varies, so too will the rate charged to the small business.

The bank will also take back a promissory note signed on behalf of the corporation and co-signed or guaranteed by the corporation's principals and their spouses. In addition the bank will probably demand back a security interest in the receivables, fixed assets, and inventory of the corporation in order to secure the debt. A security interest creates a lien on the debtor's assets so that if the debtor or the guarantor do not pay, the lender can take the assets covered by the security agreement and sell them to satisfy the debt. Security interests may be created in many ways, but the most typical in commercial situations is the filing of a *financing statement* and a UCC-1 form with the county clerk in the county where the pledged property is located. Having a security interest means that the bank will have the first call, even ahead of other corporate creditors, on those assets pledged by the corporation to secure the loan. The bank will also have a call on the guarantors in the event that the corporation defaults.

As you can see, there are an almost infinite number of methods for capitalizing a corporation. Each variation has implications for other areas of the corporation's existence. Many of these implications have to do with taxation, and it is to this subject that we will now turn our attention.

Chapter 2

Taxation of Corporations and Their Shareholders

The taxation of corporations and their shareholders is an enormously complex area of the law. In discussing it, the most basic thing to remember is that the law recognizes corporations as separate entities from those who own them, the shareholders. This factor gives shareholders their limited liability, but it also creates a series of peculiar tax problems, both for the corporation and for its owners. Some of the major tax issues confronting corporations and their shareholders are highlighted in this chapter.

To begin with, corporations are generally taxed on their own taxable income (which is, basically, gross revenue minus deductions), just as individuals are taxed on theirs. The corporate tax rates range from 15 percent on the first $50,000 of taxable income to 25 percent on the next $25,000 of taxable income to 34 percent on taxable income in excess of $75,000. In addition, there is a 5 percent surtax on all taxable income between $100,000 and $335,000. This means that corporations with taxable income in excess of $100,000 are really paying 39 percent on the excess until they reach a total taxable income of $335,000, at which point the rate drops back to 34 percent. The effect of the surtax is that a corporation with a taxable income in excess of $335,000 is paying a flat rate of 34 percent on all of its taxable income.

To the extent that any of this taxable income is distributed to shareholders as dividends, the shareholders are taxed on this distribution at their personal income tax rates. This problem has come to be known as "double taxation," the taxation of the same pool of money at the corporate level and again at the individual level. Corporations and shareholders and their lawyers and accountants are always looking for ways to avoid double taxation legally. Moreover, they look for legal ways to avoid or to delay taxation upon particular corporate transactions. In fact, the catchword of lawyers, accountants, and sophisticated business people concerning taxation has always been *deferral*, the putting off through careful planning of current taxation until some future time.

In this chapter both of these issues, the double taxation of corporate profits and the deferral of taxation, will be examined at various stages in the corporate life. The tax treatment of incorporation itself will come first; the taxation of the going concern, including methods of limiting that taxation, follows. Tax issues relating to the shareholders will be discussed, including methods of limiting these taxes. Also addressed is the tax treatment of the dissolution and liquidation of the corporation and how such acts affect the shareholders' tax status. As always, however, please keep in mind both the complexity of this subject and its ever-changing nature. Moreover, every state has its own way of taxing various transactions, and state taxation may also have a serious impact on a transaction. Therefore, before you make any plans that depend upon, or are materially affected by, the tax treatment of the transaction, be sure to consult a qualified tax expert for advice.

TAXES ASSOCIATED WITH CORPORATE ORGANIZATION

Generally speaking, the creation of a new corporation is not a taxable event. Investors (the principals) can usually contribute capital to the corporation and receive shares of stock in exchange without there being any recognition of gain (or loss) under the tax laws. This is true regardless of whether the business being incorporated is brand new or one that previously operated in some other organizational form. In addition, the shares obtained by investors in a closely held corporation may be entitled to favorable tax treatment in the event the corporation is not successful. This section will examine both of these situations.

Initial Capitalization and Recognition of Gain

Before discussing the tax consequences of capitalizing the corporation, some basic tax concepts should be defined and discussed. First, the concept of *recognition of gain* requires a brief explanation. The issue arises when an investor transfers property rather than cash to a corporation in exchange for its stock. Assume, for example, that an investor transfers to the corporation a piece of property that he or she originally purchased for $10,000 but that now has a fair market value of $20,000. When the corporation accepts the property, it receives an asset worth $20,000. In exchange for the property, the corporation gives the investor 100 percent of its shares. If no other money or property has been contributed to the corporation, these shares are worth $20,000 (the value of the corporation). The shareholder has "realized" a gain of $10,000 by transferring the property to another entity and being "paid" the fair market value of that property.

To make the concept somewhat clearer, let us suppose the investor transferred the property to a buyer for $20,000 in cash. Obviously, the investor made a $10,000 profit, which would be taxable. Similarly, if the investor had transferred the property for a painting worth $20,000, he or she would have realized the $10,000 gain by purchasing a $20,000 painting for land that had cost only $10,000. Therefore, our original investor has realized a $10,000 gain by exchanging the property for shares in a corporation that have a value in excess of the investor's *basis* (which usually is the equivalent of the original cost of an item plus improvements made to it and less depreciation attributable to it) in the property transferred. The tax question then is whether the gain "realized" by the transfer of appreciated property in exchange for stock will be "recognized" by the IRS.

As mentioned earlier, the gain that a taxpayer *realizes* in a transaction is only subject to taxation if that gain is *recognized*. Generally, gains that are realized by a taxpayer are recognized under the tax code and are taxable. There are, however, several sections of the code that exclude certain realized gains from taxation. Among the sections providing for the nonrecognition of gain are Sections 351 and 357 of the Internal Revenue Code (IRC). To determine whether a particular gain relating to the capitalization of a corporation will be recognized, one must apply the tests found in these two sections of the tax code.

Basically, these sections provide that in order to avoid the recognition (and, thus, the taxation) of the gain, the following requirements must be met:

1. For the exchange to be tax free for any particular transferor, he or she must receive *only* stock or securities in exchange for the property.

2. Transferor(s) of the property must be in control of the corporation to which it was transferred immediately after the transfer.

3. Corporation must not assume any liability of the transferor or accept from the transferor property that is subject to liabilities (with some exceptions to this latter proscription).

What this test requires in practical terms is first that the transferor transfers property, including cash, rather than services or promises of future services. After the transfer, the parties transferring property, as a group, must be in control of the corporation. Here, *control* means that the parties who transferred property must hold at least 80 percent of all *combined* voting power in the corporation and at least 80 percent of the shares in *each class*, if any, of nonvoting stock in the corporation. Furthermore, the transferor seeking nonrecognition of gain must receive in exchange for the property *only* stock or certain long-term debt instruments of the corporation, not cash or other property. Similarly, the transferor seeking nonrecognition must not have transferred personal liabilities to the corporation. These latter two tests, as opposed to the control test, allow some transferors to a new corporation to obtain nonrecognition status while others are denied. In addition, these tests permit a transferor to have part of his or her gain qualify for nonrecognition and the remainder of the gain be subject to taxation.

If the transfer of property to the corporation meets the tests for nonrecognition of gain, the next question is how will the transfer be treated by the IRC. Essentially, the Code permits each party to take what it received in the transaction at the same basis as the basis of the property he or she transferred as of the time of the transfer. Therefore, the transferor will take the stock or securities he or she receives at the same basis he or she had in the property transferred. Similarly, the corporation will take the property it received at the transferor's basis in it as of the time of the transfer. These transactions involve a *postponement* of taxation until the property taken by the corporation or the stock or securities taken by the transferor are sold. At that point, there will be a tax assessed against the corporation or the transferor on the excess of the item's sale price over its basis.

If the transfer of property does not qualify for nonrecognition of gain (or qualifies only in part), the results are somewhat different. For the transferor, there will be a tax on the gain recognized from the transfer. This will be the excess of recognized gain over the transferor's basis in the property. The shareholder's basis in the stock or securities taken from the corporation will then be adjusted upward by the amount of gain recognized. If the shareholder received any cash from the corporation or if the corporation assumed any of the shareholder's liabilities, the shareholder's basis in the stock will be reduced by the amount of cash received or the amount of liabilities assumed. The basis of the property transferred to the corporation will be the transferor's basis in the property at the time of transfer, plus any gain recognized by the transferor. The effect of these adjustments to the basis of the stock or securities in the hands of the transferor is that when he or she resells them, there will not be a tax on profits that had already been subject to tax.

For instance, if property with a basis of $10 but a fair market value of $25 is transferred to the corporation for $25 worth of stock and the gain does not meet the nonrecognition tests, the transferor will be subject to a tax on the $15 gain. If the transferor later sells the shares for $30, he or she should be subject to taxation only on the previously untaxed gain of $5 (the difference between the $25 value of the stock when obtained by the transferor and the $30 sale price). This is accomplished by increasing the transferor's basis in the stock by the amount of gain that was previously taxed (this is the $15 excess of the value of the stock when originally obtained [$25] over the transferor's basis in the property transferred [$10]).

These tax rules apply to start-up corporations as well as to corporations set up for the purpose of conducting a business previously run by a sole proprietor or a partnership. In either case, it should be a relatively simple matter for the organizers to ensure that the transfer of capital to the corporation will be a tax-free event. There is another section of the IRC that can provide tax benefits to shareholders if proper planning takes place. These are the benefits under Section 1244 of the Code.

Section 1244 Stock

New corporations are generally very high risk investments for the initial shareholders. If the corporation does not succeed, the shareholders will suffer losses, either through the liquidation of the corporation or through the sale of their stock at a price below what they paid for it. The shareholders may deduct the losses suffered but normally only as *capital losses*: A capital loss must first be offset against the taxpayer's capital gains, if any. The excess loss in any year can be used to offset the taxpayer's ordinary income but only up to a maximum of $3,000 per year. Any remaining excess loss can be carried over to the next tax year, when the same procedure is applied anew. Under these circumstances, it could take a shareholder quite a long time to recoup his or her loss through the tax write-offs.

The longer it takes to recoup a loss, of course, the less valuable will be the benefit to the shareholder/taxpayer. In order to help investors recoup some of these losses more quickly, Section 1244 of the code was enacted. It allows certain losses due to the failure of the corporation to be treated as ordinary rather than capital losses. The effect is to allow investors to use the losses to offset ordinary income each year in an amount much greater than would be the case with capital losses.

To qualify for Section 1244 treatment, the shareholder claiming the loss must be an individual or a partnership who has held the stock continuously from its issuance until the loss. The stock may be either common or preferred. In addition:

- The stock must have been issued in what is known as a *small business corporation*. This is a corporation in which the total of the paid in capital and surplus (including the amount contributed for the 1244 stock) does not exceed $1 million.

- It must have been issued for money or property (other than securities) and not for services or the promise of services.

- During the five years prior to the loss, the corporation in which the stock was issued must have derived more than half of its revenue from its business activities and not from passive sources, such as investment income. Investment income is income derived from such things as dividends, interest, rents, and royalties.

If the stock qualifies as 1244 stock, any loss suffered by a shareholder on the stock can be deducted from the shareholder's ordinary income up to a maximum of $50,000 per year for a separate return and $100,000 annually for a joint return. If there is a loss in excess of what can be used in a particular year, the excess can be carried forward to the next tax year and be applied against that year's income, up to the annual limits, and so on, until the loss is fully deducted. The benefit to the shareholder of this situation over that of deducting capital losses is clear, and simple planning is all that is necessary to assure its availability.

Although it is the shareholder who receives the direct benefit of Section 1244 treatment, the corporation is also a beneficiary, albeit indirectly. The benefit to the corporation is a result of the reduced financial risk faced by shareholders in the event of the failure of the corporation. Since the shareholder's investment can be written off against his or her ordinary income, often in the same year as the loss, the shareholder is guaranteed by the tax system a significant savings, even in the face of the total worthlessness of his or her stock. For instance, assume a shareholder invested $25,000 in a small business corporation that has gone under, leaving the corporation's stock completely worthless. If the rules found in Section 1244 did not apply, the shareholder could deduct the $25,000 by first offsetting any capital gains he or she might have had for that tax year. If there were no capital gains, the shareholder could deduct only $3,000 of the loss from his or her ordinary income and carry the balance forward to be deducted in subsequent years. If there were no capital gains in subsequent years to offset the loss on the corporate stock, it would take the shareholder nine years to write off the entire loss. The application of Section 1244, however, allows the shareholder to write off the entire loss in the very first year. If the shareholder were in the highest personal income tax bracket (currently 33 percent), the federal and state write off could save the shareholder between 40 percent and 50 percent of the loss (depending on the state tax bracket of the shareholder).

To illustrate this point, let us assume a flat 33 percent federal and a flat 10 percent state income tax rate and the availability of Section 1244 treatment. Assume also that the shareholder has a taxable income of $100,000 before deduction for the loss on the corporate stock. Without Section 1244, the taxpayer would be liable for $32,333.33 in federal tax ($100,000 – $3,000 allowable deduction for the loss = $97,000 x 33% = $32,333.33) and $9,700 in state tax ($97,000 x 10%). The total tax would be $42,033.33. With the application of Section 1244, however, the tax will be reduced significantly. Because the entire $25,000 loss is deductible immediately, the taxpayer's taxable income is reduced to $75,000, leaving a federal tax of $25,000 and a state tax of $7,500 for a total tax of $32,500. This is more than $9,500 less than the total without the use of Section 1244. This savings, in effect, reduces the shareholder/taxpayer's loss to $15,500 rather than $25,000. This reduced risk is a major selling point when the small corporation seeks to raise capital, particularly from outside investors.

TAXATION OF THE GOING CONCERN

As has already been mentioned, a corporation is treated by the law as an individual and, therefore, is subject to taxation on its own income. While there are several differences between the tax rules applicable to individuals and those applicable to corporations, the fundamental system and method of taxation is the same. Each taxpayer, whether corporate or individual, will determine its gross income, subtract from gross income its allowable deductions, thus arriving at its taxable income, and then apply the appropriate tax rates to determine the tax due. This section will discuss some of the differences between the corporate tax laws and those applicable to individuals and will point out ways in which the corporate laws can be used to reduce tax obligations and otherwise benefit the shareholder.

Subchapter S Status

Among the most common and well known of the tax-saving devices available to closely held corporations and their shareholders are the benefits available under subchapter S of the IRC. Under the sections in this part of the Code, most of the problems associated with the double taxation of corporations and shareholders can be eliminated. As you will recall, corporate income is often subjected to two levels of federal income taxation. The first is at the corporate level, when corporate tax rates are applied to the taxable income of the corporation. The second is at the individual level, when some or all of the remaining after-tax profits of the corporation are distributed to the shareholders as dividends. Subchapter S essentially eliminates taxation at the corporate level by treating the corporation for most tax purposes as if it were a partnership. Partnerships are not, themselves, taxable entities, and profits and losses of partnerships are passed through them directly to the partners in proportion to their interest in the partnership. These profits or losses then become part of each individual partner's tax picture for the year. Among the advantages of this status, besides the elimination of corporate income taxes, is the fact that any losses suffered by the corporation may be able to be used by its shareholders to offset their income from other sources. There are rules, known as the *passive loss limitations*, that may reduce the current impact of these pass-throughs, but they are, ultimately, available to the shareholder of a subchapter S corporation.

There are also several disadvantages to subchapter S status. The most significant of these is that the shareholders will be taxed on their share of corporate income, even if that income is not distributed to them but is re-invested in the business. Furthermore, many of the fringe benefits, such as health or life insurance, that are deductible in the standard subchapter C corporation are not deductible for any shareholder who owns 2 percent or more of the S corporation. Other disadvantages of subchapter S status concern the limited organizational flexibility of the corporation. To qualify for subchapter S status, the corporation must have only one class of shares and may not have corporations or partnerships as shareholders. In addition, the total number of shareholders in the corporation is limited to 35 (although for most corporations this will not be a significant restraint).

Since there are already several books for business people and for nonspecialist professionals concerning subchapter S corporations on the market, this section will give only a brief overview of the subject. It will address the requirements for achieving subchapter S status, the advantages and disadvantages of the status, and the procedures for applying for it.

In order for a corporation to be able to elect subchapter S status, it must meet *each* of the requirements set out in IRC Section 1361. These requirements are that

- the corporation must be a domestic corporation

- there may be only one class of stock

- there may be no more than 35 shareholders

- there may not be as a shareholder a nonresident alien

- each shareholder must be either an individual, an estate, or certain kinds of trusts.

There are also some corporations that can meet each of these tests but are still "ineligible" for subchapter S status. These include certain banks, insurance companies, or "affiliated" corporations.

A corporation that wants to achieve subchapter S status must apply to the Internal Revenue Service on Form 2553. In order to be operative for a particular tax year, the election must be filed prior to that year or by the fifteenth day of the third month of that tax year. The election form must include or be accompanied by the signed consents of each of the shareholders. The IRS will respond to the application in writing, usually within several weeks after receiving it.

Assuming eligibility for the status, determining whether to apply for subchapter S treatment requires careful consideration. There are several advantages to obtaining this status other than the obvious avoidance of double taxation. As was mentioned earlier, profits and losses pass through the corporation directly to the shareholders; therefore, if the corporation has losses, particularly paper losses (such as depreciation) permitted by the Code, the shareholders may be able to take advantage of these to offset their other income. Of course, all such losses are subject to the passive loss limitations (which were designed to reduce the benefit of losses from "passive" activities—such as leasing rental property—that a taxpayer may claim) applicable to each taxpayer. Similarly, since the tax on corporate earnings is based on the tax rate of each individual shareholder, the owners of stock in an S corporation could give some of the stock to their children over the age of 14. The effect of this transfer would be to split corporate income among the children of the family. The children are likely to be taxed at a lower rate than are their parents, leading to an overall reduction of the tax imposed on the earnings of the corporation.

As was mentioned, there are also several disadvantages to subchapter S status. The most significant disadvantage is the taxation of shareholders for corporate profits that are not distributed to them but are retained by the corporation to meet its own needs. As an example, imagine a subchapter S corporation with two shareholders, the first owning two-thirds of the corporate stock and the second owning the remaining one-third. If the corporation had gross income of $100,000 and deductible expenses of $70,000, the $30,000 taxable income would be ascribed to the two shareholders in the following manner: The first would be charged with $20,000 of the profit and the second with $10,000. These amounts would be added to the shareholders' personal incomes and would be taxed at their personal rates.

Suppose, however, that the corporation was in a developmental stage or in the process of expansion. In these situations it is likely that the corporation would not distribute its income to the shareholders but would retain it to meet its own corporate needs. The shareholders would, nevertheless, still be responsible for the tax on this profit. The shareholders would have to dip into their own resources to meet the tax obligations imposed upon them due to the taxable income earned by their subchapter S corporation. This unpleasant reality is the most obvious reason that shareholders need to think carefully before determining to apply for subchapter S status.

Other drawbacks are not as obvious but are, nonetheless, significant. The disability of shareholders who own at least 2 percent of the sub S corporation to deduct the cost of certain fringe benefits is an important disadvantage. In the standard subchapter C corporation, the cost of fringe benefits is deductible to the corporation, thereby reducing its taxable income. Moreover, the shareholder/ employee will generally get these fringe benefits without being subject to a tax on their value. This is true even though the shareholder would not be able to deduct the cost of the fringes if he or she purchased them individually or through a partnership. Since fringe benefits can make up a significant percentage of an employee's compensation package, the inability to deduct their cost can have substantial tax consequences for the corporation.

The S corporation is also limited as to the number and type of shareholders it may have and as to the type of stock it may issue. While the limitation of no more than 35 shareholders is often insignificant (due to the fact that most small corporations have far fewer than this number of shareholders anyway), the limitation as to who can be a shareholder is more restrictive. Because corporations and partnerships are prohibited from holding shares in a sub S corporation, an entire class of potential investors is eliminated. Similarly, since there may be only one class of shares in a sub S corporation, the flexibility offered to the organizers by the possibilities of preferred stock is also eliminated. In addition, there are a number of more technical drawbacks, many having to do with the treatment of corporations that have changed from sub C status to sub S status.

What is clear is that subchapter S treatment *is* advantageous to corporations that expect to experience losses in their operations. It is also advantageous when the corporation will have enough cash available for distribution to shareholders to cover the tax obligations brought on by the corporation's earnings. As far as the capitalization of the corporation is concerned, for subchapter S to be available, the corporation must be able to be funded with only a combination of common stock and debt. Since outside investors are often wary of investing in the common stock of start-up corporations, this requirement may mean that the principals will be the sole source of the equity capital. This is true even though Section 1244 treatment is available to an investor and can be helpful in selling the common stock to outside investors.

Deductible Corporate Expenses

While subchapter S offers the avoidance of the double taxation to which subchapter C corporations are exposed, it is not the only method of avoiding tax at the corporate level. If a corporation has deductible expenses of the same magnitude as its income, there will, of course, be little or no tax imposed at the corporate level. Careful financial planning can take advantage of these deductible items to reduce or eliminate taxable income at the corporate level while still giving the shareholders the benefit of these corporate expenditures. Among the most common of the devices available to reduce corporate income are:

- capitalization of the corporation by the shareholders with a combination of equity and debt

- leasing by the shareholders to the corporation of space and equipment needed in the corporation's business

- payment to shareholder/employees of the highest reasonable salaries

- establishment of the most generous permissible fringe benefit package for shareholder/employees.

This section will discuss each of these devices and the tax consequences associated with them. Remember, since each corporation has different circumstances and needs, there is no single set of tax-saving activities that can be universally applied. Moreover, the IRS has the right to disallow certain claimed deductions if they are fraudulent. The IRS may also disallow them even if they are not fraudulent but are unreasonable under the circumstances. In the aftermath of such a disallowance, the taxpayer may be faced with increased taxes, interest charges on the overdue balance, and, in some cases, penalties. If the taxpayer wishes to challenge the disallowance, there are appeal rights within the IRS and, if those fail, access to the federal District Court or the Tax Court. Each of these avenues offers the opportunity to redress a wrongful disallowance, but each also involves the expenditure of a significant amount of time, energy, and money. It would, therefore, be much wiser to plan your expenditures carefully and to document them with complete and accurate records.

Corporate Capitalization with Debt

Earlier, in a discussion of the capitalization of a corporation, the distinction was made between debt instruments and stock. It was pointed out that stock meant ownership in the corporation and offered the shareholder a chance to increase his or her wealth through the increase in the value of the corporation. It was also pointed out that if the corporation performed poorly and was liquidated, the shareholders would be the last to be paid off and that the common shareholders are the last of the shareholders to be paid. Debt holders, on the other hand, are in a much more secure position as far as the return of their investment is concerned. On the other hand, an investment in a debt instrument is one that offers no opportunity for growth. The debt holder will be paid his or her interest before any shareholder can receive a dividend on his or her stock. In the event of a liquidation, the debt holder will be repaid the amount owed before the shareholder can receive from the corporation a return of his or her capital. If there is not enough money to pay the debts or if the debts are paid but there is not enough to pay the shareholders, the unpaid (or partially unpaid) shareholders have no recourse (unless they allege mismanagement by the corporate directors or officers) and will lose their investment. Keep in mind that in such a situation, Section 1244 stock may be a significant benefit to these shareholders. On the other hand, the debt holder will not participate in the growth of a successful corporation. If the corporation does particularly well, the value of the note held by a lender does not increase nor, in the typical case, does the rate of interest payable on that note.

In many closely held corporations, the shareholders also lend money to it. When this occurs, many of the negatives associated with holding debt instruments do not apply. For instance, the shareholders will participate in the growth of the corporation through their stock ownership. They will receive regular payments from the corporation, whether denominated as interest or as dividends, through their holding of debt and equity. Moreover, as creditors, they may be protected from some of the risks of their investment because they will be eligible to receive a distribution on liquidation of the corporation, along with the other creditors, before the shareholders are repaid. If there is not enough money to pay even the creditors, the advantage to being in the shareholder/lender's position is clear. In the status of lender, a shareholder will receive funds as a creditor that he or she would not have received as a shareholder. Therefore, part of their contribution to the corporation may be returned to them by investing it as debt. As was mentioned in Chapter 1, in order to put such a contribution in the best possible light, all of the formalities of a loan should be observed. There should be a board resolution authorizing the corporation to borrow and a promissory note evidencing the debt. Interest should be charged, and the terms of the note should be observed. Finally, the ratio of shareholder-held debt to equity must be reasonable so that the IRS will be less likely to call the interest a constructive dividend.

Another major advantage of having the principals contribute capital partly as equity and partly as debt is associated with the tax consequences for the corporation of this structure. As you may recall from the discussion of capitalization, dividends that are distributed to the shareholders are not deductible expenses for the corporation, but payment of interest to debt holders is. This is true, with some limitations, even if the debt holders are also the shareholders in the corporation. The benefits of this consideration can best be illustrated by an example.

Suppose a subchapter C corporation had been capitalized with $400,000 of equity. Suppose also that in the current year, the corporation has gross income of $100,000 and deductible expenses of $70,000. The $30,000 excess is, of course, taxable to the corporation. If it distributes all (or any part) of the after-tax excess to the shareholders, they will be taxed on their portion of the distribution. If, instead of capitalization of $400,000 of equity, the shareholders contributed $150,000 of equity and the balance of $250,000 through a loan to the corporation bearing interest at the rate of 10 percent per year, the tax situation of the corporation would change dramatically. There would still be gross income of $100,000, but the deductible expenses would be increased because of the interest paid to the shareholders on their loans.

The interest paid to the creditor/shareholders would be $25,000 (a loan of $250,000 x 10% interest). The corporation's deductions increase by $25,000, and its taxable income decreases by a like amount. Therefore, the corporation would have $100,000 income and $95,000 in deductible expenses, leaving a taxable income of only $5,000. The shareholders would receive from the corporation the same amount (and, perhaps, even more) as they would have received from the dividend distribution. They will, of course, be taxed on what they receive, regardless of whether it is interest income or a dividend. There will not, however, be a corporate tax on the amount distributed as interest. The effect of this is to save a significant amount of money for the corporation and its shareholders. The corporation that was fully capitalized with equity would pay a tax of $4,500 on its $30,000 taxable income ($30,000 x 15%). If the balance of $25,500 were distributed to shareholders who were each in the 28 percent tax bracket, they would pay a total of $7,140 in tax on the dividend. Thus, the total tax on the $30,000 corporate profit would be $11,640.

If the corporation had been capitalized with the combination of debt and equity just described, the tax picture would be quite different. The corporation would already have paid out $25,000 in interest to the shareholders, which would leave taxable income of only $5,000. The corporation would pay a tax of $750 ($5,000 x 15%), leaving an after-tax profit of $4,250 to distribute ($5,000 – $750). When added to the $25,000 interest payment, the shareholders will have received $29,250 of the corporation's gross income. They will be taxed at the rate of 28 percent on this income, which will result in a tax obligation of $8,190 ($29,250 x 28%). They will, therefore, have paid a total tax on income derived from the corporation of $8,940. This amount is a savings of $2,700 over the tax on corporate income and distributions based on a capitalization of 100 percent equity.

The process of combining debt and equity in a corporate capitalization is known as *thin incorporation*. It involves capitalizing a corporation with the highest ratio of debt to equity that would be reasonable under the particular circumstances of the corporation. If the debt is held by the shareholders of the corporation, the IRS will be concerned that the debt is just another form of equity and the interest payments nothing more than camouflage for nondeductible dividends. The tax code gives the IRS the power to examine such situations and to disallow as a *constructive dividend* some or all of the deductions associated with the debt. The Code sets out several factors to be considered in determining whether there truly was a loan by a shareholder to the corporation, including:

- whether there is a written instrument containing the corporation's unconditional promise to pay a sum certain by a particular date or on demand

- whether the debt is subordinated to or has a preference over other indebtedness of the corporation

- the overall ratio of corporate debt to equity

- whether the debt is convertible into stock

These factors should, once again, underline for the principals of a corporation the importance of observing corporate formalities when lending to the corporation. They also should serve as a reminder not to overstep reasonable bounds of sound financial planning.

An additional advantage to the organizers of using debt to capitalize the corporation occurs if and when the corporation becomes very successful. At that point the corporation can start returning capital to its investors. One advantage of the repayment of debt is that it is a tax-free event, whereas the redemption of stock (which is another way of returning capital to shareholders) may involve undesirable tax consequences. For example, assume a subchapter C corporation earns significant profits that the shareholders wish to take out of the corporation. The obvious methods to achieve this end is for them to declare a dividend or to increase their salaries and/or fringe benefits. When their salaries and fringes are already near the limit of what the IRS will accept as "reasonable," this avenue is fraught with risk. If the IRS were to disallow the deduction for increased compensation, the corporation could be subject not only to additional taxation but also to penalties for its invalid deduction and interest on its underpayment of taxes. Declaring a dividend would not, as we know, give the corporation a deduction and would result in the double tax that most corporations and shareholders try hard to avoid.

A method that would satisfy both the shareholders' need for cash as well as their desire to avoid taxation on the distribution is the repayment of debt by the corporation. The corporation's interests are not injured since we are assuming it is in a financial position to make some form of distribution anyway. The shareholders' interests are also protected. They can receive the repayment without it affecting their ownership interest in the corporation because no stock is involved in the transaction. Furthermore, since they are merely receiving what they had previously loaned to the corporation, there is no income involved and, therefore, no tax. There is, of course, a long-term effect in that the corporation, by repaying debt, is reducing the amount it will pay out in interest, thereby reducing its deductions, and, all other things being equal, increasing its taxable income.

Shareholder Leases to the Corporation

Generally speaking, rent paid by the corporation for items used in its business activities is deductible. This is true even if the rent is paid to a shareholder of the corporation. The issue for the allowance of this deduction (when the claimed payment was made to a shareholder) is whether the rent being paid is reasonable. This is essentially asking the question, "Would a corporation dealing at arm's length with a lessor expect to pay the rent being charged?" If the answer is yes, the deduction will be allowed. If the answer is that a corporation dealing at arm's length would pay less, the excess rent will be disallowed as a deduction. Similarly, if the rent for a particular item is reasonable in amount but the item is one not really used by the corporation, the deduction will be disallowed. The effect of a disallowance is that the tax owed by the corporation will be increased, and interest and penalties will be added to the bill.

Nevertheless, if the shareholder owns property that the corporation needs for its business, the shareholder should consider leasing it to the corporation rather than contributing it in exchange for shares of stock. If the corporation has enough working capital to conduct its business and enough income to pay the rental fees, the use of a lease gives the shareholder added protection against loss. It also gives the corporation a tax deduction for the expenditure. The deduction has the effect, as does the deduction for the payment of interest on a debt, of reducing the corporation's income. This reduces its tax liability while allowing it to make a distribution of its revenue to its shareholders. There is an added advantage in that the shareholder may be entitled to deductions on his or her tax return for the depreciation and/or maintenance costs associated with the property leased to the corporation. This would shelter some or all of the income derived by the shareholder from the lease. In some cases, it might even shelter other income of the shareholder, thus making the alternative of leasing property to the corporation one clearly worth exploring.

Assume you own items that are needed by your corporation and you are willing to make them available to it through a lease. Aside from the tax advantages to the corporation and, through it, to the shareholders, there may also be advantages to the lessor of the property. The main benefit to the lessor is the possibility of taking a deduction for the depreciation of that property. The IRC permits a deduction for loss due to the ordinary wear and tear and obsolescence of a capital asset (one with a useful life of more than one year) used in a trade or business or held for the production of income. Property that is leased to the corporation may be considered held by the lessor for the production of income even if the leased property is not normally used in the lessor's trade or business. The amount of the deduction in any year and the number of years during which the lessor may depreciate the property depend on the nature and value of the property and the date when it is first put into service. In addition, the passive loss limitations added to the code in the Tax Reform Act of 1986 might effect the immediate usefulness to the lessor of the depreciation deduction.

Despite the technicalities of the tax law, the benefits of leasing can be significant. For instance, if a shareholder has an extra room in his or her home, the room could be leased to the corporation as its office. The corporation would pay the shareholder a fair market rent for the space (which would be deducted from the corporation's income). This would, as has already been observed, result in a distribution to the shareholder without the intervention of the corporate tax. Furthermore, since the building (or the part of the building) where the office space is located is a capital asset, it may be depreciated. The shareholder/lessor may deduct from his or her personal income an amount permitted by the IRC. This deduction may be large enough to shelter all or part of the rental payment made for the space by the corporation.

For example, if the rental payment were $300 per month ($3,600 per year), the shareholder would have an additional $3,600 per year in income, which would be subject to personal income taxation. If, however, he or she were able to claim in that same year a deduction for the use of the space, of, hypothetically, $3,000, the increased income *subject to tax* would be only $600. The shareholder would still have received the full $3,600, but the deduction for depreciation would have wiped out, on paper, most of the rental income. I use the phrase *on paper* because in most cases involving the depreciation of real property (buildings) there is no actual loss in value because of wear and tear. In fact, generally speaking, real property continues to *increase* in value over time.

The depreciation deductions taken previously will ultimately be *recaptured* upon the sale of the property. This is accomplished by reducing the lessor's basis in the property by the amount of depreciation claimed and taxing the gain, represented by the difference between the adjusted basis of the property and its sale price. Recapture will not occur until the sale of the property, which may be years down the road, and, as we know, tax deferral is a major element of tax planning. If the lessor provides the corporation with a capital asset other than real property (a delivery truck, for instance), the depreciation deduction will still be available. In this case, though, there probably will be an actual loss in the value of the asset due to its wearing down. If that is so, there may be no problem concerning the recapture of the deductions since the asset will most likely be scrapped or sold for less than its adjusted basis.

It is also possible that the deduction for depreciation will exceed the income derived from the leasing of the asset. In such a case, the lessor may be entitled to use the excess deduction to offset income from completely separate sources. This is what is known as a *tax shelter*, although the availability of such devices has been severely curtailed by the Tax Reform Act of 1986. This Act was the culmination of a long effort by the IRS and Congress to close various loopholes in the law that had allowed certain taxpayers to avoid paying what was considered their fair share of taxes. Nevertheless, the Act still permits the sheltering effect of depreciation deductions in several instances, and shareholders would be wise to determine if they are able to take advantage of those instances.

There is also a nontax advantage for a shareholder who leases property to his or her corporation. As you recall, the limited liability offered to shareholders protects them from personal liability for the acts of the corporation. They can only lose their investment in the corporation. If the corporation's assets are not sufficient to pay its liabilities, the creditor cannot seek additional compensation from the personal assets of the shareholders. If a shareholder has contributed property to the corporation in exchange for shares, that property belongs to the corporation and is available to be used in meeting the corporation's obligations. If, however, that property was only leased to the corporation, it remains the property of the shareholder and cannot be taken by a creditor. Thus the shareholder insulates himself or herself even further from the liabilities of the corporation.

Salary and Fringe Benefits

Another avenue for reducing the taxable income of a corporation while still providing benefits to its shareholders is for the corporation to establish the most generous salary and benefit package reasonable under the circumstances. Among the factors used in determining what is reasonable are the following:

- corporation's financial condition
- packages provided by comparable corporations in the same geographic area
- whether the package is commensurate with the shareholder's duties and activities within the corporation.

If the deduction is disallowed, the corporation, as we know, will be assessed additional tax as well as interest and penalties. The shareholder who receives the benefits, in many cases, will not be affected by the disallowance because the amounts received have been taxed as income, regardless of the "unreasonableness" of the amount. Of course, if the shareholder received excess fringe benefits or the personal use of corporate property, he or she may be assessed an additional amount as tax for this extra "income."

If a company is doing well financially and the duties of its executives are growing, deductible increases in compensation may be acceptable to the IRS. The increase could be a simple raise in salary or a bonus for a particularly useful performance by the executives. It could also be granted as the provision or expansion of health, life, or disability insurance for the executives or payment for or provision of on-site child care for employees' children. Increased compensation also often is channeled to shareholder/employees through the creation of a pension or profit-sharing plan or by an increase in the corporation's contribution to an existing plan. In any of these instances, the amounts paid provide a benefit to the shareholder while generally being deductible for the corporation. A detailed discussion of these methods of compensating shareholder/ employees is included in Chapter 3, Executive Compensation.

There are special rules concerning the deductibility of many of these items, regardless of whether the employee is also a shareholder. For instance, life insurance premiums are only deductible, assuming the coverage is otherwise reasonable, when the employee, not the employer, is the beneficiary of the policy. Similarly, if the corporation provides employees with the use of corporate property, such as an automobile, and the property is used by the employee for both business and personal purposes, only part of the cost of providing the property may be deducted by the corporation. Generally, the amount that may be deducted is the percentage of the expense associated with the property that corresponds to the percentage of business use of the property by the employee. In fact, it is possible that the personal use of corporate property by the employee will be treated as income to that employee to the extent of the personal use. A qualified tax advisor can help you develop a benefit package that takes maximum advantage of the deductions permitted by the tax code.

CORPORATE PENALTY TAXES

In addition to the corporate taxes regularly assessed against a corporation's income, the tax code includes several taxes and penalties that could impact heavily on closely held corporations. This section will discuss some of the more significant ones and their effect on corporations and shareholders—in particular, the Accumulated Earnings Tax and the tax on Personal Holding Companies. Both of these concepts were devised to limit shareholders who attempted to utilize corporations to avoid taxation on personal income. Changes in the tax laws, primarily changes found in the Tax Reform Act of 1986, have reduced the value of some of the tax avoidance schemes these provisions were designed to eliminate.

Nevertheless, the provisions continue to have vitality and are actively applied by the IRS.

Accumulated Earnings Tax

This tax was developed to keep high-income shareholders from setting up and maintaining corporations for the purpose of retaining corporate earnings within the corporation. The corporate tax rate was, until changed by the 1986 Act, significantly lower than the personal rate, which meant that less tax would be assessed against corporate income than if the same business was conducted in an individual capacity. In addition, the double tax on these earnings could be avoided by retaining the earnings in the corporation and not distributing them as dividends to the shareholders. The earnings would be allowed to accumulate until the shareholder sold the stock of the cash-rich corporation for a price that reflected its increased asset value. The proceeds of the sale of stock would be taxed at long-term capital gains rates that were also significantly lower than income tax rates until changed in 1986. Thus, the shareholder was able to avoid personal *income* taxation on what was in effect the distribution of corporate earnings.

If the shareholder did not wish to sell the corporation, he or she could achieve a similar avoidance of tax by merely keeping the corporate profit within the corporation until it was more beneficial to draw it out. This might be when the shareholder retired or otherwise had a reduced income and was in a lower tax bracket. Alternatively, it might be in a year when the shareholder had extraordinary deductions that would shelter some or all of the distribution of the accumulated earnings. In either event, the shareholder, through manipulating the timing of corporate distributions, could avoid much of the negative tax effect of double taxation.

Changes in income tax rates that make the highest corporate rate higher than the highest individual rate have reduced much of the benefit of accumulating earnings. Furthermore, the long-term capital gains rate is now the same as the highest personal income tax rate (other than the application of the individual surtax). These changes make it considerably less desirable to set up a corporation for the purpose of accumulating earnings. The penalty tax against a corporation for accumulating earnings in any year for the purpose of avoiding income tax is another major deterrent against such an accumulation. The tax may be imposed on all but a few specific types of corporations if the corporation was created or is used to avoid income tax for its shareholders and does so by accumulating its earnings "beyond the reasonable needs of the business." The tax on the accumulated earnings is in addition to the regular corporate tax and is designed to eliminate the benefit of unnecessary accumulations.

The essence of this tax is to keep corporations from retaining their profits in any tax year in amounts beyond what is necessary for their current or anticipated business needs. It is not intended to have a negative impact on business expansion or on other financial plans developed by the corporation's board or its officers. In fact, the statute creating the tax provides for a minimum amount of earnings, $250,000, that can be accumulated without penalty regardless of business purposes. This amount may be increased by funds needed for legitimate business activity. The regulations implementing the accumulated earnings tax also list several business purposes that have been accepted as legitimate reasons for accumulations. The list is illustrative and not exhaustive in that other purposes may also qualify for corporate accumulations without application of the penalty tax provisions.

According to Section 1.537-2(b) of the Internal Revenue Regulations, accumulations for the following purposes do not incur the penalty tax:

- business expansion and asset replacement

- acquisition of another business

- retirement of business debt

- funding inventory and operations

- investment in or loans to suppliers or customers.

The courts have expanded this list with decisions approving accumulations to protect against labor strife, fund retirement plans, and meet potential business or economic risks, among other things. Again, the expansion of allowable accumulations brought on by court decisions is not exclusive, and a corporation can attempt to prove that its accumulation had a legitimate business purpose independent of those recognized by the regulations or by the courts.

The question of whether the accumulation was reasonable depends on the facts and circumstances of each individual corporation. The courts are reluctant to impose their views on a corporation over those of the corporation's board of directors, but they will examine the business and financial history of a corporation charged with unreasonable accumulations to determine their purpose. If the accumulations are found to be unreasonable, a tax of 28 percent (which equals the highest individual rate) will be imposed on that part of the accumulation deemed to be unreasonable (known as *accumulated taxable income*). This is *in addition* to the regular corporate tax already imposed on the corporation's income.

Accumulated taxable income essentially means a corporation's taxable income (as adjusted) minus a *dividends-paid deduction* and minus the accumulated earnings credit. The dividends-paid deduction makes sense because any dividends actually paid (which, you will recall, are not a deduction for the corporation and do not reduce its earnings) would have been subject to the double tax and were clearly not accumulated to avoid taxation of shareholders. The tax code also allows *consent dividends* to be included in the dividends-paid deduction. These are amounts retained by the corporation that shareholders consent to have treated as dividends even though they have not been distributed. The amount of the consent dividend will be allocated pro rata among the shareholders and will be subject to tax at the shareholder level. Each shareholder will be credited with contributing additional capital to the corporation in an amount corresponding to his or her share of the consent dividend. This has the effect of increasing his or her basis in the corporation, which will have an impact if and when the shares are disposed of by the shareholder.

There is also a reduction of the corporation's taxable income by the accumulated earnings credit. This is the amount, discussed earlier, that a corporation may accumulate without penalty regardless of its need for the funds. The credit is determined by taking the greater of *a*) $250,000 or *b*) that part of the corporation's earnings for the tax year that is retained for reasonable business purposes. The $250,000 is a total credit and includes newly retained earnings as well as any accumulated earnings already existing at the beginning of the tax year.

An example will help illustrate the application of this tax. A corporation has a taxable income of $300,000 in a particular tax year. At the beginning of the current tax year it had retained earnings from prior years of $150,000. If it paid out dividends of $100,000 in the current year and retained the remaining $200,000, it would have total accumulated earnings at the end of the tax year of $350,000 ($150,000 carryover earnings and $200,000 current-year earnings). If the corporation had no reasonable business need for these funds, it would be subject to the accumulated earnings tax. To calculate the tax, determine earnings from the current year, which are $300,000. From this, subtract the amount of dividends paid, which was $100,000, leaving an accumulation of $200,000 for the current year. From this amount, subtract the accumulated earnings credit. In this case the credit would be $100,000 ($250,000 credit minus the amount of prior accumulations which, in this situation, is $150,000). Therefore, the accumulated taxable income would be $100,000 ($200,000 accumulated earnings minus the $100,000 credit), and the tax would be $28,000 ($100,000 accumulated taxable income times 28 percent).

Using the same example, if the corporation had a valid business purpose for some or all of the funds, the accumulated taxable income would be reduced by the amount allocated for that purpose. For instance, assume that the corporation intended to purchase several machines to replace existing equipment and for expansion. The cost of this machinery is $275,000. The corporation will use the $200,000 remaining after the payment of the dividend and a part of the earlier accumulation to purchase the machinery. In this case the calculation of the accumulated taxable income, if any, is slightly different. Again, there will be a taxable income of $300,000 and a dividends-paid deduction of $100,000. The accumulated earnings credit will then be the larger of the minimum credit (here, the same $100,000 as calculated before) or the amount retained for business needs ($275,000). Since this amount is larger than the minimum credit, it is used to offset accumulations. Because the accumulations in the current year were only $200,000, the credit will entirely eliminate the accumulation, leaving no accumulated taxable income.

Personal Holding Company Tax

The concept of the personal holding company tax was developed many years ago for a purpose similar to that of the accumulated earnings tax. The tax on personal holding companies was designed to prevent certain taxpayers from using a corporate shell to avoid personal income taxes. The personal holding company was set up so that it earned rather large sums that were taxed at the then more favorable corporate rates. The shareholders could then determine whether and when to distribute any of this income.

The types of corporations subject to the personal holding company tax are much more limited than those subject to the accumulated earnings tax. Typically, they are those set up to hold the personal assets or investments of their shareholders or to shield professionals (including athletes and entertainers) from personal income derived from the use of their skills or talents. Nevertheless the result of applying this tax is much the same as in the accumulated earnings situation (although personal holding companies are not subject to that tax). There is a tax (at the rate of 28 percent) in addition to the normal corporate income tax imposed on the undistributed income of a personal holding company. This tax, together with the reduced personal tax rates and elimination of the long-term capital gains benefits, have reduced the value of the personal holding company to shareholders.

A personal holding company is defined in Section 542 of the Internal Revenue Code. To be classified as a *personal holding company*, a corporation must meet each of two tests. The first is that at least 60 percent of its adjusted ordinary gross income for any year must come from what are essentially passive investment sources. The term *adjusted ordinary gross income* means gross income less several deductions that are designed to segregate the corporation's income from actual operations from income derived from passive investments. Then, if the corporation's income from such items as dividends, interest, rents, royalties, mineral rights, copyrights, compensation for the use of corporate property by its shareholders, and certain personal services contracts equals at least 60 percent of the adjusted ordinary gross income, the first part of the test will have been met.

The second aspect of the test is whether at any point within the last half of the corporation's tax year more than 50 percent of the stock (determined by value) of the corporation was owned, directly or indirectly, by not more than five individuals. This part of the test becomes complicated only when the ownership of stock is indirect. This might be through family members or business associates or through other corporations controlled by a shareholder. If one has an option to purchase stock, he or she is deemed to own it. Similarly, if one owns securities in the corporation that are convertible into stock, these will be treated as if they were stock.

In computing the tax to be paid on the undistributed portion of the personal holding company's income, first determine the corporation's taxable income. From this amount there are a number of special adjustments pursuant to Section 545 of the Code. These include certain additional deductions as well as the elimination or reduction of various otherwise allowable deductions. From this adjusted income, the corporation may subtract a dividends-paid deduction. This deduction includes the amount of dividend actually distributed as well as the amount consented to. In this regard, the deduction is the same as that relating to the accumulated earnings tax. An additional item that may be included in the dividends-paid deduction is the excess of any dividends paid in the prior two years over the corporation's income for those years.

Section 547 of the Code provides one final avenue by which the personal holding company can avoid the penalty tax on its undistributed income. This involves a distribution of some or all of that income after the tax liability for it has been established. This *deficiency dividend* can eliminate some or all of the liability for the personal holding company tax. It cannot, however, avoid the interest or penalties that might be associated with the imposition of that tax. In order to qualify for the deficiency deduction, the dividend must be paid to shareholders within 90 days after it is finally determined that the corporation owes the tax. After the dividend has been paid (and within 120 days of the determination of liability), the corporation may file Form 976 to claim the deduction. If the deduction entitles the corporation to a refund, it must be claimed within two years from the determination of liability.

Clearly, these two taxes, the accumulated earnings tax and the personal holding company tax, present significant problems to the corporation. They can, however, be avoided with planning. In each case, distributions will generally eliminate the tax liability of the corporation. Determining how much of a distribution is necessary requires careful attention. Planning may also permit the avoidance of the tax without a distribution. If a corporation has legitimate business needs, it can accumulate earnings to satisfy those needs. Similarly, the definition of a personal holding company is quite narrow. With appropriate care, corporations could be structured in ways that accomplish some of the purposes of a personal holding company without being liable for the penalty tax. Because of the complexity of the issues, consult a qualified tax advisor before you undertake such tasks as attempting to legitimately avoid the accumulated earnings and personal holding company taxes.

CORPORATE LIQUIDATIONS

A *corporate liquidation* involves the cessation of the business of a corporation, the winding up of its affairs, and the distribution of its assets. This is distinct from a *dissolution*, which is the termination of the corporation's legal existence. Assuming a corporation has assets remaining after the payment of its debts and obligations, these assets will be distributed to its shareholders, either in cash or in property. If the liquidation is complete, the distribution will be treated as if the corporation bought back (redeemed) its stock from its stockholders. The shareholders will therefore be subject to the capital gains tax on any gain or loss realized in the transaction. If the liquidation is only partial—that is, the corporation keeps more of its assets than are needed merely to wind up its affairs—the distribution will be treated as any other dividend, and shareholders will be taxed on the receipt of ordinary income.

It should be pointed out here that the determination as to whether a distribution is a *liquidating dividend* (that is, a distribution to shareholders in complete liquidation of the corporation) can only be made after the IRS evaluates all the facts and circumstances of a particular situation. While the tax code does not require any formal corporate resolution or plan of liquidation or even an actual redemption of stock or dissolution of the corporation, each of these items, alone or in combination, is evidence of the complete liquidation of the corporation. The major advantage to shareholders of having a distribution treated as a liquidating dividend is that the distribution will typically be taxed as a capital gain rather than as ordinary income. The benefit of this fact has been significantly reduced by the elimination of the favorable tax treatment formerly given to long-term capital gains. Nevertheless, some benefit to shareholders still exists, particularly the ability to offset such gains by capital losses on a dollar-for-dollar basis.

The tax to shareholders on a liquidating dividend may be on top of a tax to the corporation for income or capital gain obtained by it on the sale of its assets to a buyer. This is true regardless of whether there is actually a sale to third parties or merely a *constructive sale* (at the fair market value of the property) to the shareholders. The constructive (or fictitious) sale to shareholders is a further example of the double tax that has been mentioned throughout this chapter and earlier in the book. It is also a change from the pre-1986 tax law.

Under the older law, a corporation might avoid recognition of gain upon a sale of its assets if it underwent a complete liquidation within 12 months thereafter. The shareholders would then be taxed on their portion of the distribution, either as income or as capital gain, depending on the nature of the assets sold by the corporation. Since the repeal of that provision, both the corporation and the shareholder may be subject to tax: the corporation, for the sale of its assets, and the shareholder, for receipt of the distribution.

The tax to the shareholder on the distribution is based on the difference between his or her basis in the stock and the amount distributed. If there is an excess of distribution over basis, this amount is subject to tax at the capital gains rates. If the shareholder bought shares of the corporation at different times and for different prices, each block of shares must be treated independently to determine the gain or loss from their redemption. Where property is distributed to the shareholder as part of the liquidating dividend, that property is valued at its fair market value for the purpose of determining gain or loss. If the property transferred is subject to liabilities that the shareholder assumes, these liabilities will reduce the fair market value of the property distributed. This, in turn, reduces the amount realized from the distribution, which will affect the amount of tax due.

The corporation will also be taxed on the distribution. It will be treated as having recognized gain or loss upon the sale in complete liquidation of its assets to third parties *or* upon the liquidating distribution of its property to its shareholders. In the first instance, the corporation will recognize gain or loss based upon the difference between the sale price of an asset and the corporation's adjusted basis in it. While this is normal tax treatment concerning the sale of any business property, it is contrary to prior law. Until the Tax Reform Act of 1986, corporations that sold all of their assets prior to a complete liquidation could take advantage of provisions of the law that allowed them to avoid recognition of gain. Since those provisions have been repealed, both the corporation and the shareholder are subject to tax on the liquidation. In fact, the corporation is taxed on the gain it realizes on property distributed to its shareholders pursuant to the liquidation. All distributed property is deemed to have been sold to the shareholders at its fair market value. Once again, the gain on the sale is determined by subtracting the corporation's adjusted basis in the property from the property's fair market value at the time of the distribution.

There are a number of problems associated with the income and loss of liquidating corporations and their shareholders. These include how to treat assets that cannot be adequately valued at the time of distribution or those that continue to provide income after the liquidation. There are also special problems associated with the liquidation of a subsidiary and the treatment of liabilities and deductions of the liquidating corporation. Each of these problems, as well as others not mentioned, are complex and require specialized knowledge and experience. The warning found throughout this book that expert guidance must be sought before undertaking complex transactions applies here as well. The costs in terms of time, energy, and money associated with an improper liquidation are too great for you to treat it casually.

Chapter 3

Executive Compensation

An important question that arises in closely held corporations is how to compensate managerial employees. This question is more difficult to answer than it might at first appear. Several groups within a corporation may be competing for a share of the income. While there are a variety of laws to determine who is entitled to what, most compensation decisions are based on economic factors within the corporation and among the shareholders and other corporate constituencies. Employees who are not shareholders in the corporation want the highest possible salaries, whereas shareholders prefer that large amounts be set aside for distribution, in one form or another, to themselves. In addition to these internal tugs of war, the federal and state tax authorities are interested in finding the largest possible taxable income in the corporation from which to derive the greatest possible tax revenue.

Obviously, all of these competing factors cannot be met at the same time. Therefore, the ability to maneuver through the maze of interest group desires, legal requirements, and practical realities is a critical skill for the corporate insider. Indeed, the identification of corporate goals concerning the distribution of its revenue pie is only the first step. The implementation of those goals requires a good grasp of the available options and careful planning as to which ones to utilize in a particular corporate situation. This chapter will present some of the more significant options, along with a discussion of their attributes. Because many of the choices will be heavily influenced by tax considerations, these considerations will be highlighted in the discussion. They should be understood in the context of the overall tax situation of the corporation and its principal shareholders.

Among the most common forms of executive compensation are salaries, bonuses, expense accounts, and fringe benefits such as health, life, and disability insurance. In addition, corporations often provide their employees with pensions, profit-sharing plans, stock options, and other forms of deferred compensation. Before deciding whether to use one or more of these items and in what proportions, the principals of a corporation will need to examine all of the factors involved, including:

- composition of the executive and nonexecutive employees

- whether management is comprised of corporate shareholders or outsiders

- need for and likelihood of securing and retaining nonstockholder employees and executives

- financial condition of the corporation and its shareholders
- tax consequences of any particular choice.

As has already been mentioned, tax considerations play a major part in determining how to compensate employees. Many forms of compensation that are tax deductible to the corporation also may not be immediately (if ever) taxable to the employee. If the compensation paid to employees is deductible, the taxable income of the corporation will, of course, be reduced. If the employees who receive the compensation are also its shareholders, they will have successfully reduced or avoided the double taxation that is normally applicable to corporate distributions.

To give an example, suppose a corporation whose shareholders were its only employees took in gross revenue of $200,000 for a particular year. If it had deductible expenses (other than employee compensation) of $90,000, the corporation would have a taxable income of $110,000. This would result in a tax obligation of $26,150, leaving $83,850 for distribution as dividends to shareholders. If, however, the corporation provided salaries and fringe benefits for its shareholder employees in the amount of $75,000, the corporation could also deduct the $75,000 from its gross income. This would leave a taxable income of only $35,000 ($200,000 gross income – $90,000 noncompensation expense – $75,000 compensation expense = $35,000). The tax would be only $5,250, as opposed to the $26,150 in tax owed without the deduction. This would leave $29,750 available for distribution as dividends to shareholders. When this amount is added to the $75,000 they received as compensation, the shareholders took $104,750 out of the corporation and saved $20,900 in corporate taxation in the process.

Of course, not all corporations are as simply constructed as the one in the previous example. Many times, the shareholders are not employees, or there are employees in addition to the shareholders. In such cases, the compensation paid to the employees will still generally be deductible to the corporation, and, therefore, beneficial to the shareholders. They will not, however, receive the direct dollar-for-dollar benefit indicated in the example.

Two final points ought to be raised before going into a description of individual forms of compensation. First, state corporation laws often prescribe who may be compensated, for what services they may receive compensation, and in what form it may be provided. In earlier days, for instance, directors were often prohibited from receiving any compensation from the corporation, even if they also served as corporate officers. It was thought that directors were insiders with significant financial interests in the corporation that they were protecting. No additional compensation beyond the profits generated by good management was deemed to be necessary. In addition, the performance by directors of the duties of officers was considered merely to be part of their obligation to the corporation and, again, not separately compensable. As more and more companies utilized the services of "outside" directors, those without substantial (or any) stock holdings in the corporation, the rules concerning the compensation of directors changed. Today, many state corporation laws permit compensation of directors, and clauses providing for compensation frequently appear in corporate Articles of Incorporation and bylaws.

The second preliminary item involves the tax treatment of compensation. In order for any compensation to be deductible, it must be "reasonable" in amount. The Internal Revenue Service is entitled to review any deduction claimed by the corporation for compensation to employees. The purpose of the review is to determine whether the compensation is really a form of disguised dividend to shareholders. This issue only arises when the compensation is being paid to shareholders. Because dividends are not deductible and compensation generally is, many corporations have attempted to use a compensation format for what was really a distribution of corporate profits.

In determining what is *reasonable compensation*, the IRS will look at the compensation paid in relation to a variety of factors, including:

- size and nature of the corporation

- services performed by the shareholder

- qualifications of the shareholder to perform the required services

- compensation paid for comparable services by similarly situated corporations in the geographic area

- general economic conditions

- relationship of shareholder salaries to the salaries of other employees of the corporation

- relationship of salaries to shareholdings (i.e., Is the salary of a 50 percent shareholder twice as large as the salary of a 25 percent shareholder?)

- whether the corporation pays any dividends.

Even in the early days of a corporation's existence, there should be a provision for executive compensation. Many times, there is not enough money to pay the principals a salary. Nevertheless, it may be a good idea to allow the salary to accrue on the books of the corporation, even if it is not paid, in order to create a history of compensation for when times improve. This is because as conditions change, so may the compensation paid to shareholder employees. As the corporation's sales or product line grows, or the managers take on more responsibility, their compensation can increase accordingly.

If the IRS determines that the amounts paid by the corporation to its shareholders as compensation are unreasonably high, it will disallow some or all of the deduction. When this occurs, the tax obligation of the corporation increases. In addition, the corporation becomes liable for interest and penalties on the additional tax. The tax due from the shareholder, on the other hand, generally remains unchanged because he or she pays a tax on the amount received, regardless of whether it was called a dividend or compensation.

SALARIES, FEES, AND BONUSES

The most basic form of compensating employees is providing salaries for their services. When the payments are made to employees who are neither shareholders nor related to the shareholders, there is rarely a question about their reasonableness. This issue does arise, however, in closely held corporations where the main employees are the shareholders or their relatives. Where these corporations are taxed under subchapter C of the Code (nonsubchapter S corporations), the IRS has been on the alert for attempts to disguise dividends by casting corporate profits in the form of executive compensation paid to shareholder/employees.

Among the most important issues that the IRS examines is whether there really were services performed for the corporation. This is because the deductibility of compensation depends, initially, on there having been something done for the benefit of the corporation. The tax law requires the payment to be "ordinary and necessary" within the business and reasonable in amount. The "ordinary and necessary" restriction means that the item being deducted must be necessary for the proper conduct of the business and must be ordinarily expended by businesses of the same kind.

Salaries for management personnel are clearly deductible if

reasonable. Shareholders who are employees of their corporations are entitled to pay themselves at the highest reasonable rate, given the financial condition of the corporation and the rate paid to others with comparable duties by other businesses. This means that a shareholder should do some investigating before arbitrarily setting a salary level for himself or herself. The investigation can take place through other local business people, the chamber of commerce or a trade association, or with an accountant or attorney familiar with the local business community.

Another way that shareholders can legitimately take deductible dollars out of the corporation is by hiring family members to fill corporate positions. As long as the family member is actually performing a job and the amounts being paid are reasonable for the position, the compensation paid is deductible. This is particularly useful when the employee is an unemancipated child of a shareholder (assuming that this does not violate local child labor laws). If the child does not earn significant amounts from the corporation, he or she might not be required to file a tax return. Even if a return is required, the child may claim available deductions, including the standard deduction, to offset his or her income. Thus, even when there is taxable income, it will be taxed at a rate that is probably lower than that of his or her parents. This form of *income splitting* keeps income in the family while taxing it at a lower rate than if it were earned by the shareholder parents.

Since income splitting may draw the attention of the IRS, it is important for the corporation to protect itself against IRS attempts to disallow such deductions. Among the precautions that the corporation may take are the following:

- making all salary or wage payments directly to the employee or to the employee's bank account

- having documentation of the employee's hours of employment

- having at least a general description of the employee's position or of the tasks performed

- being able to show that the tasks and expenditures were ordinary and necessary

- having an articulated basis for having established the rate of pay for the employee

In closely held corporations where the shareholders are also the directors, shareholders often take payments from the corporation in the form of director's fees. These are fees paid to the directors of the corporation for serving in that capacity and for attending directors' meetings. The fees, of course, are income to the recipient, but they may be deductible to the corporation. In order to be deductible they must, as with other forms of shareholder compensation, be reasonable in light of the size and nature of the corporation, the director's involvement in its affairs, the frequency of meetings, and the difficulty of the tasks the director is asked to perform.

In addition, shareholders who have professional skills, such as accountants or attorneys, often provide their services to the corporation. If these services are outside the scope of their employment with the corporation, these shareholders may generally charge the corporation a fee for the services. Once again, the fee must be reasonable in light of the task and what it would cost to obtain the service elsewhere. This practice is not unlike a shareholder leasing property to his or her corporation at the fair market rental price of the item. It provides a method of taking funds from the corporation and paying them to the shareholder that is deductible. Even though the shareholder will have to pay tax on the income, he or she has eliminated the double tax that would apply if the distribution were a dividend.

It is also possible to compensate employees through the use of *bonuses*. These are payments made in excess of the normal compensation obligation of the employer. They are usually distributed when a corporation has a particularly good year or as a reward for a particularly good performance by one or more employees. Often, whether to provide bonuses and, if provided, their amounts are not determined until the end of a tax year. At that time, the financial and tax condition of the corporation is more readily discernable, which provides the principals with the opportunity to manipulate corporate finances by eliminating some profit in the form of bonuses to shareholder/employees. The IRS is, again, particularly sensitive to this ploy, especially when the amount of the bonus to each shareholder is proportionate to his or her percentage of stock ownership.

HEALTH AND LIFE INSURANCE

Health, life, and disability insurance are among the most valuable and sought after fringe benefits employers provide to their employees. The cost of these benefits if the employee had to pay for them individually would be extremely high and, under current law, would generally not be deductible. When provided by the corporate employer, however, the cost of these benefits is normally deductible to it, and the cost is generally excluded from the income of the employee. The premiums or other costs of these plans are deductible if they are "ordinary and necessary" business expenses and are reasonable in amount. They also must meet certain nondiscrimination rules established pursuant to the Tax Reform Act of 1986. Since these are commonly provided benefits by employers to their employees, the ordinary and necessary element of the deductibility test should be easily met. The issue of the reasonableness of the amount implicates the same considerations discussed previously in relation to salaries. The nondiscrimination rules will be discussed in some detail later in this chapter.

As has already been mentioned, the costs to employers of providing these benefits are generally not includable in the income of the employee. In addition, amounts received by the beneficiaries of employees are also excludable, in most cases, from their income. The factors that must be examined in determining whether the proceeds of these plans are excludable from the income of the recipient vary, depending on the nature of the plan. With medical and accident reimbursement plans, the exclusion applies to amounts paid or reimbursed not in excess of the cost of care and not attributable to amounts taken by the employee as a medical expense deduction in the prior year. For instance, if an employee had medical costs of $5,000 in 1990 that he or she claimed as a deduction on his or her 1990 tax return, the reimbursement in 1991 of that $5,000 expense will be treated as income in 1991. If the employee was able to deduct (due to limitations on medical expense deductions) only $2,000 of the medical expense in 1990, the reimbursement of the full $5,000 in 1991 would result in only $2,000 of income (the amount of the prior year's deduction), with the remaining $3,000 being excluded.

With group term life insurance, the premiums paid by an employer are, once again, normally deductible from its gross revenue. They are also excluded from the income of the employee to the extent that the amount of coverage provided in the group policy does not exceed $50,000 for that employee. If an employee has coverage in excess of that amount, the premium for the excess will be treated as income to the employee and, as such, is subject to tax. For a group term life insurance plan to qualify for the employee exclusion, it must cover at least 10 full-time employees or, if the company has fewer than 10 employees, the plan must cover all insurable employees of the company. It must also meet the nondiscrimination requirements set up under the Code.

In order for a corporation to deduct the premiums of group term life insurance, the policy must be designed to cover employees. This is true even if the real purpose is to cover the shareholders. When there are shareholder/employees, the policy must cover them as *employees*. If it appears that the coverage is for the shareholders as shareholders, it will look as if the premium is merely a distribution of a dividend disguised as a business expense.

Life insurance premiums (outside of the group term context) on the life of corporate officers or key employees, are considered additional compensation of the insured. To the extent that the amount of total compensation to the insured is reasonable, and if the corporation is not the beneficiary of the policy, the premium is deductible to the corporation. The premium amount is, however, treated as income of the insured and subject to taxation. As with the proceeds of health insurance policies, the proceeds of a life insurance policy are not includable as income of the beneficiary if they were paid because of the death of the insured.

QUALIFICATION AND NONDISCRIMINATION REQUIREMENTS

In order to keep corporations from setting up tax-preferred benefit plans that discriminate in favor of highly compensated employees, the tax code, in Section 414, provides for several rules to reduce the advantages of such plans. A *highly compensated employee* is defined as an employee who, at any point during the tax year in question or the preceding tax year:

- owned at least 5 percent of the employer (i.e., owned at least 5 percent of the stock of the corporation)

- received from the employer more than $75,000 annual compensation (with annual adjustments based on an inflation index)

- received from the employer more than $50,000 annual compensation (with index adjustments) and was among the employer's top 20 percent employees by compensation

- was an officer of the employer and earned more than 150 percent of the amount allowed to be added by the employee to a defined contribution pension plan.

Qualification Requirements

In order for a benefit plan to qualify for favorable tax treatment, it must meet certain threshold requirements. The value of employer-provided benefits must be included in an employee's income unless:

- the plan is in writing

- the employees' rights under the plan are legally enforceable

- the employees receive reasonable notice of the benefits available to them under the plan

- the plan is maintained for the exclusive benefit of the employees

- the plan was established with the intention of its being indefinitely maintained.

The obvious purpose of these qualification rules is to reduce the possibility of an employer establishing an illusory plan that benefits only the shareholders or other favored persons. The requirement of a written plan with enforceable employee rights speaks directly to that issue. Similarly, employees must know about the benefits available in order to take advantage of them. If the employer fails to notify all but a few selected employees of the plan's benefits or existence, the plan has no value to the unnotified employees. The fact that the plan must be designed to benefit employees also keeps employers from providing tax-favored benefits to shareholders who do not work for the corporation. Finally, the requirement that the plan be intended to last indefinitely will reduce the likelihood of annual manipulation of finances and employment.

Assuming a benefit plan meets these general requirements, at least some of the benefits provided to employees may be excluded from the employee's income. An important factor in determining how much of the benefit may be excluded is whether the plan discriminates in favor of highly compensated employees.

Nondiscrimination Requirements

The nondiscrimination rules were designed to discourage employers from setting up benefit plans that favor highly compensated employees over rank-and-file workers. In many closely held corporations, where the shareholders are the most highly compensated employees, a discriminatory plan would have the effect of favoring the shareholders. If not restricted, such a plan would allow shareholders to make tax-free distributions to themselves of amounts that would otherwise be treated as dividends and taxed at both the corporate level and in the hands of the shareholders. The rules, therefore, treat as income to the highly compensated employee the discriminatory amount of the coverage or benefits provided under an otherwise qualified benefit plan.

In order to avoid this undesirable consequence and be found to be nondiscriminatory, a plan must meet two tests; an eligibility test and a benefits test. To be nondiscriminatory, a plan must meet the following requirements:

- At least 50 percent of all eligible employees must not be highly compensated.

- At least 90 percent of all not highly compensated employees must be eligible for coverage under the plan.

- The not highly compensated employees would receive a benefit that is at least 50 percent of the largest benefit available to highly compensated employees.

- There is nothing in the plan as to eligibility that discriminates in favor of highly compensated employees.

The nondiscriminatory benefits test is met if the average employer provided benefit received in a plan year by not highly compensated employees is at least 75 percent of the average benefit received during that period by highly compensated employees.

There are a variety of rules to determine how to calculate these percentages and which employees may be disregarded in making the calculations. There are also alternative rules that can be elected by small employers in order to mitigate the application of the non-discrimination rules. Finally, an employer who has only highly compensated employees is excused from the application of the nondiscrimination rules for any year in which it has no not highly compensated employees.

OTHER FRINGE BENEFITS

An employer may also provide a variety of other tax-favored benefits to employees, such as:

- employee discounts
- "working condition" fringe benefits
- "no additional cost" services
- de minimus benefits.

These benefits are all typical of items that may be included by employers in employee compensation packages. Furthermore, assuming the nondiscrimination rules are observed and certain other tests are met, each of these items may be deductible (or merely not taxed) to the employer as well as excluded from the income of the employee.

Employee discounts are a well known form of benefit. Many employers, particularly retailers, permit their employees to purchase the goods or services of the employer at a discount from the price charged to the general public. Theoretically, the amount saved by the employee could be treated as income in that the employee obtained an item of a certain value, say $100, for only $75. After the transaction, the employee is $25 ahead. Nevertheless, no income will be recognized, and no tax will be assessed.

Working condition fringe benefits are property or services provided by an employer to an employee for business use. Basically, if the employee could have taken a deduction for the item if he or she had paid for it, it will qualify as a working condition fringe. A common item that fits this category is a company car provided to an employee for business purposes. To the extent the car is used for business, the value of the use of the car is not included in the employee's income, and the cost of providing it is deductible from the income of the employer. To the extent the employee uses the car (or any provided property) for personal reasons, the value of that use will be treated as income to the employee and is subject to tax.

No additional cost services involve services that the employer provides to the public for a fee that an employee is entitled to use at a reduced cost or for free. If, in allowing an employee to use this service, the employer incurs no substantial additional cost over what it would incur without such use, the value of the service will not be treated as income to the employee. An example of this might be an employer who operates a private bus line in the city for which it charges riders a fare but lets its employees ride for free. If this benefit for employees does not result in substantial additional costs to the employer, the benefit will qualify for exclusion from employee income.

De minimus benefits are those incidental benefits that are too small or too costly and inconvenient to monitor. Typical ones include using the office phone for personal calls or copying personal papers on the office coping machine. The cost and effort to monitor and report these items is deemed to be unreasonably high, and, therefore, the value of these benefits is not included in income.

Each element of compensation and fringe benefit discussed up to this point can be found in the structure of many closely held corporations. They help to attract and retain employees for the corporation at a cost that is partially subsidized by the government through the tax savings attached to them. When the employees are also the shareholders of the corporation, these devices help to turn a part of the corporation's taxable income into a tax-free distribution to shareholders. Keep in mind that in order for the deductions for these items to be allowed by the IRS, they must be ordinary and necessary expenses of the corporation and reasonable in amount. If they are, the problem of the double taxation of corporations can be greatly reduced while giving the shareholders the benefits of corporate earnings. It is also important to note that many of the benefits discussed above would not be deductible if the principals ran their business as a partnership or sole proprietorship. In addition, much of the tax benefit of these compensation devices is lost for the holders of more than 2 percent of the stock in a subchapter S corporation. Therefore, in deciding on a choice of form for your business, consider carefully the tax advantages and disadvantages of incorporation.

EMPLOYEE BENEFIT PLANS

The remainder of this chapter will deal with somewhat more sophisticated forms of executive compensation, known generically as *employee benefit plans* or *deferred compensation*. Deferred compensation is designed to put off some of an employee's compensation until a future time. Often a means to fund one's retirement or other future activities, it is also a way, if done properly, to reduce the tax obligations of both the employee and the corporation. Deferring compensation can be achieved in many ways but the most common include:

- pension plans
- profit-sharing plans

- employee stock ownership plans

- cash or deferred arrangements.

Each type of plan is different in substantial ways from each other type and may also have significant internal variations. The rules applicable to the qualification of these plans for tax-favored treatment are very complex and would take a whole volume to describe and explain. The goals for this section are less ambitious than a complete analysis of the law concerning each type of plan. It will focus, instead, on the nature of each plan, its advantages and disadvantages, and on the basic rules pertaining to its operation and the tax treatment accorded it. Choosing which plan, if any, is appropriate for your corporation and how to implement it depends on a number of factors unique to your business. You will need an experienced hand to guide you through the maze of rules found in the Employee Retirement Income Security Act (ERISA) and the tax regulations. Meeting these requirements, however, is crucial so that your plan will receive the tax treatment that makes it such a valuable compensation device.

General Qualification Requirements

There are several requirements that apply to all tax-favored employee benefit plans. Some of these have already been encountered in relation to other employee fringe benefits; others are specifically related to the investment aspect of these plans. Among the basic requirements for tax-favored treatment are the following:

- The plan must be in writing.

- Its terms must be communicated to the employees.

- It must be exclusively for the benefit of employees or their beneficiaries—this means that there must be predetermined contributions by the employer or predetermined benefits for the employee and that investments made by the plan administrator must be prudent.

- The plan must be established to be permanent and continuing.

- Any trust administering the plan must be a U.S. entity.

If an employee benefit plan is "qualified," the employer's contributions to the plan will be deductible, and they will not be included in the income of the employee. The value of qualification, therefore, cannot be overestimated, nor can the disadvantage of not qualifying. Most employers who are about to establish a new plan or amend an existing one seek an advance ruling from the IRS to determine whether their proposed action will meet the requirements for a tax-favored plan. The request for a determination letter from the IRS may be made on IRS Form 5300 if the plan is a defined benefit plan or Form 5301 if it is a defined contribution plan. There are a number of additional forms and schedules that must be attached to the application for an advance ruling but the time and effort required are well spent in exchange for the knowledge that your plan qualifies or specific information as to how it fails to qualify.

PLAN DESCRIPTIONS

As mentioned previously, each type of employee benefit plan is different and often serves different purposes. This section will describe the basic elements of the major types of plans and the internal variations possible within a plan type. It will also discuss some of the benefits and drawbacks of each plan or variation.

Pension Plans

Pension plans were designed specifically to provide a fund for employee retirement. They are often administered by the employer, by a trust established for that purpose, or by an insurance company. The employer makes a predetermined annual contribution that is invested and allowed to accumulate. An employee is usually entitled to contribute additional amounts to the plan, on a tax-favored basis, from his or her pay. Then, when an employee covered by the plan retires, he or she may draw out his or her share of the ac–cumulated funds, either in a lump sum or as an annuity payable over the rest of his or her life. As opposed to the funding of a profit-sharing plan, the employer's pension plan contribution cannot depend upon the profits of the company. Instead, in order to receive tax-favored treatment, the contributions must be calculable in advance. In this regard, there are two basic forms for a "qualified" pension plan: a defined contribution plan and a defined benefit plan.

A *defined contribution plan* is, as its name suggests, a plan in which the employer's contribution is defined for each year. The contribution may be a fixed amount or an amount determined by a pre-established formula. One formula that is often used is a contribution based on a uniform percentage of each employee's salary. Each employee will have a separate "account" in his or her name from which his or her retirement benefits will be derived. Unlike a defined benefit plan, the amount of retirement benefits in a defined contribution plan cannot be determined in advance. They are a function of the amount contributed to each employee's account, the investment success of the contributed funds, and the number of years the employee is a participant in the plan.

The *defined benefit plan* operates on a somewhat different premise. Here, the amount of the benefit is defined in advance, and the employer must make an annual contribution that varies, depending on actuarial information. This information, compiled and analyzed by an actuary hired by the corporation, will indicate how much the employer has to contribute in any year in order to meet the vested retirement rights of employees in the plan. The factors to be considered include the number and age of the employees, the compensation levels, and the projected earnings of the contributed funds.

For example, a plan might provide for employees to receive at the normal retirement age an annual payment of 15 percent of their highest average salary for any three consecutive years of employment. Assume a corporation has two employees with similar salaries for the three-year period. This would mean that, barring future salary changes, each would be entitled to approximately the same pension benefit. If one employee has thirty years of employment left before retirement, and the other has only ten years until retirement, the current contribution necessary to give the older employee the same retirement benefit as the younger one would be much greater. This, of course, is because there is less time to accumulate the funds necessary to meet the pension obligation.

There are, of course, advantages and disadvantages to each form of pension plan. With a defined contribution plan, the employer knows exactly what has to be contributed each year (there is an upper limit of the lesser of $30,000 or 25 percent of the employee's compensation). Because there are no surprises based on the profitability of the company or on actuarial determinations, the plan is relatively simple to establish and maintain. On the other hand, the participants in such a plan will not know how much they will receive upon retirement until they retire. This is a function, in part, of the investment success of the fund. The investment aspect of the plan may mean that an administrator will have to choose and follow the fund's investments and, perhaps, assume liability for inappropriate investments that have failed.

Alternatively, the defined benefit plan leaves an employer at some risk. Because the size of a particular year's contribution can fluctuate, depending on factors beyond the employer's control, there may be an unexpectedly large payment to be made in a year when such a contribution would be damaging to the corporation. Employees, however, know exactly what they will receive upon retirement, which makes retirement planning easier for them. These plans are often funded by the purchase of annuities, which insures that participants do not run the risk of an unexpectedly small pension due to the investment reversals of the fund. On the other hand, they do not have the possibility of surprisingly large pensions due to the investment success of the fund. Moreover, there are limits on the benefit that can be provided to any employee. The limit is the lesser of $90,000 (adjusted for inflation) or 100 percent of the employee's average annual compensation for his or her highest three-year period of employment. Finally, the defined benefit plan is more closely regulated by ERISA, which requires, among other things, that such plans be insured by the Pension Benefit Guaranty Corporation. This corporation was designed to insure that employees receive what they were promised by defined benefit plans. Plans must pay an annual premium to the corporation for this protection.

Profit-sharing Plans

Profit-sharing plans are different from pensions in several ways. Perhaps the most fundamental difference is that profit sharing plans are not necessarily designed to provide retirement income for the participant. They are devices that let employees share in the profits of the company through employer contributions to a trust fund set up for the benefit of employees. Distributions from the fund *may* come at the time of an employee's retirement, but there may be an earlier distribution of the fund, such as at the time of the employee's leaving his or her employment. As such it may tide an employee over between jobs, or it may be the capital he or she needs to purchase a home or go on a trip or start his or her own business.

The second major difference between profit-sharing plans and pensions is that pensions are based on a predetermined contribution by the employer or on a predetermined benefit to the employee. Profit-sharing plans, on the other hand, do not have such fixed requirements. They are usually funded out of the corporation's profits, although the Tax Reform Act of 1986 allows a corporation to contribute to the plan regardless of the existence of current or accumulated profits. The limit on the amount of contribution that an employer can deduct in any year is 15 percent of the aggregate compensation paid to all plan participants for that year. The employer's contributions are allocated to the accounts of individual employees, and while there is no required formula for the amount of employer contributions, there is a requirement of a definite, pre-determined formula for the allocation of those contributions among the plan participants. The goal of this requirement, of course, is to avoid discrimination in favor of highly compensated employees. There must also be a predetermined formula for the distribution of funds from the plan to employees or their beneficiaries. Employees are permitted to make additional contributions to the plan from their income, but these contributions are not deductible to the employee.

Profit-sharing plans offer many of the same advantages to the corporation and the employee as do pension plans. Employer con-tributions to a qualified plan are deductions for the corporation and are not taxable to the employee. There are some added benefits to each side as well as some disadvantages to the employee. For the company, there is the added flexibility of no predetermined amount that must be contributed or benefit that must be paid. This allows the company to gear its contribution to the performance of the company on a year-to-year basis. Employees benefit because, unlike pension plans whose funds can be withdrawn before retirement only for limited and specific reasons, profit-sharing plans permit any number of events to trigger a distribution to an employee. For instance, severance of the employment relationship is a common basis for a distribution.

Employees may also suffer a disadvantage in comparison to their rights under a pension plan. With a defined contribution plan, they know what will be contributed each year, even though they cannot predict their pension benefit at the time of their retirement. With defined benefit plans, employees know what their pension will be when they retire. With a profit-sharing plan, employees need not know what will be contributed on their behalf nor what their ultimate benefit will be. The contribution will depend on company performance, and their benefit will depend on the investment experience of the fund.

Stock Bonus Plans

Stock bonus plans are common forms of executive compensation, although they are of limited value in closely held corporations where the existing shareholders are also the employees who would participate in the plan. This is because the payment to the employee is in the form of shares of the company. If the employees already own 100 percent of the shares, adding shares to their holding does them little good. On the other hand, if a company has a need for outside employees, a stock bonus plan is one way to provide relatively inexpensive benefits. The most widely known type of stock plan is called an *Employee Stock Ownership Plan (ESOP)*. What is more, an ESOP is flexible enough to be used as a pension plan, a profit-sharing plan, or a stock bonus plan.

An ESOP is a trust designed primarily to invest in and hold *employer securities*—stock issued by the employer or a member of the same controlled group as the employer. The stock must be easily tradable on an established market. Because a closely held corporation could not, by definition, meet such a requirement, the law allows employer stock with voting and dividend rights at least equal to the highest rights available on the common stock of the employer to be used instead. The employer contributes cash or employer securities to the ESOP, for which the employer obtains a tax deduction. If the employer contributes cash, the ESOP will use the cash to buy employer securities. The securities, in either case, are credited to and held in an account for each participating employee, who is generally entitled to control the voting of his or her shares.

An employer is entitled to a deduction for contributions to a qualified stock bonus plan. The amount of the additions for any employee is limited generally to the lesser of 25 percent of the employee's compensation or $30,000. These limits may be increased for particular years to the lesser of $60,000 or the amount of employer securities contributed to the plan. This increase is permissible if no more than one-third of the employer contributions for the year in question were allocated to highly compensated employees. As is typical with qualified employee benefit plans, the amount contributed by the employer for the employee's account will not be treated as income to the employee. Finally, the rules concerning plan eligibility were recently changed to encourage wider coverage and participation of employees.

Generally speaking, small corporations run by their shareholders would have little use for a plan such as this. In addition, similar results could be had with a general profit-sharing plan or with a pension. The main advantage accrues to larger closely held corporations that are in competition for executive employees or that are trying to boost productivity through worker participation in ownership. If a corporation could use a stock bonus plan, an ESOP could be very beneficial. The corporation could contribute shares of its stock rather than cash and, so long as the stock was independently appraised, deduct its value. This means a corporation would be getting a tax deduction without the necessity of a cash outlay, a very enviable position. Of course, the corporation is giving up some of its stock that represents an ownership and control interest in the corporation. The employees are now, at least indirectly through the trust, shareholders, with all the rights that this status entails.

Cash or Deferred Arrangements

A *Cash or Deferred Arrangement (CODA)* is permitted under Section 401(k) of the Internal Revenue Code and has become known as a *401(k) plan*. A 401(k) plan, basically, is an arrangement that may be a part of a qualified profit-sharing or stock bonus plan. Under the arrangement, an employee participant may elect to take a part of his or her compensation immediately in cash or to defer a part of it through contributions to a trust. To the extent elective contributions (that is, contributions that are at the employee's option) are deferred, there is a limit on the amount of annual deferrals. The limit is $7,000 indexed for inflation per year per employee. Within the limit, however, the amount deferred will not be treated as income to the employee.

The employer and employee may each make contributions to the employee's account. Employer contributions are deductible and are not included in employee income. The limit on employer contributions is the same as would be the case with straight profit-sharing or bonus plans. The combination of employee as well as employer contributions make this a valuable benefit to the employee at a relatively low cost to the employer. The employer must report to each employee the total amount of the employee's elective contributions to the plan and the total deferred compensation to his or her credit. Distributions from the plan are allowed for death, disability, separation from employment, and plan termination.

These plans all have some advantages for a closely held corporation. They permit deductible expenditures by the corporation that may inure to the benefit of the shareholders as employees. The benefits may also be tax free or tax deferred to the recipient. As we have seen, in order for these benefits to accrue, the plans must meet several tests. In each case the plan:

- must be for the exclusive benefit of the employees

- must be reasonable in amount

- may not discriminate in favor of highly compensated employees

- must provide for the vesting of the plan benefits at various times during the employment.

The Vesting of Plan Benefits

Vesting basically means that at some time during the employment the employee's right to some or all of the benefits under a plan becomes fixed and cannot be forfeited. The tax law sets out a number of rules concerning vesting that must be met in order for a plan to receive tax-favored treatment. We will now turn to a short discussion of the vesting rules.

The law requires the complete vesting of an employee's retirement benefit upon the employee reaching the normal retirement age. In addition, there must be complete vesting of benefits due to the employee's contributions as well as vesting of accrued benefits due to the employer's contributions pursuant to one of two schedules relating to years of service. One of the schedules calls for complete vesting of benefits derived from employer contributions after the employee has completed five years of employment. The other schedule requires 20 percent vesting per year from the third through the seventh year of service. An employer can create a plan with more rapid vesting of employer-derived benefits, but there can be no slower vesting requirement if a plan is to qualify for favorable tax treatment.

There are also rules concerning how to determine years of service and the normal retirement age. Normal retirement age may be specified in the plan, but it may not be later than age 65 or after 10 years of service, whichever is later. To determine years of service, any years before an employee reaches 18 years of age need not be counted for benefit vesting purposes. Neither must the employer count years of service for years before the plan was established. Special rules apply for employees who have breaks in service. If an employee leaves the employment for one year or more and then returns, the employer need not count any prebreak service until the employee has completed one year of service after his or her return.

As you can see, the use of employee benefit plans can go a long way toward eliminating the double taxation problem of corporations while providing significant benefits to the shareholders. The different forms of plans should be evaluated in light of the corporation's cash and tax situation and in light of shareholder needs to determine the best fit with those needs. The appropriate plan should then be established with the assistance of an experienced professional. In this way the financial and tax benefits that these plans can provide will be within the reach of the corporation and its principals.

Chapter 4

Protecting Minority Interests and Dispute Resolution

In small, closely held corporations disputes frequently arise between shareholders about the management or direction of the business. When such a dispute goes beyond a mere disagreement about business details and becomes a personal feud between the principals, serious corporate issues may be implicated. Always unpleasant, such situations sometimes disintegrate into financial and legal disasters. It is, therefore, useful to plan for the possibility of serious disputes between the shareholders and to establish in advance the procedures to be used in the event they arise. It is also useful to know the duties of management toward the corporation and the rights of shareholders if those duties are not fulfilled. This chapter will discuss the duties of management; the rights of shareholders, particularly minority shareholders; and the remedies, both corporate and judicial, that shareholders may employ in the event of a significant corporate dispute.

DUTIES OF MANAGEMENT

The rights of shareholders are connected very closely to the duties owed to them by the corporation and by its managers, who are the directors, the officers, and, often, the majority (or, controlling) shareholder(s). These people are known as *fiduciaries;* that is, people in a position of trust in relation to their beneficiaries. As such, these fiduciaries owe two main obligations to the corporation and to its shareholders and are liable to them for any failure to carry out these obligations. This is true even though corporations and those individuals that comprise them are protected by the concept of limited liability that was discussed earlier in this book. That concept, it may be recalled, casts liability for corporate acts on the corporation itself and not on its owners or employees. This limited liability acts to protect corporate personnel from liability to third persons. It does not, however, protect them from liability *to the corporation.*

The obligations owed to the corporation by its fiduciaries are known as the *duty of care* and the *duty of loyalty.* The duty of care requires that in making corporate decisions, the fiduciary exercises that degree of care that a reasonably prudent person would use in similar circumstances. The duty of loyalty requires that the fiduciary put the corporation's interest above his or her own in any situation in which those interests come into conflict.

Duty of Care

The duty of care is really nothing more than a requirement that corporate fiduciaries not be negligent in making corporate decisions. Fiduciaries are not required to be *correct* about each decision they make, but they are required to consider each issue with the degree of care that its importance warrants. This may mean that they must inquire about unknown facts or conduct an investigation or retain experts to advise them on particular subjects. If they act prudently but make the wrong decision, they are not liable to the corporation or the shareholders for the effects of that decision. They are protected by the so-called business judgment rule, which shields fiduciaries from liability for their bad decisions if those decisions were made in the good faith exercise of the fiduciaries' business judgment. Fiduciaries will be liable to the corporation, however, if the corporation is injured by their incorrect decision and it is found that the fiduciaries did not use due care in the exercise of that judgment.

As an example, suppose the corporation was approached with the opportunity to purchase an expensive new machine. If the board or the president investigates and determines that the machine is one that will enhance the corporation's competitive position, they may consider buying it. Before the decision is finalized, it would normally be appropriate for the buyer to investigate the experience others have had with the machine and to determine if the sales price is reasonable. It might also be helpful for the buyer to determine whether there is any new technology on the horizon that would make the machine obsolete or inefficient. Will there be a pool of workers who are skilled in running and maintaining the machine? Will replacement parts and mechanics be available to repair it? These questions and others would be asked by most reasonable buyers.

If the directors or president did ask those questions and got satisfactory answers, they will be protected from liability if the machine does not produce the desired results or the costs associated with it turn out to be higher than was reasonably foreseeable. They will also be protected if the results of their investigation are incorrect, so long as the investigation was reasonable when conducted. Even if the corporation suffers serious losses due to the purchase of the machine, the fiduciaries will not be liable for the loss. On the other hand, if these questions were not asked and the fiduciaries made no investigation, they might be liable to the corporation for the losses it suffered. Remember, the question of whether the fiduciary used due care is answered by determining whether the amount of care used was the amount a reasonable person would use in decisions of like magnitude. It is measured as of the time of the decision and not in hindsight. Moreover, it is not measured by whether the decision was correct or whether someone else would have decided differently.

Duty of Loyalty

The duty of loyalty is really comprised of several distinct subparts. Nevertheless, the essence of the duty is that a fiduciary, whenever his or her personal interests come into conflict with those of the corporation, must pursue the best interests of the corporation rather than his or her own. The conflicts between the fiduciary's private interests and those of the corporation usually arise in one of three ways. The first, known as *self-dealing*, occurs when the fiduciary contracts directly with his or her corporation. This may be to obtain goods or services from it or to sell goods or services to it. The second area of conflict involves the problem of *interlocking directorates*. This situation arises when a director of one corporation is also on the board of another corporation and the two corporations engage in one or more transactions with each other. The third problem develops when a fiduciary competes with his or her corporation to obtain a benefit that neither currently has but that both desire. This situation is regulated by a rule known as the *corporate opportunity doctrine* and is, perhaps, the most complex of the three situations.

Be aware that it is not illegal for a fiduciary to deal personally with his or her corporation, either directly or through another corporation with which he or she is associated. In fact, it is often very useful for a corporation to deal with its fiduciaries or with the fiduciary's other corporations. Moreover, it is not always impermissible for a fiduciary personally to pursue a benefit that he or she knows would also benefit the corporation. Determining what is allowed and what violates the duty of loyalty is a difficult question. The following discussion will indicate some of the problems and some guidelines about avoiding them.

Self-dealing

Self-dealing is an issue that is common in closely held corporations. When such a corporation needs additional capital, it usually turns to its principals (who are almost always in a fiduciary relationship with it) for a further infusion of equity or, as is often the case, a loan. Similarly, there may be employment contracts between the corporation and its principals (and their families), and the principals might also be hired and paid for special services rendered to the corporation that go beyond the realm of their corporate duties. In addition, principals often sell or lease property to the corporation and receive financial benefit from doing so. Finally, when a corporation has prospered, the principals may decide to withdraw some of its earnings in the form of a loan from the corporation to themselves personally. These loans, if properly documented and approved, may not be subject to income tax in the hands of the principals and will usually be on favorable terms to the borrower. These and other examples of self-dealing are common and often serve the interests of the corporation as well as those of the principal very well. The question of their legality depends on an examination of several factors.

The first factors, whether the laws of the state of incorporation allow self-dealing, has lost some of its importance over the years. At one time, self-dealing was absolutely prohibited, but today all states permit a fiduciary to deal with his or her corporation on certain terms. Essentially, the regulatory scheme of the states in addressing self-dealing is that the fiduciary in question must, before acting, make full disclosure to the corporation of his or her interest in the transaction. Most states permit the interested fiduciary to participate in the discussion of the transaction and even to vote on it (assuming the fiduciary is in a voting capacity). In practice, however, fiduciaries who are in this situation often disclose their interest but abstain from any vote.

The second factor to be examined is whether the corporate charter or bylaws prohibit self-dealing. It would be very unusual, indeed, to see such a prohibition in the organizational documents of a modern corporation. In fact, most such documents, if they speak to the subject at all, specifically authorize transactions between the corporation and its fiduciaries. A typical clause permitting self-dealing follows.

> *No contract or transaction between the Corporation and one or more of its directors or officers, or between the Corporation and any other corporation, partnership, or entity in which one or more of the directors or officers of the Corporation are directors or officers or are financially interested*

shall be void or voidable solely by virtue of such position or financial interest. This provision shall apply irrespective of the director or officer's presence or vote at the meeting where such contract or transaction is approved provided that:

a) The transaction is fair and reasonable to the corporation;

b) the interested director or officer has fully disclosed his or her interest in the contract or transaction; and

c)there are sufficient votes of disinterested directors to approve the contract or transaction without counting the vote of the interested director or officer.

The first factor is the most difficult to resolve. In order for a self-dealing transaction to be valid, the transaction must be objectively fair to the corporation as of the time it was made. This does not mean that the transaction had to benefit the corporation but that at the time it was made, an independent reasonable person with knowledge of the facts could have approved the transaction on behalf of the corporation. Remember that a corporate fiduciary does not guaranty the outcome of any decision but does warrant that he or she used due care in reaching the decision and put the corporation's interest above his or her own. Of course, these factors will only come into play if a corporate transaction does not work out well for the corporation. In that case, a minority shareholder or director (one who voted against the transaction) seeks to recover for the corporation the damages it suffered due to the fiduciary's breach of loyalty in a self-dealing transaction.

Interlocking Directorates

An *interlocking directorate* occurs when a director (or other fiduciary) of one corporation is a fiduciary of another corporation. When these two corporations deal with each other, the same kind of problem exists as in a situation of self-dealing. The director has split loyalties, and this problem is complicated in that the director owes a duty of loyalty to both corporations. A similar problem also arises when a director of one corporation is a shareholder in the other. In this case, as in self-dealing, the personal interests of the director are often pitted against those of his or her corporation. In all of these situations, the rules pertaining to self-dealing also apply. The director must disclose his or her competing interest and act in the best interest of the corporation. When both corporations expect and have a right to this loyalty, however, the director is placed in a difficult position.

The test of fairness also applies to these situations, and fairness is, once again, judged as of the time of the transaction and through the eyes of a fictional reasonable person with neutral interests. As with self-dealing, it is not the success of the transaction that is judged but its fairness to the corporation at the time it was undertaken. Moreover, it is only when the deal goes awry for one of the parties that the fiduciary's loyalty is ever questioned. A transaction can be fair to both parties, even if it does not turn out well for one of them. If this is the case, the fiduciary will be exonerated. If, however, he or she favored one of the parties and the disfavored party suffers as a result, the fiduciary will be liable to the injured corporation to the extent of its damage. In addition, once the injured corporation shows that the fiduciary had a competing interest (that is, that there was an interlocking directorate or self-dealing situation in the transaction), it will be incumbent on the fiduciary to demonstrate the fairness of the transaction to the complaining corporation, not the corporation's obligation to show it was unfair.

Corporate Opportunity Doctrine

The third area in which a fiduciary's loyalty to the corporation may be challenged is when he or she seeks for himself or herself an opportunity that should properly belong to the corporation. An obvious example would be a situation where the corporation has identified a piece of property that it needs to acquire to improve its business. If the fiduciary obtains that property and offers it to the corporation at a higher price, the fiduciary has clearly breached his or her duty to the corporation. The duty also would be breached if the fiduciary merely kept the property for himself or herself and never offered it to the corporation. Unfortunately, most situations are not so clear. The question, "When is an opportunity the corporation's and when is it one that a fiduciary can pursue for himself or herself?" is difficult to answer.

Courts have struggled with this problem for decades. On the one hand, it is important to maintain loyalty to the corporation. On the other, if a fiduciary is so restricted in pursuing his or her own interests, it might be difficult to induce qualified, energetic people with varied financial interests to be corporate directors or officers except in their own companies. Because this very financial sophistication, energy, and business contacts are what make the fiduciary valuable to the corporation, there must be some appropriate middle ground to accommodate the needs of each party. The law has attempted to develop such a middle ground by using the concept of "expectancy." When the corporation has an expectancy in a particular opportunity, it belongs to the corporation, and if a fiduciary usurps it, he or she has breached the duty of loyalty.

The term expectancy, itself, is rather difficult to define. It clearly does not mean that the corporation must have already identified a particular opportunity it intends to pursue. For instance, in the earlier example of the piece of property needed by the corporation, that property does not have to be specifically identified. If the board has discussed the need to purchase a piece of property meeting certain criteria and a director goes out and finds such a piece of property and purchases it for himself or herself, this may be enough to breach the duty. I say "may" be enough because there are other factors that must be examined before such a determination can be made.

One of these factors is whether the corporation could have made the purchase itself. If it does not have the funds available and could not obtain them, it can have no expectancy in the land. Similarly, if the corporation had already decided not to pursue this particular opportunity or if the land was somehow not appropriate for the corporation, these too, would eliminate an expectancy. If it is found that a fiduciary has breached the corporate opportunity doctrine, he or she may be forced to turn the opportunity and any profits earned from it over to the corporation. He or she will also be required to make up any losses suffered by the corporation due to the usurpation of the opportunity.

RIGHTS OF MINORITY SHAREHOLDERS

Since it is normally the case, particularly in closely held corporations, that majority shareholders control the board of directors, many of the duties of management discussed in the previous section are particularly useful in protecting the interests of minority shareholders. Minority shareholders are those who do not have the voting power to elect a majority of the board of directors. If a board acts contrary to the wishes of the majority shareholder(s), the majority will quickly remove them from office and replace them with more compatible directors. The minority, while it does not have such a practical solution, is not without recourse altogether. A variety of corporate and judicial remedies are available, although some of them are quite confrontational and expensive. This section will lay out the rights that the minority has and several dispute-resolving devices. Many of these are based on careful planning and are preventative rather than remedial. Others are reactive and often involve costly litigation. Clearly, initial planning for dispute-avoiding or -resolving systems would be preferable.

Because the minority usually is not in a position to establish corporate policy, its main concerns involve the honesty of management, protection of its investment, and freedom from oppression. These issues break down into very discrete problems. For instance, the minority want to be sure that corporate profits are not being siphoned off into salary, perks, or benefits for management personnel. They want management to pursue corporate goals, rather than their own interests, and to act to improve corporate performance. Finally, they expect corporate decision making to be geared to those ends and not toward "freezing them out" of the corporation.

The problem of siphoned-off corporate profits is not an uncommon one. The possibility of dividends and the increase in the value of the corporation depend upon showing satisfactory and growing profits; therefore, any decrease in profits generally works to the disadvantage of the shareholders. If, however, those profits are diverted from the corporate treasury into the hands of management, and the management personnel are members of the majority group (or associated with it), the majority is clearly profiting at the expense of the minority. This diversion of funds is often accomplished by increasing the salaries of management or by increasing or creating new benefits for such personnel. The effect is to decrease the profits of the corporation and put what would have been the minority's share of those profits into the hands of the majority.

Similarly, the majority might make decisions that favor their own interests at the expense of the minority. When this happens, it raises issues concerning the duties owed by corporate fiduciaries to the minority shareholders. For instance, if the majority has an interest in another business that has dealings with the corporation (that are particularly beneficial to the other business), they may again be siphoning off corporate profits that, nevertheless, give them financial benefit. On a more subtle level, the majority can obtain a higher price per share for the sale of its stock than can the minority. This higher price is known as a *premium for control*, and is not, *per se*, illegal. Owning a majority of the stock of a corporation allows the owner to control it, and that control may be a valuable commodity. Nevertheless, the majority may not sell the control of the corporation at a premium to one whom he or she has reason to believe will not act in the corporation's best interests.

Finally, the majority may try to freeze out the minority. This is often attempted through a recapitalization, in which the financial structure of the corporation is revised or manipulated to the benefit of the majority interests. An extreme example would be an attempt to dilute the financial interests of the minority shareholders.

Suppose that there are two shareholders: one owning 600 shares and the other owning 400 shares of the corporation, which is the total of all authorized shares. Assume the corporation is worth $100,000, making each share worth $100 ($100,000 divided by 1,000 = $100). The value of the majority's holding is $60,000, while the minority's is worth $40,000. If the majority assumes that the minority will not make a further investment in the corporation, it may, based on that assumption, cause the corporation to issue new shares. It will accomplish this by having the board amend the Articles to create the additional authorized shares and issue them. If it issues the shares at a price far below their true value, the effect will be to injure the minority not only by lowering the minority's percentage interest in the corporation but also by lowering the value of its holding.

To continue with the example, suppose there are 1,000 new shares issued at only $10 per share. If pre-emptive rights apply, each shareholder will have the first right to purchase his or her proportionate share of the new offering. If, however, the majority's gamble is correct and the minority does not purchase its share, the majority can then purchase all of the issue for a price of $10,000 (1,000 shares at $10 per share). The result would be twofold: First, the majority would now own 1,600 shares of the 2,000 shares outstanding, or 80 percent rather than 60 percent of the corporation's stock. Second, the value per share of the corporation would have dropped from $100 to only $55. This is because the corporation, which was worth $100,000, has had $10,000 of net assets added to it. Therefore the value of the corporation has increased by $10,000. However, the number of shares has increased by 1,000, making a total of 2,000 shares outstanding. Dividing the value of the corporation by the number of outstanding shares gives a value per share of $55 ($110,000 divided by 2,000). The 400 shares of the minority, which were worth $40,000 before the recapitalization, are worth only $22,000 after it. This is true despite the fact that the corporation has increased in value. If, on the other hand, the shares had been purchased at their fair value, the second 1,000 shares would have cost the majority $100,000 ($100 per share times 1,000 shares). This would have increased the total value of the corporation to $200,000, and the value of the shares would have remained at $100 each ($200,000 divided by 2,000). The minority's interest would thus have retained its $40,000 value (400 shares times $100 per share), and although its percentage of ownership would have diminished, the financial value of its holding would not.

This system of recapitalization is often used to force minority shareholders to sell out to the majority at an unfavorable price. The majority may be attempting to sell the whole company to an outside buyer and wants to be rid of a potentially troublesome shareholder, or it may just be seeking to maximize its control or financial interest. In any event, the process, which is known as "freezing out" the minority, is a breach of the duties that corporate fiduciaries owe to minority shareholders in the corporation. As such, it is actionable by the minority, who can attempt to have the recapitalization declared void or to recover damages for any loss they suffered due to it.

This is not to say, however, that a recapitalization is never permissible. In fact, many recapitalizations are necessary or desirable for the financial health of the corporation. The problem arises when the recapitalization is attempted where there is no legitimate business reason and it does harm to the minority shareholders. If there is a business reason and the terms of the recapitalization are fair, the fact that a minority shareholder is injured in the process is not actionable. Fiduciaries do not guarantee the success of each decision nor do they shield all shareholders from injury from a particular decision. The duty of the majority (and of all fiduciaries) is only to act in the best interests of the corporation and to use due care in the process, not to protect each shareholder against injury from otherwise legitimate decisions.

PREPLANNED DISPUTE RESOLUTION

Recognizing that there are several areas in closely held corporations where disputes are likely, prudent organizers often set up mechanisms in advance that are designed to address and, they hope, to resolve those disputes. This section will point out several of the common areas of serious dispute and some of the mechanisms that can be used to head them off or to provide a context for their resolution.

Building dispute-resolution techniques into the fabric of a

closely held corporation is an important consideration for its organizers. In smaller corporations, where there is a close identity between ownership and management, the possibility of dispute is far greater than in corporations where ownership is dispersed and distant from management. In the latter situation, management often functions in isolation from the shareholders. In the closely held corporation, however, this is rarely true. Differences of opinion or even of style between the principals often arise that, in the absence of a mechanism for resolving them, may lead to serious corporate discord and conflict. The product of such dissension may be deadlocked corporate decision making as well as financial losses for the business. If the downward spiral remains unchecked, litigation and dissolution of the corporation are possible.

Disputes in closely held corporations typically arise in the following areas:

- right to manage the corporation

- deadlock in decision making

- transactions involving the shares of the corporation.

The most basic of these potential disputes is deciding who among the various shareholders is to manage the affairs of the corporation. If there is no clear majority shareholder (as when two shareholders each own 50 percent of the stock), deadlock is possible. Where higher than majority vote (i.e., 2/3 majority) is required in order to pass corporate resolutions, even a shareholder with 60 percent of the stock may not be able to put through corporate resolutions and control the corporation. On the other hand, where there *is* a shareholder with enough shares to determine the outcome of corporate votes, the minority shareholders will want to protect their access to the decision-making process and, if possible, build in controls to give them some power over the direction of the corporation.

Participation on the Board

Assuring minority shareholders a voice in corporate governance is the least complex of the various dispute resolution mechanisms. It is accomplished by providing a method for the minority to place at least one person on the board of directors or other governing body of the corporation. Generally, this is done through the technique of a *shareholders' agreement* (which is nothing more than a contract between the shareholders), in which each shareholder contracts to vote for the other (or for his or her nominee) for the board of directors. In this way, each shareholder, assuming no other shareholders enter the corporation, is assured of election to the board. In addition, the agreement as well as the Articles and bylaws can provide that no new shareholders will be admitted to the corporation unless they commit themselves to the shareholders' agreement and to electing each shareholder to the board. A sample provision assuring minority shareholders a place on the board follows:

> *Each of the undersigned shareholders agrees that so long as he or she remains a shareholder in the Corporation, he or she shall vote his or her respective shares for the election of the following persons, so long as they remain shareholders of the Corporation, as directors of the Corporation:*
> *1) _____*
> *2) _____*
> *3) _____*

Avoiding Deadlocks on the Board

A corollary to the problem of minority representation on the board is the problem of a deadlock on the board or among the shareholders. Most shareholders would agree that a deadlock should be avoided. Therefore, if there is a board of directors for the corporation (many states no longer require boards in closely held corporations), it might be wise to provide for an odd number of directors, with the deciding vote in the hands of a person agreed upon in advance by each shareholder before any conflict has arisen. Where there are two equal shareholders, they could create a three-person board on which each of the shareholders hold one seat and the third seat is held by a mutually agreed upon person. If both shareholders agree on a particular item, they will, of course, vote together and move on. If they disagree and cannot come to an accommodation, the third director will decide the matter by voting with one or the other of the shareholders. Similarly, if there is no board of directors and the shareholders manage the corporation directly (which is permitted under the corporation statute of several states), the shareholders could arrange for the third person to have one share of stock. The third person would, again, be in a position to break a deadlock between the two major shareholders.

Where there is to be a board, this method of dispute resolution requires that the Articles or bylaws provide for an odd number of directors. The shareholders would then enter into a shareholders' agreement in which they would agree, among other things, to elect each other and the third person to the board. In order to be able to keep an agreed-upon third person on the board (the third person may become disabled or die or may not want or be able to continue as a director), the third person should not be named but be described as, for instance, the president of the local chamber of commerce or the corporation's attorney or banker. The agreement might also provide for second or third choices (again, by description) in the event the first choice declines to serve.

Another way to accomplish the seating of a third person on the board would be to provide for an additional shareholder and give him or her one share of the corporation. Depending on the answer to various tax questions (which concern the desirability of subchapter S tax status), this share may be of the same class as the other shares or may be of a different class with very circumscribed voting and financial rights. In such a case, there would still be a shareholders' agreement in which the shareholders agree to vote themselves onto the board. Again, the deadlock would be broken. Keep in mind, however, that the broken deadlock might be at the expense of one of the main shareholders. That fact might increase strife within the corporation, but it might also force the disagreeing parties to compromise rather than face the possibility of complete defeat on an issue.

Arbitration and Mediation Agreements

Another way to deal with disputes is to provide for compulsory arbitration or mediation to resolve them. These methods avoid the necessity of having a nonprincipal regularly involved in the affairs of the corporation. On the other hand, they involve slower processes and potentially expensive ones. In essence, *arbitration* is the submission of a dispute to a private person who listens to evidence and argument on both sides and then renders a decision to resolve the dispute. The arbitrator's function is much like that of a judge, and an arbitration hearing has many of the characteristics of a trial. It is, however, much less formal than a court trial and is generally speedier and cheaper. Nevertheless, it does require some time, energy, and expense to complete. The American Arbitration Association, a well-known organization that conducts many complex arbitrations, has a set of rules that govern its hearings and procedures. It also maintains a large roster of arbitrators in many fields of activity.

Mediation is somewhat different than arbitration. In this process there may not be a hearing or even a decision. Instead, the mediator attempts to assist the parties to reach a settlement themselves. The mediator will often listen to each side, many times without the other side present, and will attempt to find areas of agreement or of compromise for the parties to explore. There are no formal rules for mediation, and almost anyone, such as a mutual friend or respected individual, can act as a mediator. Professional mediators are trained in methods designed to get parties to see the benefit of agreement and to help them find a basis on which to agree. The costs of this process are generally less than those of arbitration, and it is less formal and less time-consuming. It is also not guaranteed to resolve the dispute. Unlike arbitration, where the parties are bound to a decision reached by the arbitrator, mediation does not result in a decision by any third party. Nothing requires the parties to agree or binds them to a decision. If they do not come to an agreement themselves, the dispute remains unresolved.

The mechanics of establishing an arbitration or mediation requirement for dispute resolution are relatively simple. The shareholders can, through a shareholders' agreement, bind themselves to go through an arbitration process (the result of which may be binding on the parties or merely advisory) or through mediation. If such a provision is included in a shareholders' agreement, a court will enforce it in the event one party to a dispute refuses to comply. Moreover, if the parties have agreed to binding arbitration, a court, in all but the most unusual situations, will enforce the decision of the arbitrator.

Examples of typical clauses that establish the arbitration or mediation requirement follow:

ARBITRATION CLAUSE: Should any dispute or controversy as to the meaning, interpretation, or performance of this Shareholders' Agreement arise between any parties hereto, any such party may require that the dispute or controversy be submitted for binding arbitration, to be conducted in the city of _____, according to the rules and procedures of the American Arbitration Association then in effect. Judgment upon an award resulting from such arbitration may be entered in any court having jurisdiction thereof.

MEDIATION CLAUSE: Should any dispute or controversy as to the meaning, interpretation, or performance of this Shareholders' Agreement arise between any parties hereto, any such party may require that the dispute or controversy be submitted to mediation by a panel of mediators to be selected as follows. Each party to the dispute shall select a person to be a member of the panel and the persons so selected shall select one additional person who shall chair such panel. The procedures for the mediation shall be established by the mediation panel.

Buy/Sell Agreements

One of the prime concerns of the shareholders of a closely held corporation is who else will be a shareholder in the corporation. As has been mentioned, there is often a close relationship between ownership and management of such a corporation; therefore, the identity of the new shareholders is of some significance to the existing shareholders. Because of this fact, there are often *transfer restrictions* attached to the shares of closely held corporations. These restrictions usually require that any shareholder who wishes to sell his or her shares must offer them first to the corporation and, if the corporation does not agree to buy them back, to the remaining shareholders in proportion to their existing holdings. Similarly, if a shareholder receives an offer to purchase his or her shares from outside the corporation, the shareholder is typically obligated to give the corporation and, if the corporation declines, the other shareholders, the right to match the offer. These two restrictions help to preserve the composition of the corporation and allow new members to join the corporation only when they have been approved by the existing shareholders.

These restrictions, however, do not permit the preservation of the existing composition in all circumstances. For instance, when a shareholder dies, his or her shares pass into the control of the decedent's personal representative and then are divided among the heirs of the deceased shareholder. This process puts the shares into the hands of shareholders with whom the remaining shareholders have not agreed to go into business and whom they had no opportunity to approve. To avoid this situation, shareholders often include "buy/sell" agreements in their shareholders' agreements. The buy/sell agreements set out certain circumstances in which the remaining shareholders or the corporation have the right to require a shareholder to transfer his or her shares to them or to the corporation. Although some would call a requirement that the shares be sold to the corporation a *stock retirement agreement*, for the purpose of this discussion the term *buy/sell agreement* will be used to cover either or both of these situations.

Any event that places the shares of an existing shareholder into the hands of a nonshareholder as a matter of law can trigger a buy/ sell agreement. This includes transfers that were not voluntarily made by the shareholder but were made pursuant to legal requirements. Included in this definition, of course, is the death of a shareholder. Also included are such events as his or her bankruptcy, insanity, or any other disability that would place the shareholder's affairs in the hands of a trustee or conservator. In such a case the buy/ sell agreement sets out the procedures by which the corporation or the shareholders can purchase the shares. It also typically sets out a formula for establishing the price to be paid for the shares as well as the terms of payment.

Among the problems the corporation or the shareholders face in exercising their rights pursuant to a buy/sell agreement is how to fund the purchase of the shares. Small corporations rarely have the luxury of a surplus of available cash with which to make the purchase. Therefore, a system must be put in place that will provide the funds when needed. This may be accomplished through the establishment of a sinking fund or through the purchase of life or disability insurance on each shareholder with the corporation named as beneficiary. Then, if the shareholder dies or becomes disabled, thus triggering the buy/sell agreement, the corporation will have the cash to purchase the shares.

The buy/sell agreement could also establish a pay-out period for the purchase of the shares. For instance, the buyer might make a down payment of a certain percentage of the purchase price, paying the balance over a predetermined period at interest. This arrangement allows the buyer to maintain a better cash position but means that the seller must wait to be paid, which may be a hardship if the shareholder who died or became disabled was the main breadwinner in his or her family. Each party to the buy/sell agreement must consider carefully how best to accommodate the needs of the corporation, his or her own needs, and family needs in the event that he or she is the one who is forced to sell.

Another situation that might be used to trigger the buy/sell agreement deserves some attention: It is the resignation or discharge of a shareholder/employee. In many small corporations, the principals consider it important that all shareholders participate directly in the operation or management of the business. When a shareholder is no longer participating, the remaining shareholders may want to purchase the shares owned by that shareholder. This situation becomes more difficult when the departing shareholder was discharged. The freezing out of a minority interest might be implicated in such an action by the corporation.

The remaining issues to be discussed concerning the buy/sell agreement are the timing of the events and the price to be paid for the stock. While it is generally possible to establish a price or price formula that can be used no matter which circumstance triggers the buy/sell agreement, each type of triggering event may have a different time frame in which the corporation and shareholders must act.

For instance, the timing of the right to purchase the shares of a deceased shareholder would probably be set so as to begin shortly after the personal representative of the decedent was appointed by the court. On the other hand, it would be some time before it could be determined whether a disabled shareholder could return to his or her duties with the corporation. In such a case the time frame for the buyer to exercise his, her, or its rights might be set at some number of months after the shareholder became disabled. If the disability were of the sort to require the appointment of a trustee or conservator to handle the affairs of the shareholder, the timing should be set, as in the case of a deceased shareholder, to begin after the appointment of the trustee. The timing requirements would change again in the event that a shareholder resigned from the corporation or was discharged. Here, the parties would presumably want the timing to be accelerated. Since the departing shareholder is immediately available to complete the transaction, speeding up the process should present few practical problems.

Keep in mind that in each of these cases the question of timing is intertwined with the shareholders' and the corporation's ability to pay for the shares to be purchased as well as their desire to do so. For instance, it is possible that an outside buyer (assuming the shareholders and corporation declined to purchase the shares) might be someone who would be an asset to the business and whom the other shareholders would welcome as a colleague. The *right* to buy the shares does not *require* the shareholders or the corporation to buy them.

Determining the price of the shares is a somewhat difficult exercise. Valuing a business, complicated at any time, becomes significantly more difficult when the valuation is an attempt to predict the future worth of the company. Making such a prediction is precisely what the shareholders are doing in creating a price for the buy/sell agreement. No shareholder knows when the buy/sell agreement will be triggered or whether he or she will be the seller or one of the remaining shareholders of the buying corporation. Clearly, the corporation will have an interest in buying available shares at the lowest possible price, but each shareholder will have an interest in securing the highest possible price in the event he or she is forced to sell.

The shareholders, therefore, have an incentive to moderate their demands and to arrive at reasonable solutions to the pricing problem. These solutions generally take the form of one or more formulas to establish the price of the shares at any particular time. Often, there is what is known in computer parlance as a "default" solution, which means that the parties will be left to negotiate the terms of the sale and purchase of the shares, but, in the absence of an agreement within a specified time, the default solution, found in the buy/sell agreement, will apply.

The pricing formulas found in the buy/sell agreements can be tied to any of several factors. For example, the formula might provide for a return of the shareholder's capital investment, together with a premium of a certain percentage per year for each year the corporation was in business until the purchase. Formulas might also be tied to the "book value" of the shares. *Book value* is an accounting concept that prices the company according to its net asset value as shown by its books. Thus, one would total up the value of the corporation's assets as carried on its balance sheets or other financial records and subtract from this figure its total liabilities as shown on the books. The result would be divided by the number of shares outstanding in order to arrive at a figure for the book value per share.

The advantage of this system of valuation is that it is very simple and inexpensive to use. The data upon which it is based are already available to the corporation through the normal entries in its financial books. The disadvantage of using this method is that the accounting principles for valuing assets are quite different from the methods used in the marketplace. Moreover, factors such as "good will" or "going concern value" are usually figured very conservatively. In order to get a more accurate reading of the value of the company, shareholders have attempted various other formulas. One of them is a figure based upon a multiple of corporate earnings or of gross revenue.

Over time, people involved with the purchase and sale of businesses have recognized that within a particular industry and geographic area, there is a relationship between the sales price of a business and the profit it earned in the year prior to the sale or between that price and the gross revenue it received during the year. For instance, a manufacturing company in the Midwest might sell for 10 times its earnings (profits). Thus, if the company made a profit of $100,000 during the last year, it would sell for $1 million. Similarly, if such a company normally sells for 1.2 times its gross revenues and it had receipts of $800,000, the sales price would be $960,000 ($800,000 x 1.2). Historical demands largely govern the choice of index (profit or revenue). If a particular industry is usually judged by revenues rather than profits, that would be the measure that would normally be employed, and vice versa.

Once again, there are advantages and disadvantages to this method. The advantages are tied to speed and to the minor expense involved. The disadvantage is that the formulas are based on a typical company in the field and not on the particular company in question. For instance, if the company has particular elements of value that are unique to it, such as a new contract that will produce significantly increased revenue and profit in the next year, these will not be accounted for in the formula. In order to cure this defect, parties sometimes call for an appraisal of the company. This is probably the most accurate method of valuing the company (short of putting it on the market and seeing what independent buyers would pay for it), but it is also the most time-consuming and expensive.

An *appraisal* involves bringing in an outside expert who is experienced in determining the value of businesses. The appraiser will use a variety of methods, including several that have been discussed here, to calculate the value of the company. By looking at historical relationships between income and value; by identifying the trends in the company's business fortunes; by evaluating the nature, condition, and outside usefulness of its assets; by crediting the good will of the business; and by evaluating the results of each of these examinations, the appraiser comes up with a value for the company.

Regardless of how well-intentioned and thorough the appraisal, it is still nothing more than an educated guess as to what an outside buyer would pay for the company. The marketplace is what really sets the value of a company. On the other hand, accuracy may not be the most important factor in setting a price formula for a buy/sell agreement. All parties to such an agreement have an interest in the fairness of the price and the efficient use of time and resources to arrive at it. Therefore, the shareholders might be (at least at the planning stage) willing to give up some accuracy for the benefits to be derived from a speedy and inexpensive transition once the buy/sell agreement is triggered.

Finally, many agreements, recognizing the problems associated with each of these valuation methods, call for a purchase price to be established initially and then reviewed annually. The method of arriving at such a price may be any one of those already discussed, a combination of them, or, for that matter, just agreements between the shareholders based on their own experience of the value of the corporation. Such agreements usually require the shareholders to establish in writing the price to be applied for the following year. If they cannot agree upon a price, the buy/sell agreement might provide that the last agreed-upon written price is the buy/sell price or, if the last agreed upon price is more than, for example, two years old, that it is the last price plus, for instance, 5 percent per year from the date of the last written valuation. Remember, these agreements are designed to work for the shareholders and the corporation and can be drafted to include a wide variety of devices designed to reach a fair result. A sample buy/sell agreement is included in the appendix to this chapter.

SHAREHOLDER DERIVATIVE SUITS AND CORPORATE DISSOLUTION

When disputes cannot be resolved through negotiation or pre-existing dispute-resolution mechanisms, the remaining avenues open to the minority shareholders are either to begin a lawsuit or to seek the dissolution of the corporation. Both of these are extreme remedies that should not be undertaken on a whim. This section will discuss the rationale and mechanics of each remedy and will suggest that in most cases it would be advantageous for the shareholders to find some other way to resolve their dispute.

Shareholder Derivative Suits

Shareholder derivative suits are devices by which minority interests can seek judicial redress for wrongs allegedly committed against the corporation by the majority interests. You will recall that one of the fundamental aspects of corporate existence is that it shields the owners and managers of the corporation from liability to outsiders for the wrongs committed *by* the corporation. This protection does not include wrongs done *to* the corporation by the shareholders, directors, or officers. In fact, the duties owed by fiduciaries to their corporation (which were discussed earlier in this chapter) are enforced, in the last instance, by the corporation suing the fiduciary who breached the duty and caused it harm. Because the duty is owed to the corporation, it is the corporation that must bring the suit to recover for injuries done to it.

Unfortunately, it is often members of the majority position who commit the wrong, and it is very unlikely that they will vote to have the corporation bring a lawsuit against themselves. In order to vindicate the corporation's rights, therefore, the law has developed the concept of *shareholder derivative suits*. Basically, this concept allows a shareholder to bring a suit in the name of the corporation in order to protect a corporate right or to remedy a wrong done to the corporation. The shareholder is the one who instigates the suit and prosecutes it, but the real beneficiary of the suit is the corporation, not the shareholder. This is distinct from the situation when a wrong is done to the shareholder himself or herself, such as when the corporation declares a dividend but does not pay it to a particular shareholder.

The theory behind derivative suits is that a shareholder, being distinct from the corporation, claims rights of the corporation only derivatively through it. For instance, assume a shareholder owns 25 percent of the stock of a corporation. If that corporation earns a $1,000 profit, the shareholder has no direct claim to $250 (25 percent of the profit). Instead, he or she must wait until the corporation decides, if it ever does, to declare a dividend of all or part of that profit. Similarly, if the corporation suffers a loss of $1,000 because a third party has breached a contract with it, the shareholder cannot sue in his or her individual capacity to claim the $1,000 (or even a 25 percent share of it) because the contract was with the corporation and not with the shareholder. The breach injured the corporation directly and the shareholder was injured only indirectly; that is, through the reduction in the value of the corporation (and, thus, the shareholder's stock) by the amount of the loss.

Because the corporation is recognized by the law as a "person," it can sue directly for wrongs committed against it. If the wrong is committed by a third party with whom the corporation has no continuing relationship, the board of directors might, in fact, decide to have the corporation sue the wrongdoer. In that case, the suit would be the typical situation of a plaintiff (in this case the corporation) suing a defendant. If however, the wrong is committed by a third party who has some current or potential connection with the corporation, the board will be less likely to sue. When the wrong is committed by a fiduciary of the corporation, particularly one in a controlling position, the board will be *very* unlikely to vote to have the corporation sue.

In order to protect the minority against a situation where the majority refuses to institute suit in the corporate name, the law allows a shareholder (who is usually among the minority shareholders) to do so. The suit is brought in the name and for the benefit of the corporation, not the individual shareholder(s) who institute the suit. They benefit, if they prevail, by having the injury to the corporation rectified, generally by a cash award paid to the corporation by the wrongdoer. This payment will increase the value of the corporation and, therefore, the value of the stock held by the shareholders.

Although the theory concerning derivative suits is relatively simple once one is comfortable with the separate identity of the corporation, the application of the theory has caused problems for the courts for years. The most difficult issue is deciding when a suit is for the benefit of the corporation and when it is for the benefit of the shareholder, directly. The result of this inquiry determines whether a suit is derivative in nature. If it is, there are several procedural differences in conducting the suit and, of course, any judgment in the suit would go to the corporation, not to the shareholders.

The requirements for bringing a derivative suit are generally set out in a state's statutes or in its court rules. The most common requirements are that a shareholder bringing the suit must have been a shareholder at the time the alleged wrong was committed and also at the time the suit is brought. The shareholder must show either that he or she has demanded that the corporation bring the suit and has been refused or else show why it would have been futile to make the demand. Clearly, there is good reason to require one who wishes to represent the corporation in a suit to request that the corporation, itself, act in its own interest. If it agrees, there is no need for the derivative suit.

The shareholder must also show that he or she adequately represents the other shareholders of the corporation because a judgment will bind them all, even if they do not join in the suit.

Many states also require, upon a motion of the defendant, that a shareholder with a very small stake in the corporation (often this threshold is set at 5 percent of the stock or $50,000 in value) post a bond in order to continue the litigation. This expensive device is designed to keep very minor shareholders from instituting suits against their corporations in the hope of being paid off by the corporation to avoid the nuisance of a law suit. In large, publicly traded corporations, attempts to receive such payoffs have become known as "green mail" and have been in the news over the last several years.

In addition to the posting of a bond, many states have instituted rules requiring judicial approval of any settlement of a derivative suit before judgment. The rationale here is similar to that of requiring a bond. It is thought that once a suit is begun, the courts should supervise any settlement to protect the interests of the corporation and its other shareholders. Otherwise, the suit could be dismissed, and the wrongdoers could pay the individual shareholder(s) who brought the suit an inordinately high price to "buy" their shares in the corporation. Therefore, any proposed settlement of derivative suits, once they have been filed, must be presented to the court for a hearing as to its fairness.

Interestingly, because the corporation is not voluntarily bringing the suit as the plaintiff, it must be brought involuntarily before the court as a defendant. The court must have jurisdiction over the corporation because the court will be adjudicating the corporation's rights. This is somewhat confusing because the plaintiffs are not suing the corporation but are trying to represent the corporation in a suit against someone else. In fact, the title of the case on the court papers will be something like the following:

> *Jacki Bruce,*   )
> *suing derivatively on behalf of XYZ, Inc.,*   )
> *Plaintiff*   )
>   )
> *vs.*   )
> *XYZ, Inc.*   )
> *Daniel Doe,*   )
> *and Rhonda Roe,*   )
> *Defendants*   )
> _____)

This caption indicates that shareholder Jacki Bruce is suing on behalf of XYZ, Inc., for some wrong done to it. Because this is a derivative suit, the corporation has apparently refused to bring the suit itself. It is named as a defendant in the suit in order to bring it before the court so that its rights can be adjudicated. Also named as defendants are the persons whom the plaintiff believes actually committed the wrong against the corporation. If the plaintiff is successful, a judgment will be entered against Daniel Doe and Rhonda Roe and in favor of XYZ, Inc. The corporation will collect the judgment, and Ms. Bruce's interests will have been vindicated by the restoration of the corporation to its pre-injury position.

Derivative suits play a role in closely held corporations that can be both constructive and destructive. On the constructive side, they are a means by which minority shareholders can protect their rights against overreaching by the majority. The fact that the shareholders have this weapon in their arsenal may even increase the possibility of negotiated settlements of internal disputes. As long as the right to sue and the realistic possibility of using it exists, the minority shareholders have some leverage to protect their interests and, in many cases, the interests of the corporation.

On the other hand, such suits are often evidence of how intractable the internal situation in the corporation has become. They are also very destructive of the corporation's business. Aside from the great expense of litigating such a suit, an enormous amount of time and energy must be devoted to maintaining it. This time and energy will be taken from what is normally given to conducting the affairs of the corporation. In addition, the instituting of a derivative suit makes public the problems within the corporation. All of these factors will have a negative impact on the corporation and on its ability to conduct its business. While such suits are not necessarily the death knell for the corporation, they often do inflict wounds from which the corporation will not recover. Therefore, the desirability of pre-existing dispute-resolution devices cannot be over-emphasized. They can help avoid major disputes; help resolve them if they occur; and help to narrow the issues (and, therefore, the time, energy, and expense) if litigation cannot be avoided.

Dissolution

Perhaps the ultimate injury to be wrought by dissension within a corporation is its involuntary dissolution while it still has the potential to prosper. When a dispute leads to a deadlock within a corporation or when the relationships between the principals is such as to make it impossible for them to work together, dissolution may be the result. Most states provide for two types of dissolution: voluntary and judicial. Voluntary dissolution normally requires the vote of the shareholders, whereas judicial dissolution may be obtained by dissatisfied shareholders for various reasons, including oppression of the minority by the majority, deadlock, or mismanagement. A third type is the time-honored *dissolution in fact*. This occurs when a corporation, usually one without assets, merely stops functioning. The shareholders, officers, and directors abandon it and fail to file the annual reports required by the state. After a period of nonfiling, the state will generally revoke the charter of the corporation, thereby terminating its existence.

Voluntary dissolution

State statutes providing for *voluntary dissolution* of corporations set out the procedures that must be followed in order for the corporation to dissolve. The board of directors must adopt a resolution recommending to the shareholders that the corporation dissolve. The board then calls a meeting of the shareholders and gives them notice that its purpose is to vote on the board's recommendation that the corporation should dissolve. Once the shareholders accept the recommendation, the corporation files a document indicating its intent to dissolve with the appropriate state official. The document normally will include the following information:

- name of the corporation
- names and addresses of its officers and directors
- resolution of the shareholders authorizing dissolution
- number of shares outstanding and any provisions concerning voting by classes of shares
- vote, including the vote by class if class voting is required, for and against the resolution to dissolve.

Upon filing this document, the corporation ceases doing business except as is necessary to wind up its affairs. This usually means it may continue to collect its accounts receivable and to begin assembling and liquidating its assets. It may also complete work in progress but may not take on any new work. It must pay its debts or make provision for their payment. Keep in mind that these events do not dissolve the corporation or end its existence. Dissolution only occurs when the affairs of the corporation are wound up and it files its Articles of Dissolution.

The Articles of Dissolution, like the Articles of Incorporation, is a document that is filed with the state. It has a profound effect on the corporation because it is the document that ends the corporation's legal existence. These Articles contain information about the corporation and its winding up:

- name of the corporation

- that it has filed a certificate of intent to dissolve and the date of that filing

- that the debts of the corporation have been paid or adequate provision has been made for their payment and discharge

- that the remaining property of the corporation has been distributed to the shareholders according to their rights and liquidation preferences

- that there are no lawsuits pending against the corporation or that adequate provision has been made for the payment of any judgment that may be entered against it in a pending suit.

Once this document is filed, the state official will issue a certificate of dissolution, at which time the corporation ceases to exist.

Involuntary dissolution

The other method of dissolution and, generally, the more devastating one, is *involuntary dissolution*. This procedure may be undertaken in most states when one or more shareholders who do not have sufficient votes to effect a voluntary dissolution are convinced that the problems within the corporation are insurmountable and insoluble. The basis for their suit will usually be that there has been mismanagement of the corporation or oppression of the minority or, in some cases, deadlock in the decision-making apparatus. These shareholders will ask the courts to intervene and to order the dissolution of the enterprise. The courts traditionally have been reluctant to do this because it puts them in the middle of an internal struggle between the shareholders. They are being asked to substitute their judgment as to the best interests of the corporation for that of the board of directors—elected officials who, presumably, know the corporation and its best interests better than any outsider could. Therefore, the courts are not required to order a dissolution upon a request by the minority interests. Instead, they will examine each case on its own merits and determine whether there are grounds for a dissolution and, if so, whether the interests of the parties and of the public are better served by denying the request and requiring the corporation and its shareholders to resolve their internal difficulties.

An involuntary dissolution proceeding is normally instituted by filing a petition with the courts. Even though state laws may differ on this subject, usually the petition must allege, among other things:

- that the petitioners are shareholders of the corporation

- that there has been some serious wrong committed against the corporation, the minority shareholders, or the public or that the corporation is deadlocked

- that the petitioners have sought relief from the corporation and failed to receive it or that seeking such relief would be futile.

If the court orders dissolution of the corporation, it may require the board to present a plan of dissolution that makes provision for the payment of the corporation's debts and for a fair distribution of its remaining assets to the shareholders. If the court finds that there has been some wrongdoing by the corporation's management that has harmed the corporation or the minority shareholders, the court may award damages to the injured party(s) as well.

Because the time of the suit may not be a propitious time for the termination of the corporate business and the liquidation of its assets, the courts will normally try to find another avenue of resolving the dispute. The problems brought on by involuntary dissolution may also act as an incentive to the shareholders to work out their differences in some less intrusive way. Once again, the importance of pre-existing dispute-resolution mechanisms cannot be overemphasized. They may provide a satisfactory method of heading off the drastic response of a shareholders' suit for involuntary dissolution.

APPENDIX 4.1
BUY/SELL AGREEMENT

This agreement, dated _____ _____ , 19 _____ , is between
_____ and _____ (collectively known as the Shareholders). In order to promote the interest of the Corporation and to assure its orderly operation, the Shareholders agree as follows:

1. (a) The Shareholders agree that they will not transfer, assign, sell, pledge, hypothecate, or otherwise dispose of the shares of stock owned by any of them, or the certificates of stock representing their interests, unless such shares of stock shall have been first offered to the Corporation according to the provisions of this Section. Such offer shall be made in writing and shall remain open for the Corporation's acceptance for a period of 30 days. In the event the Corporation wishes to accept the offer, it must agree in writing to purchase the entire amount of stock offered and shall at that time make a down payment of 10 percent of the purchase price. The balance of the purchase price shall be paid as provided in Section 1(e) of this agreement. If the Corporation should choose not to purchase the shares within 30 days, they shall then be offered to the remaining Shareholders on a pro rata basis. Such offer shall be made in writing and shall remain open for a period of 30 days. In the event any Shareholder wishes to accept the offer, he or she must agree in writing to purchase any or all of his or her pro rata portion of shares and make a down payment in the amount of 10 percent of the purchase price. The balance of the purchase price shall be paid as provided in Section 1(e) of this agreement. If any Shareholder should elect not to purchase his or her pro rata portion, or should purchase less than the full amount, the remainder shall be offered for a period of thirty (30) days to the other Shareholders on a pro rata basis. The amount of stock that remains unpurchased after this offering to the Shareholders shall be freely transferable and no longer subject to the provisions and limitations of this agreement.

(b) In the event any Shareholder receives a bona fide third-party offer to purchase his or her share, he or she shall provide to the other Shareholders the offer, in writing. Such Shareholders shall have 30 days from his or her receipt of the offer to agree to match its terms for the pro rata purchase of the offered shares. If any Shareholder declines to purchase the shares or if 30 days have elapsed since his or her receipt of the offer without his or her having responded to it, the offering party shall be free to transfer the shares to the third-party offeror.

(c) The Shareholders agree that upon the death of any of them, the executors, administrators, or legal representatives of the deceased shall, within 30 days after qualification as such, offer to sell to the corporation, all the shares of stock in _____, Inc., owned by the deceased at the time of his or her death. Such offer may remain open for 30 days from the corporation's receipt of said offer. In the event the corporation declines to purchase such shares or the time permitted for its acceptance of the offer has lapsed without acceptance, the executors, administrators, or legal representatives of the deceased shall offer the shares, pro rata, to the remaining Shareholders, who each shall have 30 days from their receipt of the offer in which to accept. The price per share and payment terms shall be as provided in Sections 1(d) and (e) of this agreement.

(d) For the purposes of this agreement except as provided in Subsection 1(b) hereof, the purchase price per share shall be determined by dividing the capital contributed by a selling Shareholder (or his/her assigns, decedent, etc.) by the number of shares held by such Shareholder and multiplying the quotient by 1.15 per year (or part of a year) from _____ _____ , 19 _____ , to the date of sale. For the purpose of this agreement, _____ and _____ shall be deemed to have contributed four hundred thousand ($400,000) dollars each.

(e) The purchase price as provided in Paragraph 1(d), shall be paid as follows: 10 percent in cash within 30 days after the acceptance of the offer to purchase shares of the Corporation. The balance shall be evidenced by a promissory note payable in three annual installments. Interest at the rate of 10 percent shall be calculated on the outstanding balance. The Corporation or any accepting Shareholder reserves the right to prepay the whole or any part of the amount owed without penalty.

2.   The parties agree that they will take no action nor dispose of their stock in such a way as to cause the termination of the Corporation's ability to be taxed as an electing small business corporation under Subchapter S of the Internal Revenue Code of 1954.

3.   Each stock certificate of the Corporation shall contain the following information:

Transfer or pledge of these shares is restricted under a Shareholders' Agreement dated _____ _____ , 19 _____ , . A copy of the agreement, which affects other rights of the holder of these shares, is on file at the office of the corporation at _____ Street, Washington, D.C. 200____.

IN WITNESS WHEREOF, the individual parties hereto set their hands and seals, and the Corporation has caused this agreement to be signed by its duly authorized officers and the corporate seal affixed.

_____

_____

Chapter 5

Buying and Selling the Corporation

Corporations are odd creatures. They are recognized by the law as separate entities and, therefore, can own their own property. On the other hand, they are the property of their shareholders. When an individual wishes to sell a piece of property, he or she seeks a buyer, negotiates a deal, hands over the property, and receives payment for it. When someone wants to sell a corporation, however, it is not quite so neat and simple a proposition. One's ownership of a corporation is different from the ownership of the corporation's property. For example, let us say you incorporated a taxicab company and owned all of its shares of stock. You would be the sole owner of the corporation. If you had contributed some money (or other capital) to it in exchange for those shares, you would own the shares and the corporation would own the money. Assume the corporation used the money you contributed to buy a new taxicab. The corporation would then own the cab. If the cab were used to earn money by charging fares to riders, the money would belong to the corporation. You might get a salary for the labor you perform for the corporation, but you would be paid from *corporate* funds.

To continue our example, assume that someone wanted to buy the taxicab business from you and you were inclined to sell it. There are at least two distinct ways in which this could be accomplished. The first, and, perhaps, the most obvious one, is to sell the buyer the taxicab. The buyer could then drive it and collect fares. The second typical method of transferring the business would be to sell the stock you originally obtained for your contribution of capital to the corporation. In either case, the buyer could still drive the cab and collect fares as you have been doing. However, the two transactions just described are very different for several reasons.

If the buyer buys the taxicab, the payment for the cab would go to the corporation, the cab's owner. The result would be that you would own all the stock of a corporation that owns a sum of money. On the other hand, if the buyer purchases stock, the payment would go to you, the stockholder, and you would then own the sum of money instead of the stock. The buyer becomes the owner of the stock of a corporation that owns a taxicab.

These examples are intended to show that, as simple as the sale of a taxicab business might seem, it is filled with significant choices, each with its own legal and practical implications. For instance, would it be more advantageous, from the tax and liability exposure perspectives, for the buyer to purchase the stock from the stockholder or the assets from the corporation? What are the tax consequences of selling (or buying) assets rather than stock? How are corporate liabilities dealt with in the different transactions? The questions become more numerous and complex as the transactions become larger and more involved.

This chapter will discuss some of those questions (while others, particularly those related to taxation, will be left for other chapters) and various methods for transferring a corporate business. It will examine the advantages, disadvantages, and procedures involved in particular methods and provide some practical examples and forms to help you structure your own transaction. As always, be conscious of the great complexity involved in many of these transactions and seek the advice and assistance of a trained professional before embarking on the purchase or sale of a business. With that in mind, let us begin our discussion with an examination of a basic transaction and then venture into more complex areas.

THE SALE BY A STOCKHOLDER OF CORPORATE STOCK

Among the most common corporate transactions is the sale of stock from one person (the shareholder) to another. In a typical situation, this transaction is carried out over one of the major stock exchanges, such as the New York or American Stock Exchange. A prospective buyer (or seller) of a particular company's stock calls his or her stockbroker to place a buy (or sell) order. The order may be at a particular price or at "market" (that is, at whatever price the market fixes for the stock at the time of the sale). The broker then calls the order in to a colleague who deals in that stock (known as a *specialist*) on the floor of the stock exchange. The specialist lets it be known that he or she has a certain number of shares of the corporation to buy or to sell. When another specialist dealing in the same stock has a client on the other side of the transaction (a buyer for a seller or vice versa), a deal is made. Neither principal need ever see the other or even know his or her identity. The buyer will get a certificate indicating ownership in a certain number of shares of the corporation (which shares were turned in to the broker by the seller), and the seller gets the price of those shares (which was paid to the broker by the buyer).

As common as this transaction is (and it is repeated millions of times each day), it is not the only way that shares can be transferred. There are also private, often face-to-face, transactions between buyers and sellers. These may occur when someone wants to buy (or sell) a very large block of shares in a publicly held corporation from (or to) a particular person or group. They also frequently occur in closely held corporations; that is, corporations whose stock is owned by only one person or by a small group of people and whose stock is not actively or widely traded. These sales or purchases often take place when one of the shareholders wishes to sell out (or when an offer is made to buy him or her out) or wishes to buy out one or more of the other shareholders. They also take place when an outsider is interested in purchasing the business or a significant part of it. In fact, in a closely held corporation private sales such as these are essentially the only way to buy or sell shares because, by definition, the shares of such a corporation are not traded on a public exchange. Thus, either through personal contacts, the contacts of a friend or colleague, advertisements, or through the use of a business broker (not to be confused with a stockbroker), potential buyers or sellers are identified. Should one or more of the potential buyers or sellers be interested in pursuing the matter, a negotiation begins, its goal being a contract for the sale of the shares.

Advantages and Disadvantages of the Transfer of Shares

Keep in mind here that shares of stock represent an ownership interest in the corporation, not in its property. In the most basic terms, if someone owns 50 percent of a corporation's stock, that person owns 50 percent of the corporation. If one has a controlling interest (through stock ownership) in a corporation, a transfer of the controlling block of shares also transfers control of the corporation. However, the ownership of shares is not the equivalent of ownership of the corporation's assets. Those are owned by the corporation, itself. The distinction between the ownership of the corporation and the ownership of its assets is important for several reasons. Among them are tax and business considerations as well as the issue of liability. The tax considerations were addressed in the chapter on taxation. Business considerations will be discussed throughout this chapter, while the issue of liability will be discussed next.

A corporation, which is recognized as a "person" under the law, is liable for its actions. Therefore, it can be sued and forced to pay for its wrongdoing. When a buyer purchases a business by buying its stock, the buyer sometimes takes control of a corporation that has hidden liabilities. This means that it may be subject to potential lawsuits of which the buyer and, perhaps, even the corporation and its selling shareholder(s) are unaware. If the corporation were ultimately found to be liable for any of its prior activities, it could be made to pay damages to the injured party. While this payment would come from the corporation itself and not directly from the buyers, the buyers would be harmed due to the decreased value of the corporation they had bought. There are, of course, methods by which the problem of hidden liabilities can be minimized, but each method has its own risks attached. These solutions and their risks will be addressed shortly.

There are also advantages to buying a business through the purchase of shares. It is often the simplest and quickest method of buying a business. If there is only one or a small group of shareholders of the corporation, the negotiations may run smoother. In addition, there may be fewer levels of corporate bureaucracy to contend with and fewer state and federal regulations to comply with. As has been mentioned, business and tax reasons may also play a role in determining why the purchase of stock would be more favorable than the purchase of assets. For instance, if a corporation had significant tax losses which would benefit a buying corporation, the purchase of stock would be a way to secure the use of those losses for the buyer while the purchase of assets would leave the loss carryover with the seller.

In addition, if the buyer were a going business and was attempting to buy a business in a different field, it might not want to combine the two businesses under the same corporate umbrella. It might, instead, choose to buy the shares of the new business, thus maintaining two separate corporations, each with its own separate identity. Of course, in the last example, the buying corporation could set up a new corporation and own all of its stock. It could then cause the newly formed corporation to purchase the assets of the selling corporation, and the buyer would have accomplished by a different means the same goal of separating the two businesses. This process would, however, be somewhat more complicated than the straight purchase of the existing company's shares by the parent company.

Methods of Purchase

There are several ways in which stock can be purchased. Most simply, it can be paid for with cash. It is not unusual, however, for stock to be bought with a combination of cash and promissory notes payable to the seller whereby the purchase price for the stock is paid out over a period of time. Stock may also be purchased for property, including the stock of another corporation. In the next section we will examine in some detail the purchase of stock for a combination of cash and note. Before we begin that examination, however, a brief discussion of the purchase of stock by the payment of property would be useful.

Assume, again, that you are the sole owner of the stock of a corporation that owns and operates a fleet of taxicabs. You are interested in selling that business, and you have found a buyer who wishes to purchase it. Once you have agreed that the buyer will purchase the corporation's stock and have arrived at a value for the business, the next question to be addressed is the method of payment. Each party will have to determine what is for him or her the optimum form of payment. He or she will take into account cash needs, the appreciation potential of any property that might be transferred, and the tax consequences of each potential method.

If you agree with the buyer to accept his or her art collection in exchange for the shares of the taxicab company, the result will be that you will own an art collection while the buyer will own all of the shares in a corporation that owns and operates a fleet of taxicabs. If you agree to accept as payment some (or all) of the shares owned by the buyer of a corporation that operates a bakery, the result of the transaction will be that you own some percentage (perhaps all) of the shares in a bakery corporation and the buyer will own all of the shares of a taxicab corporation. The question of the value of the art collection in the first example or the shares of stock in the bakery is one for the buyer and seller to resolve. It is more complex in terms of calculation but otherwise the same as determining the amount of cash to pay for the stock.

The "value" of a corporation is a nebulous concept. In the end, it is only what a willing buyer would pay a willing seller where neither party was compelled to buy or to sell. Sometimes, as was discussed previously, people attempt to establish the value of a corporation by adding the value of all the corporation's assets and subtracting from this the sum of all the corporate liabilities. This form of valuation, however, may not take into account, or may not account for properly, the intangibles of the corporation, such as its "going concern" value (which is the value of having a business already operating rather than having to start up from scratch) or its "good will" (which involves its good name and the loyalty of its customers) or future prospects.

Once the parties do agree on a value for the business, they must also agree on the value of the property to be exchanged for the stock. If it is the art collection, it must be appraised. If it is the stock of another corporation, that stock must be valued in a manner similar to the valuation of the corporation being sold. In each case, the valuation process is inexact, and, ultimately, it depends on the willingness of the parties to consummate the transaction. If the seller decides before finalizing the contract that he or she does not want the art collection, even if its value is comparable to the value of his or her stock, the deal will not be made. On the other hand, if the seller wants the art collection badly enough, even though its objective value is demonstrably less than the value of the shares, the deal may be concluded. This is essentially a private transaction, and, as such, it is subject to little outside regulation other than general legal rules against overreaching, fraud, and breach of duty to others (which was discussed in Chapter 4).

The more typical transaction, as has already been mentioned, involves the transfer of shares in exchange for a combination of cash and notes. This transaction will be discussed primarily through an examination of the essential elements of the documents that normally are part of it. These documents usually include a contract of sale, a promissory note, and a security agreement. There will normally also be various warranties of the sellers as well as a noncompetition clause. There may be other documents added as exhibits to those mentioned earlier and, occasionally, additional agreements (such as an employment contract for the seller) specifically addressing issues in a particular transfer. The documents that appear in this chapter in the appendix are not intended as exact models of such documents but merely as examples that include issues to be addressed and one way to resolve them. This section will present a discussion of both a contract for the sale of stock and a contract for the sale of assets. A sample contract for the sale of assets will be included in full at the end of this chapter. It contains many of the same paragraphs as would a contract for the sale of stock as well as those specifically addressed to an asset sale. Remember, however, that if you are involved in a transaction that calls for the use of one or more of these documents, you must be sure to obtain expert advice on how to draft it to suit your particular needs.

Contract for Sale of Corporate Stock

The contract, of course, will begin by identifying the parties and the date of the contract as well as stating briefly the purpose of the agreement. The language might be as follows:

> *This agreement, made this _____ day of _____, 199_,*
> *by and between Jacqueline Puck and Michael Herman*
> *(hereinafter referred to as Sellers) and Cheverly Shepherd*
> *(hereinafter referred to as Buyer), is for the purpose of setting*
> *out the rights and responsibilities of the parties in relation*
> *to the sale of all of the stock of Jacki's Designs, Inc. (here-*
> *inafter referred to as the Corporation).*

While this paragraph has no real substantive effect on the transaction, it does contain a great deal of information and gives insight into what is to follow.

Many contracts follow this introductory paragraph with a list of some of the basic premises of the agreement (such as that the Sellers own all of the stock of the Corporation). In some agreements, this list appears as the so-called Whereas clauses. There need not be such clauses in an agreement, and many leave them out. Some contracts do not include the premises at all, and it is not necessary to do so. Nevertheless, it is a useful device to make clear on what the parties based their agreement, and it eases some of the linguistic problems in drafting the substantive terms of the agreement. A sample paragraph (without the Whereas clauses) might read:

> *The Sellers (between them) own all of the issued and out-*
> *standing shares of the capital stock (hereinafter referred to*
> *as the Stock) of the Corporation that has its principal place*
> *of business at 4299 87 St. N.W., Washington, D.C. The*
> *Corporation operates a business at that location that in-*
> *volves the development and production of works of art for*
> *sale to the public. The Sellers wish to sell and the Buyer*
> *wishes to purchase all of the Stock, and they have reached*
> *an agreement to accomplish that end. The parties now wish*
> *to reduce this agreement to writing as the definitive, final,*
> *and complete expression of the terms of the sale and pur-*
> *chase of the Stock. Therefore, in consideration of the pre-*
> *mises contained herein and the mutual promises and un-*
> *dertakings by the parties, the Sellers and Buyer hereby agree*
> *as follows:*

This clause further introduces the parties and the transaction they contemplate. It provides additional information about the corporation and leads you into the body of the contract.

The body of the contract may be divided broadly into several "articles" or "sections," each covering major points of the agreement. These sections may then be further broken down into paragraphs that deal with specific issues within each broad topic covered by the sections. For instance, Section 1 might be entitled "Purchase of Corporate Stock." Each paragraph in Section 1 might then be numbered Paragraph 1.1, 1.2, and so on, while those in Section 2 would be numbered 2.1, 2.2, and so on. One could then easily identify each paragraph and its appropriate section. Once again, it is important to remember that this is merely an example of how a contract *might* be organized, not how it *must* be organized.

Section 1 would begin with the most fundamental aspect of the agreement. Paragraph 1.1 would state that the Sellers agree to sell and the Buyer agrees to buy all of the capital stock of the Corporation. The rest of Section 1 would deal with the specific terms of the transaction. For example, Paragraph 1.2 might deal with the date and form of the transfer, while Paragraph 1.3 might lay out the details of the payment for the stock. The following examples illustrate the content of those paragraphs:

> *1.2 Delivery. On the _____ day of _____, 199_, at the offices of Buyer's attorney or at such other place as Buyer shall designate (hereinafter referred to as the Closing), Sellers shall deliver to Buyer certificates representing all of the outstanding Stock of the Corporation free and clear of all liens and encumbrances and subject to no claims by any person. Such certificates shall be duly endorsed by the owner(s) thereof or shall be accompanied by properly executed stock powers.*

> *1.3 Payment. In consideration of the transfer of shares provided for herein, Buyer shall pay to Seller at the Closing the sum of $250,000, which shall be comprised of the $10,000 Buyer has previously paid to Sellers as a deposit on the purchase together with a certified check made payable to Sellers in the sum of $90,000. The balance of the purchase price shall be paid by the delivery to Sellers of a negotiable promissory note (hereinafter referred to as the Note) in the amount of $150,000 payable to the order of the Sellers.*

> *1.4 The Note. The Note shall bear interest at the rate of 12 percent per year from the date of the closing until paid and shall be secured by the Stock and further secured as may*

hereinafter be provided in this agreement. Payments on the Note shall be made in 20 equal, self-amortizing, quarterly installments comprised of interest and principal. Such payments shall begin on January 15, 199_, and continue until the Note is fully paid on October 15, 199_. The Note shall contain an acceleration clause that shall provide that in the event a default in payment is not cured within 15 days of Buyer's receipt of notice of such default, the Note shall, at the option of the Sellers, become immediately due and payable. The Note may be prepaid in whole or in part without penalty provided that such prepayment be made only on a quarterly payment date and is in an amount equal to the quarterly payment or any multiple thereof. No partial prepayment shall reduce the amount of any subsequent quarterly payment until the Note is paid in full.

These three paragraphs contain the main details surrounding the transfer of the shares provided for in the agreement. The first establishes the method of transfer. This normally takes place at a meeting of the parties and their attorneys (known as a *closing*). At the closing, the shares of stock will be physically transferred to the buyer, and the purchase price will be transferred to the seller. You will note that Paragraph 1.2 calls for the share certificates to be "duly endorsed" or to be "accompanied by properly executed stock powers." One or the other of these are necessary because the share certificates are made out with the name of the owner of the shares written or printed on their faces. The endorsement, usually on a form printed on the back of the certificate, indicates that the owner of the shares is transferring them to someone else. Often, however, the owner does not want his or her endorsement on the certificate, itself. This is to protect against loss or theft of a fully executed certificate that would give the holder of it the appearance of ownership. Therefore, the owner will sign a separate document, known as a *stock power*, which serves the same purpose as an endorsement. This device is often used when documents have to be mailed prior to the closing. In that case, the unendorsed certificate would be mailed separately from the signed stock power, thus lessening the perceived danger. Of course, if the documents are to be signed and transferred at the closing, the risk of loss is negligible.

Paragraph 1.3 deals with the purchase price. In our hypothetical transaction, the total purchase price is $250,000, of which $10,000 has already been paid as a deposit. Deposits of this kind are usual in such transactions and are often held by the sellers' attorney to help assure the completion of the transaction. The deposit, itself, is given as a sign of the buyer's serious intent and good faith. If the buyer, without just cause, fails to go through with the purchase, one of the remedies available to the Seller is to retain the deposit.

The balance of the purchase price is to be paid at closing. In this case, it will take the form of a certified check for $90,000 and a negotiable promissory note for $150,000. As has already been pointed out, the use of promissory notes in the purchase of a closely held corporation is a common occurrence. This is due in part because the buyer may not have or want to expend the entire purchase price in cash. It is also usually an easier and less expensive process to secure financing from the seller of a business, who has an obvious interest in the deal being successful, than from a bank. The seller may also wish to have the additional income derived from the interest on the loan, which will probably be at a significantly higher rate than the seller could obtain through most other investment opportunities.

Finally, Paragraph 1.4 sets out the terms to be included in the promissory note. The note will bear interest at the rate of 12 percent per year and will be "self-amortizing" over the period of five years through 20 quarterly payments whose dates are set out in the note. The self-amortizing feature means that the buyer will be paying part of the outstanding principal with each quarterly installment. Since the amount of each quarterly payment is to be equal, it can be seen that as each payment (which includes part of the principal to be repaid) is made, the outstanding principal balance becomes smaller. Since interest is paid only on the outstanding principal balance, the smaller it becomes, the smaller the amount of interest charged on it. Again, since the quarterly payments are equal, and since the amount of interest owed gets smaller with each payment, the amount of principal repaid in each payment increases. This process continues until the debt is entirely extinguished. There are books available from most commercial bookstores that set out amortization tables so that, given a particular interest rate, a loan term, and the frequency of payments (i.e., monthly, quarterly), the periodic payment needed to pay off a loan can be determined. There are also several computer programs that will compute not only the periodic amount necessary to amortize a loan but also the amount of each payment dedicated to reducing principal, the amount allocated to interest, and the remaining principal balance at any time.

Paragraph 1.4 also includes an acceleration clause and prepayment clause. The acceleration clause allows (but does not require) the sellers to speed up the due date of the payoff of the note in the event the buyer fails to make a payment and continues not to pay after notice of default from the sellers. If the sellers exercise their right to "accelerate" the note, they will inform the buyer that the note is immediately due and payable. If the buyer does not then pay the note in full, the sellers can take advantage of any remedies available, including instituting suit against the buyer.

In this case, the sellers have an additional remedy against the buyer. Paragraph 1.4 calls for the establishment of a "security interest" in the stock. This means that if the buyer defaults in its payments, in addition to any other remedy the sellers may have, they may take back the stock and sell it to satisfy the balance due on the note. As a practical matter, there probably will not be much of a market for the shares, in which case the sellers may take the stock for themselves and return to their former ownership position in the corporation. Unfortunately, this may not be a particularly appealing solution. The sellers may have become involved in other enterprises and may have no wish to return to their former company. Moreover, it may be that the company has been run down by the buyer or is failing for other reasons, possibilities that are supported by the buyer's inability or unwillingness to pay on the note. Therefore, this paragraph provides for other forms of security that will be addressed elsewhere in the contract.

There is also a provision for the prepayment of the note. In some ways, this is the other side of the coin from acceleration. It applies if the buyer wishes to pay the note off sooner than is required. Perhaps he or she has the funds to pay off the debt or wishes to get out from under too high an interest rate, or can obtain new funds more cheaply than the cost of the existing note. The fact that the note may be prepaid without a penalty may need some explanation. When a lender agrees to make a loan, he or she expects to receive a certain amount of interest over its entire term. If the borrower pays the loan off before it is due, the lender's expectations concerning interest income will have been defeated. Therefore, lenders used to include in their loan agreements a penalty for the early payment of the debt. In today's lending market, the practice of penalizing prepayments has all but disappeared, and borrowers can normally prepay their loans without penalty.

After the fundamental terms of the transaction have been set out, the remainder of the contract will include provisions for the protection of the parties and for implementing the deal. For instance, each side will make a series of representations, warranties, and covenants running to the benefit of the other. A *representation* is a statement of the existence (or nonexistence) of a particular fact or state of affairs. For example, a seller may represent that he or she (or they) own all the outstanding stock of the corporation. This is a statement of fact to the other party. When one "warrants" a representation, he or she is saying "I stand behind the representation and will rectify any injury you may suffer if it is false." A *covenant* is merely a legal term that means a promise (as opposed to a statement of current fact). Therefore, when a seller "covenants" not to compete with the business he or she has sold, he or she is *promising* not to compete.

Among the typical representations and warranties (and remember, these are only typical examples and will change as the facts and circumstances change) of a seller of stock are:

- that the corporation was duly formed and is currently in good standing

- that its financial condition is as represented in the financial statements given to the buyer

- that there have been no material changes in its status or operation for a named period prior to the closing (this period usually encompasses the negotiations and approval of the contract and the warranty survives the closing)

- that taxes are current and no tax liens, levies, or penalties are pending or threatened against the corporation

- that future taxes have been adequately provided for

- that there is no litigation pending or threatened against the corporation

- that there are no undisclosed liabilities of the corporation

- that the corporation has good title to its assets and that they are free of liens or encumbrances.

In addition, the buyer will want a list of as well as copies of all significant contracts (including insurance policies) to which the corporation is a party and a list of each major asset owned by the corporation, along with a description of its condition. A listing of the corporation's inventory; the backlog of its orders, if any; and a list of its major customers are also normally provided to the buyer. The seller will usually warrant, if it is true, that there is no "labor trouble" pending or threatened. This phrase means that there is no strike, work stoppage or slow down, or other labor dispute that would materially and negatively affect the corporation. These clauses often include a provision by which the seller represents and warrants that the corporation's employees are not represented by a labor union and that no union is currently attempting to organize them. Similarly, the buyer will normally want information about any pension or other deferred compensation plan of the corporation as well as a representation that the corporation is current with all government reports or filings required of it.

The buyer's representations are generally less numerous than those of the seller. If, for instance, the buyer is a corporation, its principals will often have to indicate that it was duly formed, that it is in good standing, that its purchase of the seller's stock does not violate its charter or other corporate document, and that the purchase has been authorized by its board of directors and shareholders. The resolutions of each of those bodies certified by the corporation's secretary will normally be attached to the contract as exhibits. To meet the requirements of federal and state securities laws, there may also have to be a representation by the buyer that the purchase of stock is solely for the account of the buyer and is not being purchased with a view toward resale. The seller may also have to provide financial statements (if the payment is to be evidenced in part by a promissory note) and warrant that they are accurate.

The covenants of each of the parties will also be set out in sections of the contract. The covenants are, as has been mentioned before, promises of a party to act (or to refrain from acting) in a certain way in the future. Perhaps the most important covenant (from the buyer's point of view) is the seller's promise not to compete with the corporation. Clearly, the buyer would be distressed if, after buying the stock of the corporation, the seller, who was experienced in the corporation's field of business, invested in or was employed by another company in the same field and in the same geographic locations. The buyer would be justifiably concerned that the expertise of the seller would be used to benefit the new company to the disadvantage of the corporation. There would also be concern that the seller would attempt to use his or her relationship with the customers of the corporation to solicit them for the new company. To protect against these events, the buyer is likely to demand that a covenant not to compete be included in the contract.

A typical covenant not to compete might read as follows:

4.1   a) Sellers hereby covenant and agree that for the period of three years from the date of the closing, they will not, individually or together, directly or indirectly, own, operate, invest in, be employed by, or otherwise participate in any business within a 500 mile radius of the principal office of the Corporation which business engages in the design, production, distribution, or sale of any works of art.

b) Sellers shall not, during the three-year period, solicit or service any customers of the Corporation nor solicit or employ any employees of the Corporation. For the purpose of this paragraph, the term customer shall include all current customers as well as any person or entity who was a customer or was actively solicited by the Corporation as a customer at any time within the one-year period immediately prior to the closing.

Noncompetition clauses are routinely used in the sales of businesses, and they have been upheld by the courts as valid if they are reasonable in duration and geographic limitation. For instance, it would be unreasonable for a buyer to attempt to prohibit the seller of a local candy store in New York, whose selling area was comprised of several city streets, from owning or operating for a period of twenty-five years a candy store in Seattle, Washington. On the other hand, it might not be unreasonable to prohibit that same seller from owning or operating a candy store across the street from the original store for a period of one year. What will be considered reasonable depends on all of the facts and circumstances of a particular situation. There are almost no hard and fast rules in this area, although it is clear that a restriction that prohibits a person from *ever* pursuing his or her trade or profession would be unreasonable. If a noncompetition clause is found to be unreasonable, the courts will declare it to be void and of no effect. Therefore, it is in the interest of the buyer to be sure the clause he or she wants is a reasonable one.

The contract will usually include several other covenants of the seller and the corporation, such as the following:

- Sellers will make information—including books, records, reports, and properties—available to the buyer and its agents.

- Sellers will take whatever further or additional actions are reasonably necessary or advisable to consummate the sale.

- Prior to closing, the business of the corporation will be conducted in the ordinary course and consistent with its current practices.

- Accounting methods or employee benefits will not change.

- Corporation will not hire additional employees or lay off employees except in the ordinary course of its business.

- Corporation's assets will be maintained as before.

- Corporation's receivables are collectible and will be collected in the ordinary course.

Some of these covenants will be accompanied by a *liquidated damages* clause, which is a device whereby the parties to a contract predetermine an amount of damages one party must pay to the other in the event of a violation. Liquidated damages are available when the actual damages a party will suffer would be difficult to determine. In such a case, an attempt, before the fact, to agree on an amount of damages that would be reasonable under the circumstances may be used instead of actual damages. If a contract contains a valid liquidated damages clause, that clause will control the amount of the injured party's recovery. That party will not be allowed to prove his or her actual damages.

The contract may also establish certain conditions that must occur (or not occur) before the closing can take place. If these conditions are not met, the party who was to benefit from its performance may be given the right to cancel the contract. Such a clause might, for instance, read as follows:

Unless the Buyer waives their performance in writing, the Buyer's obligation to perform pursuant to this contract is conditioned on the fulfillment by the Sellers, by the time of or at the Closing, of each of the following conditions:

The contract would then go on to set out the conditions that must be met by the sellers before the buyer is obligated to perform. Some of the typical conditions include:

- representations, warranties, and covenants of the sellers shall be true or shall have been substantially performed with the sellers providing satisfactory evidence thereof

- opinion of counsel from the sellers' attorney stating that the corporation is duly authorized and in good standing; that the stock being transferred is free and clear of all liens and encumbrances; that the transaction does not violate any provision of any contract or agreement, any corporate document or instrument, or any regulation or decree of which counsel is aware; that the corporation has good and marketable title to the assets described in the exhibits to the contract free and clear of all liens and encumbrances except as otherwise indicated; and that the corporation is legally entitled to carry on its business and has all necessary licenses and permits

- statement that the corporation has the right to its premises (offices, factories, stores, showrooms, etc.) and that other contracts (such as insurance, suppliers, employment) are in full force and effect and will be continued

- statement that there has been no material adverse change in the financial condition of the corporation and that no suits, proceedings, or investigations are pending or threatened against the corporation.

The status of the corporation's financial condition will usually be tested by an examination conducted by the buyer's accountant shortly before the closing. Often, both the buyer and seller will have their accountants review the books and financial documents and take an inventory of materials on hand as well as work in progress and finished goods. There will often be a provision for a price adjustment if the examination results in a material discrepancy, up or down, in the condition of the corporation. Often, the contract will contain a provision establishing a permissible range of discrepancy. If a discrepancy within the range is found, it will be rectified with a price adjustment. If the discrepancy is greater than the permissible range, the contract often gives the negatively affected party the right to cancel the sale.

As an example, suppose the seller represents that the corporation's inventory and accounts receivable will amount to $350,000 at the time of closing. If, at that time, the buyer's financial review shows the value to be only $345,000, the buyer might be required to go forward with the purchase but would be given a reduction in the purchase price. If the examination showed a value of only $250,000, the result would be so far off from the company's projections that the buyer might not want to go through with the sale at all and would be permitted to cancel the transaction.

The parties will also normally provide for indemnification of one another. *Indemnification* in this situation is an agreed upon re-imbursement of an injured party for any unexpected liability or expense it incurs to a third party by virtue of the other party's false representations, breaches of warranties, or other acts. For instance, if the seller warrants that it owns a certain piece of machinery that, in fact, it had only rented on a short-term basis and the buyer must expend extra funds to purchase a replacement machine, the seller would have to reimburse (indemnify) the buyer for the expense incurred in the purchase. There may also be liabilities for which the seller would demand indemnity. For instance, assume the seller personally guaranteed to the landlord the payment of rent for the corporate offices. If the landlord refuses to release the seller from that guarantee, the seller would want indemnification from the buyer for any payments the seller has to make on the guarantee due to the failure of the corporation to pay the rent. The language of the clauses would be very similar. An example of an indemnity clause protecting the buyer might read as follows:

> *Sellers agree to indemnify Buyer and hold him or her harmless from and against any and all damages, losses, or expenses, including reasonable attorneys' fees, caused by or arising out of a) any breach of warranty or covenant, any misrepresentation by Sellers; b) any claims against Buyer or the Corporation in connection with the operations or own-ership of the Corporation which claims arose prior to the Closing even though the claim is first asserted after the Closing; c) any bad debts or uncollectible receivables that were on the books of the corporation prior to Closing, provided Buyer assigns such debts or receivables to Sellers for collection for their own account; d) any claims, defi-ciencies, or assessments for federal, state, or local taxes, including but not limited to income, property, and sales taxes incurred prior to closing; and e) any claims of any nature made by any licensing or regulatory agency arising out of actions or omissions of the Corporation prior to Closing.*

Aside from any special issues that must be resolved, the re-mainder of the contract will contain what is known as "boilerplate." These are standard clauses that appear in almost all contracts and deal with items such as to whom and where notices are to be sent, the fact that the written agreement is the entire agreement between the parties and that there are no oral agreements or representations on which either party is relying. The boilerplate may include a statement that there are no brokers who assisted in arranging or negotiating the deal or, if there has been a broker involved, identifying and recognizing that broker and stating who is responsible for his or her fee. There may also be a nonassignment clause that prohibits either party from transferring its rights or obligations under the contract to anyone else. This protects the parties from having people other than those they contemplated performing various duties under the contract. Finally, there may be a confidentiality or nondisclosure provision in the agreement. This is designed to protect the parties from the disclosure of confidential or proprietary information that was given in contemplation of the sale and not for general distribution.

THE SALE BY THE CORPORATION OF ITS ASSETS

The other way in which a business is normally transferred is through the sale by a corporation of substantially all of its assets. The assets of a corporation include such obvious categories as its machinery, equipment, office furniture, and supplies; its bank accounts or holdings of stock, or bonds; its supply of raw materials, goods in progress, and finished goods; its real estate (including its leases); and its vehicles. There are also less obvious assets such as its customer list; its key employees under contract to the corporation; various service contracts and insurance policies it may have; any copyrights, patents, or trademarks it owns or is licensed to use; and its good will. These assets are used in the conduct of the business and their sale, in effect, is a sale of the business. It is important to note, however, that in this case, as opposed to the sale of stock discussed previously, the corporation, not the shareholder, is the seller.

The buyer and seller each gain several advantages through the purchase and sale of assets rather than of stock. For the buyer, there is little chance that it will be saddled with any hidden corporate liabilities of the seller. The buyer also obtains some significant tax benefits. These are derived, primarily, through its ability to depreciate the newly purchased assets based upon their new purchase price. The tax aspects of an asset sale/purchase were discussed in detail in Chapter 2.

There are also some disadvantages to the purchase and sale of assets. Among them are the added bureaucracy that attends a corporation's sale of substantially all of its assets. First, a deal must be arranged between the buyer and the corporation. Once a proposed deal has been struck, it must be presented to the board for its approval. If that is obtained, state corporation laws generally require that the board's resolution approving the sale be submitted to the shareholders for their approval. The shareholders having the right to vote on this issue will then be entitled to pass upon the work done by the negotiators and the board. Some states require a two-thirds vote to approve the sale, whereas others require only a simple majority. In any event, there may be a significant time lag from the time the proposed deal is struck and its final approval, not to mention the additional risks associated with requiring approval from so many different constituencies.

Contract for the Sale of Corporate Assets

The contract for the sale of corporate assets will normally be negotiated by one or more corporate officers, usually with the assistance of an attorney. The essence of the contract is very similar to that of the contract for the sale of shares. There are, of course, several obvious differences, but the majority of the contract is designed to protect the parties from the same kinds of perceived risks and problems. Among the major differences in the documents is that in an asset deal the corporation is the seller. Also, the buyer does not obtain or become responsible for, except as specifically provided for in the contract, the liabilities or other obligations of the corporation. A clause by which the buyer assumes certain of the seller's liabilities might read as follows:

> *Buyer shall assume as per their terms or pay (at Buyer's option) those obligations and liabilities, and only those obligations and liabilities, of Seller as shown in appendix _____ attached hereto and shall, at closing, deliver to Seller documents or undertakings in a form reasonably satisfactory to Seller indicating such assumption or payment.*

The conveyance of the assets is normally accomplished through bills of sale running from the seller to the buyer (bill of sale forms can be obtained at any legal or business stationary store). These bills will normally be delivered at the closing, together with other documents evidencing transfer of items not subject to a bill of sale. For instance, if the seller holds a promissory note payable to it from a third party and the note is being transferred to the buyer, the transfer is accomplished not by a bill of sale but by an endorsement on the note that it is to be paid to the order of the buyer. Similarly, if accounts receivable of the seller are to be transferred to the buyer, the transfer is accomplished by a written assignment of the receivables.

If the buyer is going to pay for the assets over time, the seller will want to obtain the personal guarantees of the principals of the buyer (if the buyer is a corporation). The seller will also retain a security interest in the assets transferred to the buyer and as many of its other assets as possible. A *security interest* is a device whereby certain identified property of the debtor is pledged to the creditor to secure a debt. If the debtor does not pay the debt as required, the lender can sell the identified property. The proceeds of the sale go to the secured party up to the amount of the debt. Again, forms for creating a security interest can be purchased at any legal stationers. Once the forms that create the security interest are complete, they are signed by the debtor and filed with the clerk's office in the county where the subject property is located.

If the seller is a closely held corporation, the buyer may want its shareholders to be parties to the contract as well as the corporation. This will assure the buyer that there is unanimous shareholder assent to the transfer and that no shareholder will seek judicial intervention to prevent the sale. The buyer will also be likely to seek noncompetition clauses from the principals of the seller. This will protect the buyer from having those most closely associated with running the business of the selling corporation use their experience, skill, and contacts in competition with it. Finally, the contract will usually include a representation that the requirements of the Bulk Sales Act have been met.

The Bulk Sales Act

Article 6 of the Uniform Commercial Code, a commercial statute that has been adopted in every state, deals with an issue that is germane to the transfer by a corporation of substantially all of its assets. The Article is entitled "Bulk Transfers" but is commonly known as the *Bulk Sales Act*. The Act covers any transfer in bulk that is not in the ordinary course of the transferor's (the seller's) business. Therefore, if a manufacturer sold all of its inventory and all of its manufacturing equipment (what we have previously called a sale of substantially all of its assets) this would be a *bulk transfer* covered by the Act. A failure to comply with the requirements of the Act can have grave consequences for the buyer. A creditor of the seller may be able to follow the assets into the hands of the transferee (the buyer) in order to satisfy the creditor's claim against the transferor.

Among the requirements of the Act is that:

- transferee requires the transferor to prepare a signed, sworn list of the transferor's existing creditors, together with their names, addresses, and the amounts owed

- parties prepare a list of the assets transferred with sufficient detail so that they can be identified

- list must be retained by the transferee for six months or filed among public records so that it may be inspected and copied by creditors

- transferee gives notice of the sale to the listed creditors, indicating that a bulk transfer is about to be made, the name and address of the transferor, and certain information about the use of the proceeds of the sale.

The exceptions to the coverage of the Bulk Sales Act can be found in local state law. There are also variations in the terms of the Act as enacted in different states. In all states, however, the purpose of the Act is to protect the creditors of transferors who attempt to avoid their financial obligations by selling the assets of their businesses without providing for payment of their debts. The protection is achieved by providing the creditors with advance notice of the sale and in sufficient detail so that they may take action to stop it in order to protect their rights. If proper notice is not given, the creditors of the transferor are protected in that they can seek payment of the transferor's debts by attaching the property transferred to the buyer. On the other hand, if the Act *is* complied with, the buyer will be protected from action by the creditors of the seller.

APPENDIX 5.1
ASSET PURCHASE AGREEMENT

This agreement, dated _____, 19__, is between _____ (hereinafter called the Seller), the undersigned stockholders of the Seller (hereinafter called the Stockholders), and the _____ Corporation (hereinafter called the Buyer).

Whereas the Buyer wishes to purchase, and the Seller and the Stockholders wish to sell, the assets, business, and goodwill of the Seller, which is engaged in the manufacturing, distributing, and selling of various paper products and school and office supplies; and

Whereas the parties have reached an agreement on the terms of the purchase;

Now, therefore, in consideration of the premises, covenants, and undertakings set forth herein, the parties agree as follows:

1. PURCHASE AGREEMENT.

The parties hereto acknowledge that this transaction is conditioned upon and subject to the Buyer's obtaining financing from _____ Bank in the minimum sum of _____. Should Buyer fail to obtain such financing prior to the closing of title, for any reason whatsoever, except for Buyer's failure to use its reasonable best efforts to obtain such financing, the deposit money paid hereunder pursuant to Paragraph 2(a) of this agreement shall be immediately refunded to the Buyer, and this contract of sale shall automatically be null and void and of no further force and effect.

Subject to the contingency just mentioned, Buyer agrees to purchase and the Seller and the Stockholders agree to sell, at the closing, the assets of the Seller, including the use of its name and telephone numbers, as listed in Appendix _____ (attached hereto and made a part hereof) for:

a) The payment by Buyer of $325,000 (in the manner set forth in Paragraph 2, below); and

b) The payment or assumption by Buyer of certain specified outstanding obligations and liabilities of the Seller as set forth in Paragraph 4 below.

2. PAYMENT OF PURCHASE PRICE.

The payment of $325,000 as required by Paragraph 1 above shall be made as follows:

a) $25,000 shall be paid by Buyer to the Seller upon the signing of this agreement. Said sum shall be held in escrow by _____ in an interest-bearing account pending Closing.

b) $125,000 shall be paid by Buyer to the Seller upon closing.

c) The balance of $175,000 shall be paid in installments on terms and in amounts as provided in Paragraph 3 herein.

Appendix 5.1 *(continued)*

d) Notwithstanding anything herein to the contrary, if Buyer, while there is any amount owing to any party hereunder, should liquidate the business or transfer substantially all its assets to a third party outside of the ordinary course of business, all such amounts owed to any such party together with accrued interest shall become immediately due and payable.

3. TERMS AND OBLIGATIONS OF INSTALLMENT PAYMENTS.

   a) The balance of $175,000 payable to Seller shall be evidenced by a negotiable instrument payable to the order of Seller and signed by Buyer. Such note shall bear interest at the rate of 8 percent per annum on the outstanding balance until paid.

   b) Payment of interest and principal shall be as follows: On the first anniversary of the Closing of this agreement Buyer shall pay to Seller (or its assignee(s), as hereinafter provided) the sum of $10,000. It is understood that the first year interest on the $175,000 will be $14,000. The $4,000 of first year interest remaining unpaid after the payment of $10,000 shall be added to the principal, making a total outstanding principal of $179,000. This amount shall be amortized over the remaining nine years at 8 percent interest payable in semiannual installments of $_____. All payments made shall be credited first to accrued interest and then to the reduction of principal.

   c) It is understood that Seller intends to dissolve within one year of the closing. Seller shall give 30 days advance notice to Buyer of such dissolution and shall provide Buyer with individual negotiable promissory notes payable to the order of each Stockholder, as listed herein, in an amount equal to his or her pro rata share of the balance of the purchase price and accrued interest, if any, outstanding on the date of such dissolution. Buyer shall, prior to such dissolution, deliver such notes, signed by an authorized officer of Buyer, to Seller in exchange for Seller's cancelling and surrendering to Buyer its note as provided in Paragraph 3(a) herein.

   d) _____ shall personally guarantee to each Stockholder their pro rata share of principal and interest up to a total guarantee of $30,000. The pro rata share of each Stockholder is as follows:

   | _____ | 70% |
   | _____ | 30% |

4. ASSUMPTION OF OBLIGATIONS AND LIABILITIES.

   Buyer shall assume as per their terms or pay (at its option) the obligations and liabilities of Seller as shown in Appendix _____ (attached hereto and made a part hereof) and shall, at closing, deliver to Seller documents sufficient to indicate such assumption or payment.

5. SECURITY INTEREST CREATED.

   Seller and Stockholders shall have a security interest in the inventory, equipment, cash, furnishings, and receivables of Buyer to secure the full and timely performance of this agreement. Buyer shall provide at Closing a duplicate executed financing statement (UCC-1) sufficient in form and content for filing in New York to create a lien on Buyer's assets together with a fully executed security agreement. It is understood that any liens so created shall be subordinate to liens on the same assets held by the _____ Bank to secure advances made by it to Buyer. It is further understood that the security agreement shall allow Buyer to use and sell the assets in the ordinary course of its business.

6. REPRESENTATIONS AND WARRANTIES OF SELLER.

    a) *Organization and Standing.* Seller is a corporation duly organized, existing, and in good standing under the laws of the State of New York. Its Certificate of Incorporation was filed in 1963.

    b) *Subsidiaries.* The Company has no subsidiaries.

    c) *Financial Statements.* The Company has delivered to the Buyer copies of its balance sheet as of October 31, 1990, and statements of profit and loss and surplus for fiscal year 1990 prepared by _____. Such balance sheets fairly present the condition of the Company as of their respective dates, and such statement of profit and loss and surplus fairly presents the results of the operation of the Company for the period stated.

    d) *Absence of Material Changes.* Since October 31, 1990, there has not been:

        (i) Any discharge or satisfaction of any lien or incumbrance, or payment of any obligation or liability (fixed or contingent) other than current liabilities included in the Company's October 31, 1990, balance sheet and current liabilities incurred since October 31, 1990, in the ordinary course of business;

        (ii) Any damage, destruction, or loss (whether or not covered by insurance) materially and adversely affecting the Company's properties or business;

        (iii) Any declaration or payment of any dividend or other distribution in respect of the Company's common stock or any direct or indirect redemption, purchase, or other acquisition of any such stock;

        (iv) Any increases in the compensation payable or to become payable by the Company to any of its officers, employees, or agents, or any bonus payment or arrangement made to or with any thereof;

        (v) Any labor trouble, or any event or condition of any character, materially and adversely affecting the Company's business or future prospect.

    e) *Title to Properties; Liens and Encumbrances.* The Company has good and marketable title to all properties and assets used in its business, including those reflected in the aforesaid October 31, 1990, balance sheet (except as since sold or otherwise disposed of in the ordinary course of business), subject to no mortgage, pledge, lien, conditional sales agreement, encumbrance, or charge except for liens shown of such balance sheet as securing specified liabilities (with respect to which no default exists). All material leases pursuant to which the Company leases any substantial amount of property are valid and effective in accordance with their terms, and there is not under any such lease any existing default or event of default or event that with notice or lapse of time or both would constitute a default.

f) *Accounts Receivable.* The Company has delivered to the Buyer an accurate list of the Company's accounts receivable as of October 31, 1990. All of such accounts receivable (after allowance for doubtful accounts in the amount of the reserve established therefore) have been collected or are collectible in the aggregate amounts thereof.

g) *Inventories.* The inventories of the Company shown on the aforesaid October 31, 1990, balance sheet, or thereafter acquired by it prior to the date of this Agreement, consist of items of a quality and quantity usable or salable in the normal course of the Company's business; and the value at which such inventory is carried reflects the Company's normal inventory valuation policy.

h) *Contracts.* The Company has no presently existing material contract or commitment except those listed on Schedule ____ hereto. True and complete copies of all contracts listed on Schedule _____ have been delivered to the Buyer. The Company has complied with all the provisions of all contracts and commitments to which it is a party and is not in default under any thereof. Such contracts shall be assigned to Buyer at Closing.

i) *Litigation.* There is no litigation or proceeding (at law or in equity or before any governmental instrumentality) pending, or to the knowledge of the Company threatened, against or relating to the Company, its properties, or business except as hereinafter stated.

j) *Tax Returns.* The Company has filed all tax returns and reports required to be filed with the U. S. Government and with the states in which the Company is qualified to do business and political subdivisions thereof and has paid in full or made adequate provision for the payment of all taxes, interest, penalties, assessments, or deficiencies shown to be due or claimed to be due on such returns and reports. To the best of the Company's knowledge, it is not required to file tax returns or reports with any other taxing jurisdictions. The federal income tax returns of the Company for all taxable years through and including _____ have been examined by the federal tax authorities and no proposed (but unassessed) additional unpaid taxes, interest, or penalties have been asserted. The Company is not party to any action or proceeding before any governmental authority for assessment or collection of taxes, nor has any claim for assessment or collection of taxes been assessed against the Company;

k) *No Violation.* Consummation of the transactions contemplated by this Agreement will not violate or result in a breach of or constitute a default under any provision of any charter, bylaw, contract, lien, instrument, order, judgment, decree, ordinance, regulation, or any other restriction of any kind to which any property of the Company is subject or by which the Company is bound.

l) *Corporate Approval.* All necessary corporate action has been or prior to the Closing will be taken to authorize this Agreement and the transactions contemplated herein. The Company will deliver to the Buyer, at or prior to the Closing, copies of the corporate minutes containing the resolutions (certified by the Company's Secretary) adopted in this connection, together with the signed waivers of notice of the meetings from each Director and Shareholder. Provided, however, that if such authorizations are not obtained, this agreement shall be null and void and of no force or effect. In that event, Seller shall return to Buyer the Deposit and all accrued interest and neither Seller nor Stockholders shall have any further obligation to Buyer.

7. COVENANTS OF THE COMPANY AND THE STOCKHOLDERS.

The Company and the Stockholders agree that, pending the Closing:

a) *Negative Covenants as to Further Operations.* They will not, unless written approval by the Buyer be first obtained:

  (i) Make any change in the Company's Certificate of Incorporation, as amended, or its bylaws;

  (ii) Declare or pay any divided or make any distribution in respect of its stock whether now or thereafter outstanding, or purchase, redeem, or otherwise acquire or retire for value any shares of its stock;

  (iii) Enter into any contract or commitment or grant any power of attorney except in the normal course of business;

  (iv) Make any change affecting compensation payments, banking arrangements, or safe deposit boxes.

  (v) Create, assume, or permit to exist (except as indicated in Appendix ___ attached hereto and made a part hereof) any mortgage, pledge, or other lien or encumbrance upon any of its assets or properties whether now owned or hereafter acquired;

  (vi) Sell, assign, lease, or otherwise transfer or dispose of any of its property or equipment except in the normal course of business; or

  (vii) Merge or consolidate with or into any other corporation.

b) *Affirmative Covenants as to Future Operations*

The Company will:

  (i) Give to the Buyer and to its counsel, accountants, engineers, and other representatives full access during normal business hours to all its properties, books, and records, and furnish the Buyer with all such information concerning the Company's operations as the Buyer may reasonably request;

  (ii) Except as otherwise requested by the Buyer, use its best efforts to preserve its business organization intact, keep available to the Buyer the services of its present officers and employees, and preserve for the Buyer the goodwill of the Company's suppliers, customers, and others having business relations with it;

  (iii) Maintain its properties in customary repair, reasonable wear and damage by unavoidable casualty excepted, and maintain insurance upon its properties and with respect to the conduct of its business in such amounts and of such kinds comparable to that in effect on the date of this agreement:

  (iv) Maintain its books and records in the usual manner on a basis consistent with prior years;

Appendix 5.1 *(continued)*

(v) Comply with all laws applicable to it in the conduct of its business;

(vi) The Company will comply with any applicable "Bulk Sales Act" and any other applicable laws as required for the valid and effective consummation of the transactions contemplated by this Agreement.

8. REPRESENTATIONS AND WARRANTIES OF BUYER.

   a) *Organization and Standing.* Buyer is a corporation duly organized, existing, and in good standing under the laws of the State of New York. Its Certificate of Incorporation was filed September 1, 1990. The copy of the Certificate of Incorporation and of its bylaws (each as amended and certified by Buyer's Secretary), which have been delivered to Seller, are complete and correct as of the date of the agreement.

   b) *Absence of Undisclosed Liabilities.* Except as and to the extent indicated herein, Buyer as of the date of this agreement had no liabilities or obligations of any nature, whether accrued, absolute, contingent, or otherwise, including without limitation, tax liabilities due or to become due.

   c) *Corporate Approval.* All necessary corporate action has been or prior to Closing will be taken to authorize this Agreement and the transactions contemplated herein. Buyer will deliver to Seller at or prior to Closing, copies of the corporate minutes containing the resolutions (certified by Buyer's Secretary) adopted in this connection together with the signed waivers of notice of the meetings from each Director and Shareholder.

   d) *Litigation.* There is no litigation or proceeding (at law or in equity or before any governmental instrumentality) pending, or to the knowledge of Buyer threatened, against or relating to Buyer, its properties or business.

   e) *Maintenance and Availability of Books and Records.* Buyer agrees, during the life of this agreement and while any money is owed by Buyer to any party hereunder, to maintain its books and records in a complete and accurate manner. All financial records and documents shall be "review" documents and shall be prepared and kept in accordance with generally accepted accounting principles. In the event of any default hereunder, Buyer agrees to make such books and records available during normal business hours to any party hereto or his, her, or its representative for inspection and copying.

9. CONVEYANCE AND TRANSFER.

   Seller shall deliver to Buyer at closing such bills of sale, endorsements, assignments, and other good and sufficient evidence of transfer and conveyance as shall be needed to effect the vesting in Buyer of good and marketable title to the assets and business sold to Buyer.

10. REPRESENTATIONS AND WARRANTIES.

   The representation and warranties of each party contained in the Agreement shall be true at and as of the time of Closing as though such representations and warranties were made at and as of such time.

11. DEFAULT.

In the event a default in the payment of principal or interest on any obligation of Buyer continues beyond 15 days after written notice from the Seller or any Stockholder(s) to whom such obligation is owed, the Seller or Stockholder(s) may, at its option, declare such obligation immediately due and payable, and the Buyer or guarantor shall pay all the cost of collection, including reasonable attorney's fees in the event the obligation is referred to an attorney for collection. During the 15-day period provided for herein, Buyer shall be entitled to cure any default.

12. INDEMNIFICATION.

13. MISCELLANEOUS PROVISIONS.

a) *Closing.* The Closing of such sale and purchase shall take place at _____ Road, _____, New York at _____ on or about _____. At the Closing, the Buyer will deliver to the Seller a certified or bank cashier's check in New York Clearing House funds in the amount of $125,000. The escrow will deliver to the Seller the deposit provided for in Paragraph 2A. The Buyer will furthermore execute and deliver to the Seller the undertaking described in Paragraph 3(a).

b) *Acknowledgement of Broker.* The parties hereto recognize and acknowledge _____ as the broker in this transaction. His fee shall be paid by the Seller from the proceeds of the sale described herein.

c) *Taxes.* The Seller and Buyer will divide equally all sales, transfer, and documentary fees and taxes, other than income taxes, if any, payable in connection with this Agreement and the conveyances, assignments, transfers, and deliveries to be made to the Buyer hereunder.

d) *Covenant not to Compete.*

(i) The Seller and the Stockholders agree that from and after the Closing they will not, directly or indirectly, own, manage, operate, join, control, or participate in the ownership, management, or control of, or be connected in any manner with, any business under any name similar to the Seller's name, and that, for a period of five years after the Closing, the Seller and the Stockholders will not in any manner directly or indirectly compete with or be interested in any competitor of the Buyer.

(ii) It is recognized by Buyer that _____ has acquired a special expertise in relation to the customers and business of Seller and that it is in Buyer's interest to secure a noncompetition agreement from _____. Therefore, in consideration of _____'s agreement not to engage, for a period of five years, in competition with Buyer in any activities currently carried on by the Company and his agreement to serve Buyer as a consultant in such areas as sales, marketing, trade shows, and day-to-day operation of the business, Buyer agrees to pay to _____ 50 percent of Buyer's annual profit between $150,000 and $300,000 for the period of three years beginning with the first full fiscal year in which Buyer operates the business.

Appendix 5.1 *(continued)*

Payment shall be made annually within two and one half months of the closing for the year of Buyer's books. _____ or his estate shall be entitled to payment as provided herein for the full three-year period contemplated by this agreement.

(iii) Should Buyer liquidate the corporation, Buyer shall pay to_____ for the remaining years, if any, of compensation, under this paragraph by determining the amount of compensation paid to _____ pursuant to this paragraph in the year immediately prior to such liquidation or transfer and multiplying it by the number of years yet to be compensated hereunder. Such compensation shall be payable immediately upon such liquidation or transfer.

(iv) If Buyer transfers substantially all its assets to a third party, Buyer may, provided it has obtained the prior written consent of _____, delegate its obligation to pay _____ as provided in Paragraph 14(e)(ii) rather than as provided in Paragraph 14(e)(iii). _____ shall not unreasonably withhold such approval.

e) *Business Expenses.* Buyer is to pay or reimburse to _____ all of his business-related expenses, provided that the expenses shall be approved as to type by Buyer. Such expenses shall include, but not be limited to, automobile expense (at the then current Internal Revenue Service rate) including travel from _____'s home to Buyer's place of business, meals, lodging, airline or railroad tickets, cab fares, and parking fees connected with Buyer's business. _____ shall keep a log and receipts for such expenses. Buyer shall also reimburse _____ for all authorized credit card charges he incurs.

f) *Survival of Representations and Warranties.* All representations, warranties, and agreements made by the Buyer, the Seller, and the Stockholders, respectively, in this Agreement or pursuant hereto shall survive the Closing. All the terms and provisions of this Agreement shall be binding upon and inure to the benefit of and be enforceable by the parties hereto, their respective heirs and legal representatives of the Stockholders and the agents, successors and assigns of the Buyer and the Seller.

g) *Law to Govern.* This Agreement is being made in New York and shall be construed and enforced in accordance with the law of that State.

h) *Notices.* All notices and approvals shall be in writing and shall be deemed to have been duly given if delivered personally or if mailed via certified mail, return receipt requested, postage prepaid to the party at his address set forth at the end of this Agreement.

i) *Counterparts.* This Agreement may be executed in any number of counterparts, each of which shall be deemed an original but all of which shall constitute one and the same instrument.

j) This writing constitutes the entire agreement between the parties hereto and no such party has relied on any oral or written statement not contained herein.

IN WITNESS WHEREOF, the parties have duly executed this Agreement as of the date first above written.

SELLER

_____

By: _____ , President

ATTEST:

_____
Secretary

BUYER

_____

By: _____ , President

ATTEST:

_____
Secretary

_____
Guarantor

_____
Stockholder

_____
Stockholder

_____
_____ , Esq., Escrow

APPENDIX 5.2
MINUTES OF MEETING OF DIRECTORS' APPROVING SALE OF ASSETS

Minutes of the meeting of the Board of Directors of Seller, Inc., held _____ , 19 _____ .

The Directors of Seller, Inc. (Seller) met by telephone on_____ , 19 _____ . Present for the meeting were _____, _____, and _____ comprising all of the members of the Board of Seller. A waiver of notice for this meeting is on file among the records of Seller.

The meeting was called to order at 10:45 A.M. by _____, who indicated that a proposed contract had been received from Buyer Corp. (Buyer) offering to purchase substantially all of the assets of Seller. The proposed contract had been distributed in advance to the Directors. He also indicated that a Plan of Complete Liquidation had been prepared for consideration, which Plan had also been distributed to the Directors.

_____ then moved the acceptance by the Directors of the Plan of Complete Liquidation and the Motion was seconded by _____. There being no further discussion thereon, it was unanimously

RESOLVED to adopt the Plan of Complete Liquidation as presented to the Directors.

_____ then moved the approval of the proposed contract received from Buyer for the purchase of substantially all of the assets of Seller and to recommend its acceptance by the Seller's Shareholders. There being no further discussion thereon it was unanimously

RESOLVED to approve the proposed contract received from Buyer for the purchase of substantially all of the assets of Seller and to recommend to the Seller's Shareholders the adoption of the same.

There being no further business, the meeting was adjourned at 11:05 A.M.

Dated_____   _____
                                        Director

Dated_____   _____
                                        Director

Dated_____   _____
                                        Director

I, _____, Secretary of Seller, Inc., a corporation organized and operating under the laws of New York, hereby certify that the foregoing is a full, true, and complete copy of the minutes of the special meeting of the Directors of Seller held by telephone on _____, 19__ at 10:45 A.M.

IN WITNESS WHEREOF, I have hereunto set my hand this _____ day of _____, 1991.

APPENDIX 5.3
SHAREHOLDER CONSENT IN LIEU OF A MEETING

I, _____, the holder of shares of stock in Seller, Inc. (Seller) and in consideration of an agreement (the Contract), dated the _____ day of _____19__, by and between the Seller and Buyer Corp. (Buyer) whereby the Buyer agreed to purchase substantially all of the assets of Seller hereby agree to the following provisions:

1. I acknowledge that I am the owner of _____ shares of stock in Seller and have not transferred any of my shares to any other person, group of persons, or entity.

2. I consent to the sale of Seller's assets as per the terms of the Contract.

3. The President of Seller is hereby authorized to execute all appropriate documents and to take all appropriate action necessary to consummate such sale.

4. I hereby release and forever discharge and by these presents do for myself, my heirs, executors, administrators, and assigns, remise, release, and forever discharge Seller and each other Stockholder their heirs, executors, administrators, successors, and assigns of and from all and any manner of action and actions, cause and causes of action, suits, debts, dues, sums of money, accounts, reckonings, bonds, bills, specialties, covenants, contracts, controversies, agreements, promises, damages, judgments, claims, and demands whatsoever, in law or in equity which I ever had, now have, or which my heirs, executors, or administrators, hereafter can, shall, or may have against the Seller or any other Stockholder for, upon or by reason of any manner, cause or thing whatsoever from the beginning of the world to the date of this release.

5. I agree that for five (5) years from the date of the closing of the transaction contemplated in Paragraph 1 hereof, I will not, within the states of New York, Connecticut, New Jersey, Massachusetts, Maine, Vermont, New Hampshire, Rhode Island, and Pennsylvania and the District of Columbia and Puerto Rico, re-establish, re-open, be engaged in, nor in any manner whatsoever become interested, directly or indirectly, either as employee, as owner, as partner, as agent, or as stockholder, director, or officer of a corporation or otherwise, in any business, trade, or occupation similar to that conducted by the Seller.

Dated: _____   _____

APPENDIX 5.4
BUYER'S PROMISSORY NOTE

$141,500.00

New York, N.Y.

September_____ , 19 _____ ,

Pursuant to that certain contract, dated September _____ , 19 _____ , between _____ (Seller) and _____ (Buyer) and in consideration thereof, Buyer promises to pay to the order of Seller, in self-amortizing installments as hereinafter set forth, the sum of $141,500.00 with interest on the unpaid balance at the rate of 8% per annum from the date hereof until paid.

1. INSTALLMENTS: On the first anniversary of this note, Buyer shall pay to Seller the sum of $8,085.71, which sum shall be applied toward the accrued first year's interest of $11,320.00. The accrued but unpaid first-year interest, in the amount of $2,680.00, shall be added to the outstanding principal balance of $141,500.00, making a total principal balance of $144,180.00.

    Thereafter, Buyer shall make 18 semi-annual payments of $11,434.01, each beginning on the first day of April, 19__, and then on the first day of each October and each April thereafter until the entire amount, with interest at 8% per annum from the date hereof, is paid.

2. DEFAULT: Default shall occur in the event of the nonpayment of any installment on its due date. In the event of default, Seller shall give Buyer written notice thereof by certified mail, return receipt requested. Buyer shall have fifteen (15) days from the date any such notice is mailed to cure said default.

3. ACCELERATION: In the event a default is not cured as hereinabove provided, the entire unpaid principal balance with interest due thereon shall, at the option of Seller, immediately become due and payable without further demand or notice. In the event of default by Buyer of any term or provision of this note, which default is not timely cured as hereinabove provided, Seller shall be entitled to collect the costs, including reasonable attorney's fees, of such collection.

    In the event of a sale, transfer, and/or conveyance of more than fifty (50) percent of the stock of Buyer, the unpaid principal indebtedness, together with interest thereon, if any, shall immediately become due and payable, without notice to Buyer.

    In the event of a sale, transfer, and/or conveyance of the stock of Buyer so that _____ owns less than fifty (50) percent of its authorized, issued, and outstanding shares and/or the sale of substantially all of the assets of Buyer outside the ordinary course of its business, the unpaid principal indebtedness, together with interest thereon, if any, shall immediately become due and payable with no demand or notice to Buyer.

Appendix 5.4 *(continued)*

4. PREPAYMENT: At any time and from time to time, prepayment, in whole or in part, shall be permitted, at Buyer's option, without penalty. Any such prepayment(s) shall be applied in inverse order of the due dates hereunder and shall not alter the due dates or amounts of future payments. Payments shall, in all cases, be credited first to accrued interest, if any, and then to the reduction of principal.

Buyer

_____

By _____, President

APPENDIX 5.5
RIDER TO SECURITY AGREEMENT

This Rider to the Security Agreement, dated September _____ , 19 _____ , between _____, Inc., Debtor, and _____, Secured Party, is for the purpose of setting out additional terms and understandings between the parties thereto. Upon execution hereof, this Rider shall be attached to, and become a part of, said Security Agreement.

1. The Security Agreement securing an indebtedness in the amount of $141,500.00, with interest, (evidenced by a promissory note of even date herewith) shall be subject to the following terms and provisions:

    Default shall occur in the event of the nonpayment of any installment of the promissory note on its due date. In the event of default, the Secured Party shall give Debtor written notice thereof by certified mail, return receipt requested. Debtor shall have fifteen (15) days from the date any such notice is mailed to cure said default.

    In the event a default is not cured as hereinabove provided, the entire unpaid principal balance with interest due thereon shall, at the option of the Secured Party, immediately become due and payable without further demand or notice.

2. It is understood that the Security Agreement shall be subordinate to liens on the same assets held by _____ National Bank to secure advances made by it to the Debtor. Should the Debtor obtain such advances from a source to replace _____ National Bank, then the Secured Party agrees to subordinate its Security Agreement to such a new source. It is further understood and agreed that the Security Agreement shall allow the Debtor to use and sell such assets in the ordinary course of its business. Should the Debtor purchase new such assets, the Secured Party agrees to subordinate its subject security agreement to a purchase money security interest for the purchase of such new assets.

3. All the terms of that certain Promissary note (the Note) between _____, as Maker, and _____, as payee dated _____ 19_____ are incorporated herein and made a part hereof. Any inconsistency between the terms of the Note and the Security Agreement shall be resolved as per the terms of the Note.

Appendix 5.5 *(continued)*

IN WITNESS WHEREOF, the Parties have respectively signed and sealed these presents the day and year first above written.

Debtor

_____

by _____, President

Secured Party

_____

by _____, President

Chapter 6

Securities Regulation

We have already discussed in Chapter 1 some of the issues involved in the initial capitalization of the corporation. As you will recall, capital may be raised through the sale of stock or by borrowing funds from the principals, from a lending institution, or, occasionally, from the public. This chapter will discuss some of the other legal requirements for raising that capital and the additional capital that a corporation may need for expansion. It will also discuss some of the issues raised when a corporation "goes public." Going public occurs when the small group of shareholders who started and developed a closely held corporation believe that it has become sufficiently successful for the public to be interested in buying its stock. The principals will then arrange to have the corporation offer additional authorized shares of its stock to the public. At the same time, the principals may attempt to sell to the public some of the corporation's shares that they hold. As one might expect, a significant amount of federal and state regulation surrounds these transactions. This chapter is designed to give you an overview of that regulatory scheme and how to comply with it.

INTRODUCTION TO FEDERAL SECURITIES REGULATION

The federal government is involved in regulating the sale of securities to the public through the use of any instrumentality of interstate commerce. A sale is in interstate commerce when the seller uses the mails or the telephone at any level of the transaction. This is true even if the sale is made to a neighbor down the street. The federal regulation is accomplished largely through an administrative agency known as the Securities and Exchange Commission (SEC), which operates pursuant to several federal statutes. The two main ones are the Securities Act of 1933 (the Securities Act) and the Securities Exchange Act of 1934 (the Exchange Act). These laws basically require that companies attempting to raise capital by selling securities provide to investors complete and accurate information about those securities.

Neither the SEC nor any other federal regulatory agency passes on the investment merits of any issuance of securities. The SEC's goal is to insure that each potential investor has access to sufficient information to evaluate the merits himself or herself. The availability of information is accomplished through a requirement that the company (called the *issuer*) make certain public disclosures about the company, its principals, finances, and business activities.

The statutes also include several antifraud provisions that may be enforced by private individuals who were injured in their purchase or sale of securities by a false or misleading statement or omission. The penalties for violation of these requirements may be severe.

The requirement of disclosure is met (subject to several exceptions that will be discussed later in this chapter) by having the issuer *register* the securities to be sold with the SEC. Registration requires that the issuer file with the SEC a registration statement that includes a prospectus (which also must be delivered to each purchaser of the security) as well as a great deal of additional information and exhibits (which, while not required to be delivered to purchasers, will be available for public inspection). It is very important to note that the process of registration is a long, complex, and expensive one that is fraught with difficulties. For the small company seeking start-up capital, or even a going concern of modest size seeking to expand, the cost of an SEC registration (which can easily run into the tens of thousands of dollars) is prohibitive. Moreover, the liability for an improper registration or for not registering when registration is required may be quite serious. Once again, therefore, the assistance of experienced professionals is needed to advise the small company about registration requirements and to assist it in preparing the appropriate documentation.

Perhaps the best way to approach the subject of security regulation is to begin by defining the term *security*. Section 2(1) of the Securities Act and Section 3(a) (10) of the Exchange Act define the term very broadly. It includes those instruments, such as stock and bonds, that are normally thought of as securities as well as a wide variety of lesser known instruments, such as profit-sharing agreements or investment contracts. For the purposes of this book, unless the context requires otherwise, we will concentrate on stock, both common and preferred, evidences of indebtedness, including bonds, debentures, and promissory notes, and debt instruments convertible into stock.

The general rule is that when a security is offered for sale, that security must be registered with the SEC. As mentioned earlier, the purpose of the registration is to have a public disclosure of information about the offering and the company and people behind it. While this is a valuable device, it is a very complex and expensive procedure, as has also been discussed. Recognizing that the expense is usually so large as to be completely outside of the capability of the small corporation and recognizing the desirability of encouraging small entrepreneurs to begin and to expand business, Congress and the SEC have developed a series of exemptions from the registration requirements. For instance, Section 4(1) of the Securities Act specifically exempts from the registration requirement "transactions by any person other than an issuer, underwriter, or dealer." This means, generally, that individuals can sell the shares they own without registering them. There are also two general types of exemptions for issuers; those that apply to a security itself and those that apply to the transactions through which the securities are to be offered. The securities that are exempt in and of themselves include:

- those issued by the federal government or by a state or municipal government

- those issued by nonprofit organizations

- certain short-term promissory notes.

The transactional exemptions have more applicability to closely held corporations, and this is the type of exemption that will be discussed in this chapter. Remember that these exemptions apply only to the federal law. The fact that there is a federal exemption for a particular transaction does not mean that the transaction is exempt from the provisions of state securities laws. These laws, known as "blue sky" laws, will also be discussed in this chapter.

TRANSACTIONAL EXEMPTIONS FROM REGISTRATION

There are several types of transactions for which the securities laws, including the rules and regulations of the SEC, provide an exemption from registration. In each of the cases to be discussed in this section, the securities transaction must be one between a corporation (or its agent, collectively known as an issuer) and a purchaser of its securities. A principal shareholder who wants to sell his or her corporate shares to the public is not covered by the exemption of the issuer. Such shareholders have to register the shares or qualify for an exemption on their own. In addition, since the available exemptions are for types of transactions, the proponent of the exemption must show, if challenged, why the transaction qualifies for the exemption. In order to assist in this regard, the SEC has promulgated several rules that, if complied with, will give the issuer a "safe harbor" from liability. Finally, regardless of whether a transaction is exempt from SEC registration, the antifraud provisions of the securities laws apply to all transactions involved in interstate commerce. These provisions also will be discussed later in this chapter. The remainder of this section, however, will be devoted to a discussion of the major transactional exemptions.

Regulation D

Regulation D (Reg D) consists of a series of rules promulgated by the SEC that set out the requirements for various exemptions from registration. There are several definitions of general applicability within Reg D, and they are set out in Rule 501. (For those with access to the Code of Federal Regulations, the citation is 17 CFR 230.501.) Among the most important are the definitions of an "accredited investor," an "affiliate," the "aggregate offering price," and "the calculation of number of purchasers."

An *accredited investor* is a person who has sufficient wealth and/or income to be deemed able to absorb the loss of his or her investment and one who has sufficient knowledge to be able to decide on his or her own whether to invest in a particular offering. The test to determine whether an individual is an accredited investor is, however, purely economic, with one exception. Therefore, a very unsophisticated person holding, for instance, inherited wealth might qualify while a knowledgeable business person who has not yet achieved wealth would not. Nevertheless, when discussing an individual, an accredited investor includes:

- any natural person whose net worth (including that of his or her spouse) at the time of the purchase of securities exceeds $1 million

- any natural person who had an individual income in excess of $200,000 for the last two years and reasonably expects to exceed $200,000 in the current year

- any person who purchases at least $150,000 of the offered securities for cash, for securities with a readily available price quote, for the forgiveness of indebtedness owed by the issuer, or for an unconditional promise to pay within five years cash or securities with a readily available price quote.

In addition, a director, executive officer, or general partner of an issuer is deemed to be an accredited investor, as is any entity that is wholly owned by accredited investors. Certain other organizations, such as banks and private business development companies, are also considered accredited investors.

An *affiliate* is a person who, directly or indirectly, controls, is controlled by, or is under common control with another person.

The *aggregate offering price* is the sum of all cash, services, property, notes, cancellation of indebtedness, or other consideration paid by the investor to the issuer for the securities. Property and services are measured at their fair market value determined by sales or some other accepted standard.

The *calculation of the number of purchasers* is relevant to the exemptions under Sections 505 and 506 of Reg D. For the purposes of those two sections, the calculation of the number of purchasers excludes:

- any relative, spouse, or relative of the spouse of the purchaser who has the same principal residence as the purchaser

- any trust or estate in which the purchaser or any of the persons related to the purchaser collectively have more than 50 percent of the beneficial interest

- any corporation or other organization of which a purchaser or his or her relatives collectively are beneficial owners of more than 50 percent of the equity securities or interests

- any accredited investor.

In addition to the definitions, there are a series of other conditions of general applicability under Reg D. For instance, while the term *offering* is not defined in the securities laws or in the regulations, it is clear that an offering takes place over time. In order to determine which securities or transactions are part of an offering for Reg D purposes, Section 502 deals with the "integration" of various sales into one offering. Because all sales in an offering must be considered when determining whether a Reg D exemption applies, an issuer must know which sales are part of a particular offering. For instance, the regulation indicates that any sales of securities made more than six months *before* the start of a Reg D offering or more than six months *after* the completion of the offering will not be considered part of that offering. During the two six-month periods, there may not be any offers or sales by or for the issuer of the same or similar securities as offered or sold under the Reg D exemption.

The SEC has set out five additional guidelines to assist parties in determining whether offers and sales of securities should be integrated:

1. Are the sales part of a single plan of financing?

2. Do the sales involve issuance of the same class of securities?

3. Have the sales been made at or about the same time?

4. Has the same type of consideration been received for the security?

5. Have the sales been made for the same general purpose?

The regulation also indicates that for a Reg D exemption to apply, neither the issuer nor any person acting on its behalf may offer or sell securities through a general solicitation or through general advertising. This includes a prohibition on advertisements, articles, or notices in the print or broadcast media. It also prohibits offers through the use of investment seminars or meetings where the attendees have been invited by general solicitation or advertising.

Any securities acquired by a purchaser pursuant to a Reg D exemption may not be resold without being registered under the Securities Act or obtaining a new exemption from such registration. It is the responsibility of the issuer to use reasonable care to assure that the purchasers of the securities are not "underwriters," as defined in Section 2(11) of the Securities Act. An *underwriter* is a person who has purchased from an issuer with a view to a subsequent distribution of the securities or who offers or sells for the issuer in connection with a distribution. The term specifically excludes any person who merely receives a commission from an underwriter that is not in excess of the usual and customary commission for such sales or distribution. If an issuer sells to an underwriter who then resells to the public without first registering the securities, the issuer, as well as the underwriter, may be liable for violation of the registration requirement. For the purpose of the regulation, an issuer includes any person directly or indirectly controlling or controlled by the issuer or under common control with it.

According to Section 502(d), the steps taken by the issuer to assure no sales to an underwriter shall include:

- reasonable inquiry to determine whether the purchaser is acquiring the securities for himself or herself or for other persons

- written disclosure to each purchaser prior to sale of the securities that said securities have not been registered under the Securities Act and therefore cannot be resold unless they are registered or an exemption is available

- a legend placed on the securities stating that the securities have not been registered and setting forth or referring to the restrictions on resale.

The reasonable inquiry requirement is usually met by the issuer obtaining from each purchaser a written commitment (called an *investment letter*) that the securities being purchased are for their own account as an investment and not for resale.

Exemptions Pursuant to Reg D

There are several bases for exemption under Reg D. Two are concerned with the size of the offering, and a third, often called the exemption for the "private placement" of securities, deals with the number and type of investors who are purchasing securities. This section will discuss the various exemptions and the requirements attached to each one.

The first exemption is for offers and sales of securities for a price not exceeding $1 million. Its purpose clearly is to assist small companies that are in the start-up stage or involved in relatively small expansions. The rules applicable to this exemption are found in Section 504 of the regulations, and if a company qualifies, the prohibitions found elsewhere in Reg D on general solicitations and advertising and on resales of securities will not apply to the offering. Moreover, there are no federal disclosure requirements for this exemption nor is there a requirement that the issuer assure itself that the purchaser is "sophisticated" in investment matters. Therefore, this is a particularly useful exemption to obtain.

The essence of the exemption is that the securities must be offered in at least one state that requires registration of the securities and the delivery to purchasers, before the sale, of a disclosure document. If this requirement is met, the exemption is valid even for sales made in states that do not require registration. The $1 million limitation on the offering applies to sales made pursuant to the offering itself and to all securities sold by the issuer within the 12 months before the start of the offering. Moreover, only $500,000 of the securities can be offered or sold in states where they are not registered pursuant to state law. The calculation of the aggregate offering price takes on critical importance here.

The SEC has provided examples of how to determine the amount eligible at any time for exemption under this provision. Suppose an issuer who is eligible under a state registration requirement sold $400,000 of its securities on June 1, 1990, and $200,000 more on September 1, 1990. This issuer would be permitted to sell only $400,000 more until June 1, 1991. The $600,000 of prior sales within 12 months of the current offering count toward the $1 million limit permitted under this exemption. If the issuer waited until June 2, 1991, to make its next sale, it would be permitted to sell $800,000 of its securities because the June 1, 1990, sale of $400,000 would no longer be within the 12-month period before the current offering. Only the $200,000 sale on September 1, 1990, would count toward the $1 million limit.

The second exemption is set out in Section 505 of Reg D. It is based, in part, on a maximum dollar amount of securities that can be sold through the offering. The rule permits an aggregate offering price of $5 million, less the aggregate offering price of all securities sold during the 12 months before the start of the offering. In addition to this limitation, the issuer must reasonably believe that there are no more than 35 purchasers for the securities. Here, the calculation of the number of purchasers plays a major role in determining whether the exemption is available. Similarly, the concept of integration is critical in determining which transactions are part of the offering, which, in turn, will permit a calculation of the aggregate offering price.

This exemption is, in some ways, more restrictive than the exemption under Section 504 that was discussed previously. The permissible number of purchasers under Section 505 is limited, which is not true with the 504 exemption. Under this exemption, unlike the 504 exemption, there are restrictions on advertising and solicitation. Moreover, there are federal informational requirements that must be met for *all* purchasers if *any* sales under this exemption are made to nonaccredited investors. These informational requirements will be discussed in more detail later in this chapter. On the other hand, the amount of money that can be raised pursuant to this exemption is much greater than under 504. Thus, companies with larger needs may still be able to sell their securities without the delay and expense associated with a federal securities registration.

Perhaps the most familiar exemption (although it is not well understood by nonspecialists) is the so-called private placement of securities pursuant to Section 506 of Reg D. This exemption is available without regard to the dollar amount of the offering. Instead, it is based on a limitation on the number of purchasers, 35, calculated in accordance with the provisions of Section 501(e), which was discussed earlier. Again, the integration rules established in Section 502(a) come into play to determine what is the offering for the application of the 35 purchaser limitation. One other element found in this exemption, which is not found in the others we have discussed, is the requirement that the issuer shall reasonably believe, prior to making any sale, that each purchaser who is not an accredited investor has, either on his or her own or through a "purchaser representative," sufficient knowledge and experience in financial and business matters so as to be able to evaluate the merits and risks of the investment.

A purchaser representative is a person:

- who is not, directly or indirectly, an affiliate of the issuer

- who has, alone or with the purchaser or with other purchaser representatives of the purchaser, sufficient knowledge and experience in financial and business matters so as to be able to evaluate the merits and risks of an investment

- who is acknowledged in writing by the purchaser, during the course of the transaction, to be his or her purchaser representative

- who discloses to the purchaser in writing, prior to the above-mentioned acknowledgement, any material relationship between the purchaser representative and his or her affiliates and the issuer or its affiliates that then exists, that is mutually contemplated, or that has existed at any time within the past two years as well as disclosing any compensation received or to be received as a result of such relationship.

As you can see, this exemption places a premium on the knowledge and experience of the purchaser or his or her ability to obtain such knowledge and experience. Accredited investors are deemed to have such knowledge and experience, but for nonaccredited investors the issuer must reasonably believe the purchaser has or has access to such sophistication. This is often accomplished by the requirement that the potential investor submit a purchaser questionnaire to be used by the issuer to meet its obligation concerning the suitability of the investment for the investor. In addition, there may be a purchaser representative questionnaire to meet the issuer's obligation in this respect. In each case, the investor and the purchaser representative are providing information and representations to the issuer about their background, skill, knowledge, and experience upon which the issuer will rely in accepting the investment of the potential purchaser. This must be done in order to qualify for the Section 506 exemption. Keep in mind, however, that once it is determined that the potential purchaser, alone or together with a purchaser representative, has the requisite sophistication, the purchaser is on his or her own as far as evaluating the investment is concerned.

The exemption under Section 506 is, perhaps, the broadest in Reg D. First, there is no limit on the amount that may be raised through the sale of securities. Second, while there is some restriction on the number of purchasers who may take securities pursuant to this exemption, this limitation applies only to nonaccredited investors. There may be an unlimited number of accredited investors among the purchasers. What is more, the limitation of 35 nonaccredited investors applies to the number of *purchasers*, not the number of people to whom the offer of purchase is made. In this regard, however, it must be remembered that a Section 506 offering *is* subject to the restrictions on general solicitations and advertising as well as the restriction on resales. Therefore, if the offer of purchase is made to too broad a group, it is possible that the offering will not be deemed private, and the exemption will not be available.

Exemptions Other Than Under Reg D

There are also several exemptions that are available under the securities laws or the SEC regulations other than Reg D. Please do not interpret their brief discussion here as a suggestion that they are not important. They are often quite useful to closely held corporations and should not be disregarded. The Reg D provisions, however, have a somewhat broader scope and often raise more complex issues. Among the most significant of the non-Reg D exemptions are those for "intrastate offerings," those for corporate recapitalizations and reorganizations, and those pursuant to Regulation A promulgated by the SEC.

Intrastate Offerings

The intrastate offering exemption is found in Section 3(a)(11) of the Securities Act. This statutory provision is amplified in Section 147 of the SEC rules. Essentially, it is available to any issuer who offers and sells securities only to residents of a single state. The issuer must also be a resident of and do business in that state. An offer to even one nonresident makes the exemption unavailable. The underlying premise for this exemption is that if an offering is limited to one state, the offerees are more likely to have access to important investment information. In addition, if the offering is limited to one state, that state has the interest and ability to regulate the offering and to protect its residents.

The uncertainties with the exemption have arisen primarily with regard to the definition of terms. Rule 147 was designed to eliminate those uncertainties. Under that rule, the term *resident*, when applied to a purchaser, means the state in which the purchaser has his or her principal residence at the time of the offer and sale. When applied to the issuer, the term means the state in which the issuer was incorporated or organized and in which it is "doing business." To determine whether the issuer is doing business within a state, the rule examines four criteria:

1. Is the issuer's principal office within the state?

2. Does the issuer derive 80 percent of its gross revenue from operating a business or rendering a service within the state?

3. Are 80 percent of its assets within the state?

4. Does the issuer use at least 80 percent of the funds raised from the offering for operations within the state?

An issuer who qualifies under this exemption will not be limited as to the amount of the offering or the number of purchasers. In fact, the purchasers will even be allowed to resell the securities if they are sold to another resident of the same state. The SEC has established a nine-month holding period before a purchaser can safely sell the securities to a nonresident. It should be pointed out that this regulation merely establishes a "safe harbor" for the offering. If the securities come within the terms of the rule, they will be deemed to be exempt. If they do not precisely meet the terms of the rule, they may still be exempt under the statute, but the issuer will be required to show the exempt nature of the offering.

Recapitalizations and Reorganizations

Sections 3(a)(9) and 3(a)(10) of the Securities Act provide exemptions that are useful in recapitalizations and reorganizations. The former section permits an issuer to exchange any security exclusively with its existing security holders where there is no commission or other payment given for soliciting the exchange. This section makes the conversion of convertible securities possible without registration. It also allows the corporation to replace existing issues of securities with another issue—either to retire more senior securities or to effect a stock split or other recapitalization. There are, however, problems of integration if the same or similar securities have been issued to the public. There are also resale restrictions on the existing security holders if they are "in control" of the issuer. If they are deemed to be underwriters, they will have to register the securities or perfect an exemption from registration before the resale.

Section 3(a)(10) applies to situations when securities are issued in exchange for claims, property, or other securities or partly in such exchange and partly for cash. The terms of the issuance and exchange must have been ordered or approved, after a hearing on the fairness of such terms, by a court or by an official or agency of the United States or by a state agency or official who is authorized by state law to grant such approval. Generally, this section has been invoked in order to expedite the settlement of private disputes, including those pursuant to shareholder derivative actions. It has also been used in corporate reorganizations. The fact of judicial supervision or that of a federal or state agency has been deemed sufficient to assure appropriate treatment of security holders and prospective security holders; therefore, no federal registration is required.

Regulation A

Regulation A is a series of SEC created rules that, taken together, provide the format and requirements for another set of exemptions from full registration. Before Reg D was promulgated in 1982, the provisions of Reg A were important in avoiding a full registration. The regulation did not, however, eliminate the requirement of a federal filing altogether. Reg A provides for what has been called a "mini registration," in that the issuer must file with the SEC an *offering statement*. The information required in the offering statement is not as detailed or extensive as that required in a registration. Nevertheless, preparing and filing an offering statement is still a significant undertaking.

In addition to permitting the shorter offering document (which must be made at the appropriate SEC regional office rather than at the SEC's national office), Reg A relieves the issuer from several of the periodic filings required of an issuer who must register its offering. Under Reg A, moreover, the issuer is permitted, in certain circumstances, to use dealers and advertisements to solicit purchasers. Another advantage of Reg A is that, unlike many of its counterparts in Reg D, there is no limit on the number of offerees or purchasers of the securities. Also, there is generally no restriction to prevent a purchaser of securities under Reg A from reselling them. Therefore, the issuer need not take steps to restrict the resale.

On the other hand, there are several similarities with Reg D and in some areas there are disadvantages to Reg A. For instance, the concepts of aggregation of price and integration of offerings apply to Reg A as they do to Reg D. Moreover, the upper limit on the aggregate offering price under Reg A is only $1 million, rather than the $5 million permitted under Section 505 in Reg D. All things considered, and despite some of the advantages under Reg A, its filing requirement, particularly when compared to the broad scope and relative administrative ease of Reg D, have reduced its importance in the sphere of registration exemptions.

A few final words should be said about underwriters and the registration and exemption process. Underwriters, as you will recall, are people who purchase from an issuer all or part of an offering of securities for the purpose of, or with a view to, reselling the securities or who offers or sells those securities for an issuer. An issuer who claims an exemption is usually under a duty to investigate purchasers to make sure they are not going to resell the securities in violation of the law. In many cases such sales are inadvertently made by a principal of the corporation or by someone acting, in good faith, on behalf of the issuer. The liability of the issuer *and* the underwriter is potentially very large. It is, therefore, of the utmost importance that the issuer, its principals and agents, and any purchasers be aware of the resale restrictions and seek expert assistance before reselling any unregistered securities of the issuer.

As to registration and exemption, the issuer is not required to file an application to obtain an exemption. Instead, the issuer and its advisors are primarily responsible for making the decision as to whether to register the offering and for complying with the terms of any exemption they believe is applicable. If they are wrong about the applicability of an exemption or about the conduct on their part necessary to comply with the law, they may be liable to the SEC and to any investor injured due to their failures. At least as far as the SEC is concerned, issuers can seek advance rulings on the correctness of their conduct prior to acting through a procedure known as the "no-action letter."

Under this procedure, an attorney for a company subject to SEC regulation may write on behalf of his or her client to the staff of the SEC about a proposed action of the client or about the availability of an exemption under certain described circumstances. The letter sets out in detail what the client proposes to do and seeks an opinion from the staff as to its legality. The staff will examine the activity described in the letter. If they find it to comply with the law, they will issue a no-action letter. This letter will state that, provided that the action taken by the issuer is as stated in its letter, the SEC will take no enforcement action against the company.

If the staff refuses to issue the letter, most attorneys will advise their clients not to proceed with the proposed activity. They do so because even if the proposed conduct turns out to be perfectly legal, the expense and delay, not to mention the risk and bad publicity, of an SEC investigation or enforcement action is generally more trouble than the proposed activity is worth. Be aware that obtaining a no-action letter does not insulate the company from liability for the described conduct. The letter has no binding effect on any person injured by the described activity, and even the SEC itself is not bound by the action of its staff. On this last point, it would be highly unlikely, however, that the SEC would move against a company who had acted in accordance with the terms of a no-action letter obtained from the SEC staff.

INFORMATIONAL REQUIREMENTS FOR PURCHASERS OF NONREGISTERED SECURITIES

As we have already seen, the essence of the federal regulatory scheme concerning the sale of securities is that complete and correct information be made available to all investors. With new issues of securities, this goal is achieved through the requirement of registration with the SEC. Registration of an offering is a way of putting significant amounts of information on the public record and of providing a good deal of that information directly to potential investors through the requirement of a prospectus.

We have also seen, however, that there are several ways to avoid the registration requirement. One may ask, therefore, how are the informational requirements of the federal scheme met in the absence of registration? The answer is that in some cases they are not met. The law does not require, for instance, that any information be given to purchasers if sales are made only to accredited investors or are made pursuant to the small offering exemption of Section 504. The rest of this section will discuss the informational requirements of offerings exempt from registration pursuant to other exemptions under Reg D. It will also discuss one of the main ways in which those informational requirements are met, the Private Placement Memorandum (PPM).

Section 502(b) of Reg D sets out in general terms the informational requirements for offerings exempt under the terms of this regulation. It begins by stating that if the issuer sells securities under Section 504 or sells exclusively to accredited investors, there are no federal requirements to provide investors with any information at all. As a practical matter, this provision is not as significant as it appears to be. In the first instance, there are very few investors who would invest in a company without knowing anything about it. Typically, the issuer or its officers provide some information to potential investors. Since the antifraud provisions of the securities laws (which will be discussed later in this chapter) continue to apply, even to otherwise exempt offerings, any misleading statement or omission that causes a loss to an investor may be actionable. Nevertheless, the lack of an informational requirement is an advantage to the issuer because much of what would otherwise be required to be provided is expensive and time-consuming to compile. In many cases it is more than an investor needs in order to make a rational decision about investing.

If the issuer sells securities under section 505 or 506 to *any* nonaccredited investor, Section 502 prescribes the type of information that must be provided to *all* investors, including the accredited investors. For most small corporations, those not subject to other SEC reporting requirements, the information that must be provided to purchasers is "the same kind of information as would be required in Part I of Form S-18." Form S-18 is one of the forms for Registration Statements under the Securities Act, and Part I requires quite a bit of information about the issuer and its principals, such as:

- risk factors associated with the offering
- use of the proceeds of the offering
- offering price and how it was determined
- plan of distribution, including the use of underwriters

- directors and executive officers, including their relationship to each other and their business experience

- security holdings of certain persons, including management

- securities being offered

- development and conduct of the business

- important property owned or used by the issuer

- interest, if any, of management and others in certain transactions of the issuer

- market in which the issuer will operate

- compensation of executives

- issuer's financial status, including the provision of its balance sheets, income statements, and other relevant documents.

As can be seen from this list and from the accompanying S-18 and PPM excerpts, the amount of required information is impressive. In addition, it often must be presented in a particular manner. Many prospectuses and PPMs, therefore, have a similar appearance and are often not carefully read by potential investors. In fact, although it is the nonaccredited investor for whom this information is provided, that investor is probably the least likely to read and digest it. This problem is compounded by the overwhelming detail included in some documents in order for the issuer, its principals, and the underwriters to avoid charges that some material factor was omitted and that the omission caused some purchaser to invest in what has become a losing deal. Some commentators have gone so far as to suggest that this fear has caused issuers and underwriters to mention even insignificant risks so that readers will become immune to the true risks of the venture that are hidden among the surplus verbiage of the document. Such a cynical view is probably inaccurate, but there is a significant exposure to liability for the persons mentioned and others who help them put together the prospectus. The next section will deal with the liabilities of the issuer, underwriters, and certain other participants in the offering process.

Liability for Material Misstatements and Omissions

Because the securities laws are premised upon disclosure to investors of the facts surrounding an issuer or any securities of that issuer, that information must be accurate and complete. In order to increase the likelihood of this, the securities laws specifically require such information and create liabilities for failing to provide it. The sections of the law that are most pertinent here are Sections 11 and 12 of the Securities Act and Section 10(b) of the Exchange Act, together with Rule 10(b) (5) of the SEC regulations. These laws run from a general antifraud and antimanipulation provision concerning the purchase or sale of any security to a specific requirement of complete and accurate information in a registration statement. For each of them, the law provides for both public and private remedies. This means that the government, through the SEC or the Justice Department, may go after violators, either criminally or civilly. It also means that private citizens who have been injured by a violation may pursue the wrongdoer and seek judicial relief in a civil action. In this section we will examine the provisions of these sections and some of their practical applications.

Sections 10(b) and 10(b) (5)

Section 10(b) of the Exchange Act makes it unlawful for any person, through the use of any aspect of interstate commerce, such as the mail or the telephone (including fax machines and computer modems), to employ in connection with a *purchase or sale* of a security any manipulative or deceptive device or practice. This rather broad statement is elucidated in Rule 10(b) (5) of the SEC regulations pursuant to the Exchange Act, which prohibits any person from:

- employing any device, scheme, or artifice to defraud

- making any untrue statement of a material fact or omitting to state a material fact necessary to make the statements made, in light of the circumstances under which they were made, not misleading

- engaging in any act or practice that would operate as a fraud or deceit upon any person.

The Act as well as the regulations implementing it apply to very specific situations: *a*) They apply only in connection with the *purchase or sale* of a security. The transaction need not be between an issuer and a purchaser (although the rules do apply to this situation). It may be between two individuals involved in a private sale. *b*) They apply when the parties have used any element of interstate commerce to achieve the sale or purchase. Even if the parties are next-door neighbors and never cross a state line, if they use the telephone or the mail for any of their negotiation, they have implicated interstate commerce, and the antifraud provisions apply. *c*) They apply when a party attempts, through a scheme, a misstatement or omission of fact, or an act or practice, to deceive or defraud another in connection with the sale or purchase of a security. The misstatement or omission must be of a *material* fact: a fact that a reasonable investor would consider important in making his or her investment decision.

These rules are designed to protect against *insider trading*, a term that has appeared frequently in the news over the past few years in connection with various stock and bond scandals. It is defined as the participation of people with knowledge of important, nonpublic information about particular securities in the trading of these securities to the detriment of those without such knowledge. As you may recall, the penalties for this type of behavior are quite severe. Several well-known investors and brokers went to prison and paid large fines to the federal government for violating insider trading rules. Many of these people were also sued by investors who dealt with the insiders and who were injured by their lack of knowledge or by the insider's manipulation of the market. The same kind of liability, although generally not on so large a scale, applies to any investor who, in connection with a purchase or sale of a security, trades on inside information, makes false or misleading statements or omissions, or manipulates a security or a market.

Liabilities Concerning Registration Statements

Section 11 of the Securities Act creates liabilities for a misstatement or omission of a material fact in a registration statement. The liabilities are created in favor of a defrauded purchaser of the securities against every person who:

- signed the registration statement (including the issuer)

- was a director of the issuer at the time of the registration

- was, with his or her consent, listed in the registration statement as about to become a director of the issuer

- is an expert who has, with his or her consent, been named as having prepared or certified any part of the registration statement or any material used in connection with that statement

- was an underwriter of the offering.

The purchaser generally need not even prove that he or she relied on the misstatement or omission. It is sufficient to show that the material misstatement or omission in the registration statement existed. In addition, no causal connection between the misstatement or omission and the purchaser's injury need be exhibited. The showing of a financial loss is enough.

This fairly strict and far-reaching net of liability is limited by several defenses available to defendants. The most obvious is that the purchaser knew at the time he or she purchased the securities that the statements complained of were false. A defendant may also defend an action by showing that the facts misstated or omitted were not material or that the decline in value was the result of factors other than the misstatements or omissions. Another defense is the statute of limitations, which requires that a suit under the section be brought within one year of the discovery of the untrue statement or the omission or within one year after the discovery should have been made by the exercise of reasonable diligence. In no event, however, may a suit be instituted more than three years after the security was offered to the public.

Finally, Section 11(b) of the Securities Act provides the so-called due diligence defense for each potential defendant other than the issuer. Basically, this defense relieves defendants of their liability if they can show that they did not know and had no reason to know that there were material misstatements or omissions in the registration statement. In this regard, Section 11(b) (3) divides the registration statement into two distinct elements: *expertised* and *unexpertised*.

The expertised elements are those parts of the registration statement that purport to be made on the authority of an expert such as an engineer, accountant (as to certified financial documents), or attorney (on issues on which they have rendered an opinion) or purporting to be a copy or extract from a report or valuation by the expert. As to these expertised parts of the registration statement, every defendant, other than the issuer and the expert whose authority is implicated, is provided with a potential defense. They may show that they had no reasonable grounds to believe, and did not believe at the time that part of the registration statement became effective, that there were material misstatements or omissions of fact.

A defense as to the unexpertised sections of the registration statement requires the defendant to prove a bit more. This defense is available to every defendant other than the issuer who, after "reasonable investigation," had reasonable grounds to believe, and did believe at the time the registration statement became effective, that the statements in the registration statement were true and that there were no material omissions. The investigation required in this section is the due diligence mentioned earlier. The nature of the required investigation is set out in Section 11(c), which states that the standard of "reasonableness" is that degree of care and effort that would be required of a prudent person in the management of his or her property. This means that the defendant must have used reasonable care in determining that the nonexpert sections of the registration were accurate and complete. Although the Securities Act makes due diligence a defense to an action by a purchaser who lost money as a result of a material misstatement or omission, it has, as a practical matter, become an affirmative obligation of those who participate in the registration process. They generally must use the care of the reasonably prudent person in investigating the company and the offering and in developing the registration statement. The issuer, on the other hand, is not able to take advantage of the due diligence defense. Even if the issuer has used great care in determining that the statements are true and complete, it will be liable if they are untrue or if a material fact has been omitted.

Liabilities Concerning Prospectuses and Communications

The liabilities created under Section 11 apply only in relation to securities that have been registered. Because most small corporations that solicit funds from outside investors attempt to obtain an exemption from registration, Section 11 is not available to purchasers of those securities. Section 12(2) of the Securities Act, however, applies to any offer or sale of a security through a facility of interstate commerce by the use of a prospectus or oral communication. Liability attaches to sellers of securities where the prospectus or oral communication by which the securities were sold contains an untrue statement or omission of material fact. The purchaser need not have relied on the misstatement or omission in making the purchase. All that is necessary is that there be such a misstatement or omission in the prospectus or oral communications by which the securities were sold.

A seller may avoid liability by showing that he or she "did not know and in the exercise of reasonable care could not have known, of the untruth or omission." This reasonable care standard is similar to, although perhaps not as high as, the due diligence test in Section 11. To be exonerated, the seller must have exercised reasonable care to assure the truth and completeness of the communications and the prospectus. At least one court, however, has distinguished between sellers who are corporate insiders and those who are not. When applied to the insiders, the court suggested that the reasonable care test of 12(2) requires essentially the same investigation as the due diligence test of Section 11.

The question of who, precisely, is a "seller" has recently been examined and largely resolved by the courts. In interpreting the term *seller* in Section 12(1) of the Securities Act, the Supreme Court in *Pinter v Dahl* said it included a person who "successfully solicits the purchase" and who was at least partly motivated by serving his or her own financial interests or those of the owner of the securities. Thus, not only may the owner or the person who actually "sold" the securities be liable but also the one who solicited the sale for personal gain (i.e., a commission) or for the gain of another (a friend, relative, or employer) may also be liable. The liability of the seller is to rescind the transaction if the purchaser still owns the securities or for the damages suffered by the purchaser if they have been sold.

The sections we have discussed, 10(b) of the Exchange Act, 10(b) (5) of the regulations pursuant to that Act, and 11 and 12(2) of the Securities Act deal with only some of the liabilities imposed upon issuers and their principals and representatives by the securities laws. These sections all deal with false or misleading statements or omissions concerning the sale or purchase of securities. Sections 10(b), 10(b) (5), and 12(2) apply regardless of an exemption from registration and can impose potentially huge liabilities on even unsuspecting participants in a transaction. These rules are in addition to the complex and occasionally overlapping rules concerning registration and exemption.

There is, however, at least one more level of complexity that must be addressed concerning the issuance of securities to outside investors. This is the maze of rules and regulations known as "Blue Sky Laws." These are the laws of the various states concerning the offer or sale of securities within their borders. As with the federal laws, state law typically requires any securities offered or sold in the state to be registered with the state or to obtain an exemption from registration. The following section will provide a brief overview of a typical state securities law. It will also address, generally, the Blue

Sky Laws applicable to securities exempt from any federal registration requirements.

BLUE SKY LAWS

Most states and territories have adopted a statute or set of statutes regulating security transactions that occur within the state. There has been some attempt over the years to unify state securities laws. In fact, 35 years ago a Uniform Securities Act was developed for adoption in the hope that the state securities laws would become uniform. Unfortunately, this has not occurred, despite the fact that several states have adopted at least some of the Uniform Act. The problem is that several important states (as far as corporate finance is concerned) have not adopted the Act, and even in those that have, there is a great deal of local variation. This means that the corporate issuer or underwriter must examine and comply with the law of every state in which a security is offered or sold. The failure to comply, once again, can subject the noncomplying parties to significant liability. This is true even if they have complied with the federal requirements.

Basically, most state laws provide for:

- registration and exemption of securities

- regulation of broker/dealers

- prohibition of misstatements or omissions of material facts.

In this regard, they are very similar to the federal laws. The state laws, however, differ from the federal laws in several important ways. Perhaps the most significant difference is that some states go well beyond the disclosure requirements of the federal law. In these states, a state agency or official passes not only on the completeness and accuracy of the disclosure concerning an offering but also upon its fairness, regardless of the fact that the information provided by the issuer is complete and accurate. This is a significant departure from the federal philosophy (and that adopted by most states) that an informed and sophisticated investor is the best judge of the desirability of an investment.

As to registration, most states provide for alternative forms of registration, depending on the nature of the issuer and whether it is also registering with the SEC. The most common methods of state registration are registration by notification, registration by qualification, and registration by coordination. Registration by coordination, where it is permitted by state law, allows an issuer who is simultaneously registering with the SEC merely to file its SEC prospectus with the state agency. Registration by notification is available only to issuers who have done business in the state for a specified number of years and who have a stable earnings history. If an issuer qualifies, it need only file information attesting that it meets the stability test and describing the securities being offered and the details of the offering. Registration by qualification is required of those issuers who do not meet the tests for the other forms of registration. In this case the issuer must file information that is similar to what must be furnished to the SEC in a registration statement. This, of course, is a major undertaking, and most corporations seek to avoid the requirement of such a registration. This would lead them to seek an exemption from the registration requirements. Once again, however, the issuer will be faced with a lack of uniformity in the available exemptions so that it might be exempt in one state while being required to register in another. Remember, the issuer must register or qualify for an exemption in every state where the offering takes place.

Like the federal statutes, most state laws create exemptions for various types of securities and also for various types of transactions. The list of exempt securities is similar to those in the federal laws. The transactional exemptions, however, are somewhat different. Many states do provide an exemption for the private placement of securities to no more than a certain number of investors within the state. On the other hand, some states require that all the investors be "sophisticated," and others put a maximum limit on the number of purchasers, regardless of whether they are within the state. The number of investors differs between the states and is sometimes less than the 35 allowed under Reg D. Another major difference between some state laws and the federal rules (and those of many other states) is that some states require an issuer to apply for an exemption. Under the federal law, the issuer makes the first determination as to whether it qualifies for an exemption and bears the burden if it is wrong. In the application states, the state agency will rule on whether the issuer qualifies before the issuance of securities in that state.

There are a variety of other differences and peculiarities, as well as great complexity, in state laws. This is even more true of the federal laws. Therefore, keep in mind that the overview presented by this chapter does not begin to cover all the intricacies of securities regulation and practice. It was designed only to give you an idea of the landscape of securities law and a recognition of the need for expert assistance in navigating it.

APPENDIX 6.1
FORM S-18
REGISTRATION STATEMENT UNDER
THE SECURITIES ACT OF 1933

OMB APPROVAL
OMB Number: 3235-0098
Expires: November 30, 1989

SECURITIES AND EXCHANGE COMMISSION
Washington, D.C. 20549

FORM S-18

REGISTRATION STATEMENT UNDER THE SECURITIES ACT OF 1933

_____

(Exact name of registrant as specified in its charter)

_____

(State or other jurisdiction of incorporation or organization)

_____

(Primary Standard Industrial Classification Code Number)

_____

(I.R.S. Employer Identification Number)

_____

(Address, including zip code, and telephone number, including area code, of registrant's principal executive offices)

_____

(Address of principal place of business or intended principal place of business)

_____

(Name, address, including zip code, and telephone number, including area code, of agent for service)

_____

(Approximate date of commencement of proposed sale to the public)

Calculation of Registration Fee

Title of Each Class of Securities to be Registered	Amount to be Registered	Proposed Maximum Offering Price Per Unit	Proposed Maximum Aggregate Offering Price	Amount of Registration Fee

SEC 1766 (2-87)

Appendix 6.1 *(continued)*

The registrant hereby amends this registration statement on such date or dates as may be necessary to delay its effective date until the registrant shall file a further amendment which specifically states that this registration statement shall thereafter become effective in accordance with Section 8(a) of the Securities Act of 1933 or until the registration statement shall become effective on such date as the Commission, acting pursuant to said Section 8(a), may determine.*

*Inclusion of this paragraph is optional. See Rule 473. (Each page of this document, including exhibits and attachments, shall be numbered sequentially from this page, as page 1, through the last page of the document.)

I. **Rule as to Use of Form S-18.**

   A. This form is to be used for the registration of securities not to exceed an aggregate offering price of $7.5 million which are to be sold for cash, installments for cash and/or cash assessments and assumptions by partners of partnership debt, by the registrant, or for the account of security holders in accordance with paragraph B, provided such registrant:

   (1) Is organized under the laws of the United States or Canada or any State or Province thereof, and has or proposes to have its principal business operations in the United States, if a domestic issuer, or Canada or the United States if a Canadian issuer;

   (2) Is not subject to the reporting provisions of the Securities Exchange Act of 1934 pursuant to Section 12 or 15(d) of that Act;

   (3) Is not an investment company;

   (4) Is not an insurance company which is exempt from the provisions of Section 12 of the Securities Exchange Act of 1934 in reliance upon Section 12(g)(2)(G) thereof; and

   (5) Is not a majority owned subsidiary of a registrant which does not meet the qualifications for use of the form, as specified herein.

   B. This form may be used for the registration of securities to be sold for the account of any person other than the registrant, *provided:* (i) the aggregate offering price of such securities by any such persons does not exceed $1.5 million and (ii) the aggregate offering price of such securities together with the aggregate offering price of any securities to be sold by the registrant does not exceed $7.5 million.

   C. For purposes of computing the $7.5 million ceiling specified above, there shall be included in the aggregate offering price of the securities registered herein, the aggregate offering price of all securities sold: (i) by the registrant within one year prior to the commencement of the proposed offering in violation of Section 5(a) of the Securities Act; (ii) by the registrant within one year prior to the commencement of the proposed offering pursuant to a registration statement filed on Form S-18; and (iii) which would be deemed integrated with the proposed offering. (*See* Securities Act Release No. 4552 (November 6, 1962) [27 FR 11316].) In computing the $7.5 million ceiling amount, the aggregate price of all securities sold which fall in more than one of the above-described categories need be counted only once.

   D. Notwithstanding the provisions of paragraph (A)(2), a registrant which has had a prior offering on Form S-18 may, during the remainder of the fiscal year in which the prior registration statement was made effective, use the form to register additional securities until the offering limit as computed in paragraph C has been met.

II. **Place of Filing**

   A. At the election of the registrant, all registration statements on Form S-18 and related papers filed with the Commission should be filed either at its principal office in Washington, D.C. or in the Regional Office for the region in which the registrant's principal business operations are conducted, or are proposed to be conducted; *Provided, however,* that if the registrant's principal business operations are conducted or are proposed to be conducted in the region covered by the Philadelphia Regional Office, the registration statement may be filed either with the Atlanta or New York Regional Office. The registration statement of any registrant having or proposing to have its principal business operations in Canada may file with the Regional Office nearest the place where the registrant's principal business operations are conducted, or are proposed to be conducted; *Provided, however,* that if the offering is to be made through a principal underwriter located in the United States, the registration statement may be filed with the Regional Office for the region in which such underwriter has its principal office.

Appendix 6.1 *(continued)*

If the application of the previous sentence would require a filing with the Philadelphia Regional Office, such filing may be made with the Atlanta or the New York Regional Office.

B. The Commission will endeavor to process From S-18 registration statements at the place of filing. However, due to workload or other special consideration, the Commission may refer processing to a different Commission office.

C. All post-effective amendments to the Form S-18 registration statement shall be filed in the office where the corresponding Form S-18 registration statement was declared effective.

III. **Application of General Rules and Regulations.**

A. Attention is directed to the General Rules and Regulations under the Act, particularly those comprising Regulation C [17 CFR 230.400 to 230.494], which contains general requirements regarding the preparation and filing of a registration statement.

B. Attention is directed to Rule 463 [17 CFR 230.463] and Form SR [17 CFR 239.61] which is required to be filed by first-time registrants under the Securities Act showing sales of registered securities and the use of proceeds therefrom. Form SR shall be filed at the same office where the registration statement was declared effective.

C. Attention is directed to Regulation S-K [17 CFR 229.001 et seq.] relating to registration statement content. Where this form specifically references an item within that Regulation, the information need only be furnished to the extent appropriate. Special attention also is directed to paragraphs (b) and (c) of §229.10 of Regulation S-K which outline the Commission's policies on projections and securities ratings, respectively.

D. Attention is directed to disclosure provisions set forth in the Industry Guides which are listed in §229.801 of Regulation S-K [17 CFR 229.801]. These Industry Guides represent Division practices with respect to the disclosure to be provided by the affected industries in registration statements.

E. Attention is directed to Rule 15c2-8 [17 CFR 240.15c2-8] regarding prior delivery of preliminary prospectuses by registrants not subject to the reporting requirements of the Exchange Act.

F. Attention is directed to From S-11 [17 CFR 239.18] which relates to the registration of securities of certain real estate companies, and particularly Item 13 [Investment Policies of Registrant], Item 14 [Description of Real Estate], and Item 15 [Operating Data] contained therein. To the extent that these items offer enhanced guide lines for disclosure by real estate entities, registrants engaged or to be engaged in real estate operations may wish to consider these items for use in a Form S-18 offering.

PART I—INFORMATION REQUIRED IN PROSPECTUS

Item 1. Forepart of the Registration Statement and Outside Front Cover Page of Prospectus.

Set forth in the forepart of the registration statement and on the outside front cover page of the prospectus the information required by Item 501 of Regulation S-K [17 CFR 229.501].

Item 2. Inside Front and Outside Back Cover Pages of Prospectus.

Set forth on the inside front cover page of the prospectus or, where permitted, on the outside back cover page, the information required by Item 502 of Regulation S-K [17 CFR 229.502].

Item 3. Summary Information and Risk Factors.

Furnish the information required by Item 503(a), (b), and (c) of Regulation S-K [17 CFR 229.503(a), (b) and (c)].

Item 4. Use of Proceeds.

Furnish the information required by Item 504 of Regulation S-K [17 CFR 229.504].

Appendix 6.1 *(continued)*

Item 5. Determination of Offering Price.

Furnish the information required by Item 505 of Regulation S-K [17 CFR 229.505].

Item 6. Dilution.

Furnish the information required by Item 506 of Regulation S-K [17 CFR 229.506].

Item 7. Selling Security Holders.

Furnish the information required by Item 507 of Regulation S-K [17 CFR 229.507].

Item 8. Plan of Distribution.

Furnish the information required by Item 508 of Regulation S-K [17 CFR 229.508], except the information specified in Item 508(c)(1), (3), and (d).

Item 9. Legal Proceedings.

Furnish the information required by Item 103 of Regulation S-K [17 CFR 229.103].

Item 10. Directors and Executive Officers.

Furnish the information required by Item 401 of Regulation S-K [17 CFR 229.401].

Item 11. Security Ownership of Certain Beneficial Owners and Management.

Furnish the information required by Item 403 of Regulation S-K [17 CFR 229.403].

Item 12. Description of the Securities To Be Registered.

Furnish the information required by Item 202 of Regulation S-K [17 CFR 229.202].

Item 13. Interest of Named Experts and Counsel.

Furnish the information required by Item 509 of Regulation S-K [17 CFR 229.509].

Item 14. Statement as to Indemnification.

Furnish the information required by Item 510 of Regulation S-K [17 CFR 229.510].

Item 15. Organization Within Five Years.

If the registrant was organized within the past five years, furnish the following information:

(a) State the names of the promoters, the nature and amount of anything of value (including money, property, contracts, options or rights of any kind) received or to be received by each promoter directly or indirectly from the registrant, and the nature and amount of any assets, services or other consideration therefor received or to be received by the registrant. The term "promoter" is defined in Rule 405 under the Act.

(b) As to any assets acquired or to be acquired by the registrant from a promoter, state the amount at which acquired or to be acquired and the principal followed or to be followed in determining the amount. Identify the persons making the determination and state their relationship, if any, with the registrant or any promoter. If the assets were acquired by the promoter within two years prior to their transfer to the registrant, state the cost thereof to the promoter.

(c) List all parents of the registrant showing the basis of control and as to each parent, the percentage of voting securities owned or other basis of control by its immediate parent if any.

Instruction. Include the registrant and show the percentage of its voting securities owned or other basis of control by its immediate parent.

Appendix 6.1 *(continued)*

Item 16. Description of Business.

(a) *General development of business.* Describe the general development of the business of the registrant, its subsidiaries and any predecessor(s) during the past five years, or such shorter period as the registrant may have been engaged in business. Information shall be disclosed for earlier periods if material to an understanding of the general development of the business.

(1) In describing developments, information shall be given as to matters such as the following: the year in which the registrant was organized and its form of organization; the nature and results of any bankruptcy, receivership or similar proceedings with respect to the registrant or any of its significant subsidiaries; the nature and results of any other material reclassification, merger or consolidation of the registrant or any of its significant subsidiaries; the acquisition or disposition of any material amount of assets otherwise than in the ordinary course of business; and any material changes in the mode of conducting the business.

Instruction: The following requirement in paragraph (2) applies only to registrants (including predecessors) which have not received revenue from operations during each of the three fiscal years immediately prior to the filing of the registration statement.

(2) Describe, if formulated, the registrant's plan of operation for the remainder of the fiscal year, if the registration statement is filed prior to the end of the registrant's second fiscal quarter. Describe, if formulated, the registrant's plan of operation for the remainder of the fiscal year and for the first six months of the next fiscal year if the registration statement is filed subsequent to the end of the second fiscal quarter. If such information is not available, the reasons for its not being available shall be stated. Disclosure relating to any plan should include such matters as:

(i) A statement in narrative form indicating the registrant's opinion as to the period of time that the proceeds from the offering will satisfy cash requirements and whether in the next six months it will be necessary to raise additional funds to meet the expenditures required for operating the business of the registrant. The specific reasons for such opinion shall be set forth and categories of expenditures and sources of cash resources shall be identified; however, amounts of expenditure and cash resources need not be provided. In addition, if the narrative statement is based on a cash budget, such budget should be furnished to the Commission as supplemental information, but not as a part of the registration statement.

(ii) An explanation of material product research and development to be performed during the period covered in the plan.

(iii) Any anticipated material acquisition of plant and equipment and the capacity thereof.

(iv) Any anticipated material changes in number of employees in the various departments such as research and development production, sales or administration.

(v) Other material areas which may be peculiar to the registrant's business.

(b) *Narrative description of business.*

(1) Describe the business done and intended to be done by the registrant and its subsidiaries. Such description should include, if material to an understanding of the registrant's business, a discussion of:

(a) the principal products produced and services rendered and the principal markets for and methods of distribution of such products and services.

(b) the status of a product or service if the issuer has made public information about a new product or service which would require the investment of a material amount of the assets of the registrant or is otherwise material.

(c) the estimated amount spent during each of the last two fiscal years on company-sponsored research and development activities determined in accordance with generally accepted accounting principles. In addition, state the estimated dollar amount spent during each of such years on material customer-sponsored research activities relating to the development of new products, services or techniques or the improvement of existing products, services or techniques.

(d) the number of persons employed by the registrant indicating the number employed full time.

Appendix 6.1 *(continued)*

    (e) the material effects that compliance with Federal, State and local provisions which have been enacted or adopted regulating the discharge of materials into the environment, or otherwise relating to the protection of the environment, may have upon the capital expenditures, earnings and competitive position of the registrant and its subsidiaries. The registrant shall disclose any material estimated capital expenditures for environmental control facilities for the remainder of its current fiscal year and for such further periods as the registrant may deem material.

    (2) The registrant should also describe those distinctive or special characteristics of the registrant's operations or industry which may have a material impact upon the registrant's future financial performance. Examples of factors which might be discussed include dependence on one or a few major customers or suppliers (including suppliers of raw materials or financing), existing or probable governmental regulation, expiration of material labor contracts or patents, trademarks, licenses, franchises, concessions or royalty agreements, unusual competitive conditions in the industry, cyclicality of the industry and anticipated raw material or energy shortages to the extent management may not be able to secure a continuing source of supply.

(c) *Segment data.* If the registrant is required to include segment information in its financial statements, such information may be disclosed in the description of business or in the financial statements. If such information is included in the financial statements, an appropriate cross reference shall be included in the description of business.

Item 17. Description of Property.

State briefly the location and general character of the principal plants, and other materially important physical properties of the registrant and its subsidiaries. If any such property is not held in fee or is held subject to any major encumbrance, so state and briefly describe how held.

Instruction: What is required is information essential to an investor's appraisal of the securities being registered. Such information should be furnished as will reasonably inform investors as to the suitability, adequacy, productive capacity and extent of utilization of the facilities used in the enterprise. Detailed descriptions of the physical characteristics of individual properties or legal descriptions by metes and bounds are not required and should not be given.

Item 17A. Description of Property—Issuers Engaged or to be Engaged in Significant Mining Operations.

(a) *Definitions:* The following definitions apply to registrants engaged or to be engaged in significant mining operations:

    (1) *Reserve:* That part of a mineral deposit which could be economically and legally extracted or produced at the time of the reserve determination. *Note:* Reserves are customarily stated in terms of "ore" when dealing with metalliferous minerals; when other materials such as coal, oil shale, tar sands, limestone, etc. are involved, an appropriate term such as "recoverable coal" may be substituted.

    (2) *Proven (Measured) Reserves:* Reserves for which (a) quantity is computed from dimensions revealed in outcrops, trenches, workings, or drill holes; grade and/or quality are computed from the results of detailed sampling and (b) the sites for inspection, sampling and measurement are spaced so closely and the geologic character is so well-defined that size, shape, depth, and mineral content of reserves are well-established.

    (3) *Probable (Indicated) Reserves:* Reserves for which quantity and grade and/or quality are computed from information similar to that used for proven (measured) reserves, but the sites for inspection, sampling, and measurement are farther apart or are otherwise less adequately spaced. The degree of assurance, although lower than that for proven (measured) reserves, is high enough to assume continuity between points of observation.

    (4) (i) *Exploration Stage*—includes all issuers engaged in the search for mineral deposits (reserves) which are not in either the development or production stage.

       (ii) *Development Stage*—includes all issuers engaged in the preparation of an established commercially mineable deposit (reserves) for its extraction which are not in the production stage.

       (iii) *Production Stage*—includes all issuers engaged in the exploitation of a mineral deposit (reserve). *Instruction:* Mining companies in the exploration stage should not refer to themselves as development stage companies in the financial statements, even though such companies should comply with FASB Statement No. 7, if applicable.

(b) *Mining Operations Disclosure*—Furnish the following information as to each of the mines, plants and other significant properties owned or operated, or presently intended to be owned or operated, by the registrant:

Appendix 6.1 *(continued)*

(1) The location of and means of access to the property.

(2) A brief description of the title, claim, lease or option under which the registrant and its subsidiaries have or will have the right to hold or operate the property, indicating any conditions which the registrant must meet in order to obtain or retain the property. If held by leases or options, the expiration dates of such leases or options should be stated. Appropriate maps may be used to portray the locations of significant properties.

(3) A brief history of previous operations, including the names of previous operators, insofar as known.

(4) (a) A brief description of the present condition of the property, the work completed by the registrant on the property, the registrant's proposed program of exploration and development, and the current state of exploration and/or development of the property. Mines should be identified as either open-pit or underground. If the property is without known reserves and the proposed program is exploratory in nature, a statement to that effect shall be made.

(b) The age, details as to modernization and physical condition of the plant and equipment, including sub-surface improvements and equipment. Further, the total cost for each property and its associated plant and equipment should be stated. The source of power utilized with respect to each property should also be disclosed.

(5) A brief description of the rock formations and mineralization of existing or potential economic significance on the property, including the identity of the principal metallic or other constituents insofar as known. If proven (measured) or probable (indicated) reserves have been established, state (i) the estimated tonnages and grades (or quality, where appropriate) of such classes of reserves, and (ii) the name of the person making the estimates and the nature of his relationship to the registrant.

Instructions:

1. It should be stated whether the reserve estimate is of in-place material or of recoverable material. Any in-place estimate should be qualified to show the anticipated losses resulting from mining methods and beneficiation or preparation.

2. The summation of proven (measured) and probable (indicated) ore reserves is acceptable if the difference in degree of assurance between the two classes of reserves cannot be reliably defined.

3. Estimates other than proven (measured) or probable (indicated) reserves, and any estimated values of such reserves shall not be disclosed unless such information is required to be disclosed by foreign or state law; provided, however, that where such estimates previously have been provided to a person (or any of its affiliates) that is offering to acquire, merge, or consolidate with, the registrant or otherwise to acquire the registrant's securities, such estimates may be included.

(6) If technical terms relating to geology, mining or related matters whose definitions cannot be readily found in conventional dictionaries (as opposed to technical dictionaries or glossaries) are used, an appropriate glossary should be included in the registration statement.

(7) Detailed geologic maps and reports, feasibility studies and other highly technical data should not be included in the registration statement but should be, to the degree appropriate and necessary for the Commission's understanding of the registrant's presentation of business and property matters, furnished as supplemental information.

(c) *Supplemental Information:*

(1) If an estimate of proven (measured) or probable (indicated) reserves is set forth in the registration statement, furnish:

(i) maps drawn to scale showing any mine workings and the outlines of reserve blocks involved together with the pertinent sample-assay thereon,

(ii) all pertinent drill data and related maps,

(iii) the calculations whereby the basic sample-assay or drill data were translated into the estimates made of the grade and tonnage of reserves in each block and in the complete reserve estimate.

Instructions: Maps and other drawings submitted to the staff should include:

1. A legend or explanation showing, by means of pattern or symbol, every pattern or symbol used on the map or drawing; the use of the symbols used by the U.S. Geological Survey is encouraged;

Appendix 6.1 *(continued)*

2. A graphical bar scale should be included; additional representations of scale such as "one inch equals one mile" may be utilized provided the original scale of the map has not been altered;

3. A north arrow on maps;

4. An index map showing where the property is situated in relationship to the state or province, etc., in which it was located;

5. A title of the map or drawing and the date on which it was drawn;

6. In the event interpretive data is submitted in conjunction with any map, the identity of the geologist or engineer that prepared such data;

7. Any drawing should be simple enough or of sufficiently large scale to clearly show all features on the drawing.

(2) Furnish a complete copy of every material engineering, geological or metalurgical report concerning the registrant's property, including governmental reports, which are known and available to the registrant. Every such report should include the name of its author and the date of its preparation, if known to the registrant.

Any of the above-required reports as to which the staff has access need not be submitted. In this regard, issuers should consult with the staff prior to filing the registration statement. Any reports not submitted should be identified in a list furnished to the staff. This list should also identify any known governmental reports concerning the registrant's property.

(3) Furnish copies of all documents such as title documents, operating permits and easements needed to support representations made in the registration statement.

Item 17B. Supplementary Financial Information about Oil and Gas Producing Activities.

Registrants engaged in oil and gas producing activities shall follow the disclosure standards specified in paragraph (c) of Item 302 of Regulation S-K [17 CFR 229.302] with respect to such activities.

Item 18. Interest of Management and Others in Certain Transactions.

Describe briefly any transactions during the previous two years or any presently proposed transactions, to which the registrant or any of its subsidiaries was or is to be a party, in which any of the following persons had or is to have a direct or indirect material interest, naming such person and stating his relationship to the issuer, the nature of his interest in the transaction and, where practicable, the amount of such interest:

(1) Any director or executive officer of the issuer;

(2) Any nominee for election as a director;

(3) Any security holder named in answer to Item 11; or

(4) Any member of the immediate family of any of the foregoing persons.

Instructions:

1. See Instruction 2 to Item 20(a)(i). No information need be given in response to this Item as to any remuneration or other transaction reported in response to Item 20 or specifically excluded from Item 20.

2. No information need be given in answer to this Item as to any transaction where:

   (a) the rates or charges involved in the transaction are determined by competitive bids, or the transaction involves the rendering of services as a common or contract carrier, or public utility, at rates or charges fixed in conformity with law or governmental authority;

   (b) the transaction involves services as a bank depositary of funds, transfer agent, registrar, trustee under a trust indenture, or similar services;

   (c) the amount involved in the transaction or a series of similar transactions, including all periodic installments in the case of any lease or other agreement providing for periodic payments or installments, does not exceed $60,000; or

Appendix 6.1 *(continued)*

     (d) the interest of the specified person arises solely from the ownership of securities of the issuer and the specified person receives no extra or special benefit not shared on a pro rata basis by all holders of securities of the class.

3. It should be noted that this item calls for disclosure of indirect, as well as direct, material interests in transactions. A person who has a position or relationship with a firm, corporation, or other entity, which engages in a transaction with the issuer or its subsidiaries may have an indirect interest in such transaction by reason of such position or relationship. However, a person shall be deemed not to have a material indirect interest in a transaction within the meaning of this Item where:

     (a) the interest arises only (i) from such person's position as a director of another corporation or organization (other than a partnership) which is a party to the transaction, or (ii) from the direct or indirect ownership by such person and all other persons specified in subparagraphs (1) through (3) above, in the aggregate, of less than a 10 percent equity interest in another person (other than a partnership) which is a party to the transaction, or (iii) from both such position and ownership.

     (b) the interest arises only from such person's position as a limited partner in a partnership in which he and all other persons specified in (1) through (4) above had an interest of less than 10 percent; or

     (c) the interest of such person arises solely from the holding of an equity interest (including a limited partnership interest but excluding a general partnership interest) or a creditor interest in another person which is a party to the transaction with the issuer or any of its subsidiaries and the transaction is not material to such other person.

4. Include the name of each person whose interest in any transaction is described and the nature of the relationship by reason of which such interest is required to be described. The amount of the interest of any specified person shall be computed without regard to the amount of the profit or loss involved in the transaction. Where it is not practicable to state the approximate amount of the interest, the approximate amount involved in the transaction shall be disclosed.

5. Information should be included as to any material underwriting discounts and commissions upon the sale of securities by the registrant where any of the specified persons was or is to be a principal underwriter or is a controlling person, or member, of a firm which was or is to be a principal underwriter. Information need not be given concerning ordinary management fees paid by underwriters to a managing underwriter pursuant to an agreement among underwriters the parties to which do not include the registrant or its subsidiaries.

6. As to any transaction involving the purchase or sale of assets by or to the registrant or any subsidiary, otherwise than in the ordinary course of business, state the cost of the assets to the purchaser and if acquired by the seller within two years prior to the transaction, the cost thereof to the seller.

7. Information shall be furnished in answer to this item with respect to transactions not excluded above which involve remuneration from the registrant or its subsidiaries, directly or indirectly, to any of the specified persons for services in any capacity unless the interest of such persons arises solely from the ownership individually and in the aggregate of less than 10% of any class of equity securities of another corporation furnishing the services to the registrant or its subsidiaries.

8. The foregoing instructions specify certain transactions and interests as to which information may be omitted in answering this item. There may be situations where, although the foregoing instructions do not expressly authorize nondisclosure, the interest of a specified person in the particular transaction or series of transactions is not a material interest. In that case, information regarding such interest and transaction is not required to be disclosed in response to this item. The materiality of any interest or transaction is to be determined on the basis of the significance of the information to investors in light of all of the circumstances of the particular transaction. The importance of the interest to the person having the interest, the relationship of the parties to the transaction to each other and the amount involved in the transaction are among the factors to be considered in determining the significance of the information to investors.

9. For purposes of this item, a person's immediate family shall include such person's spouse; parents; children; siblings; mothers and fathers-in-law; sons and daughters-in-law; and brothers and sisters-in-law.

Item 19. Certain Market Information.

Furnish the information required by Item 201(a)(2) of Regulation S-K [17 CFR 229.201(a)(2)].

Appendix 6.1 *(continued)*

Item 20. Executive Compensation.

(a) (1) *Cash compensation.* Furnish, in substantially the tabular form specified, all cash compensation paid to the following persons through the latest practicable date for services rendered in all capacities to the registrant and its subsidiaries during the registrant's last fiscal year.

   (i) Each of the registrant's five most highly compensated executive officers whose cash compensation required to be disclosed pursuant to this paragraph exceeds $60,000, naming each person; and

   (ii) All executive officers as a group, stating the number of persons in the group without naming them.

Cash Compensation Table

A	B	C
Name of individual or number in group	Capacities in which served	Cash Compensation

Instructions:

1. The Cash Compensation Table shall include:)i) all cash bonuses to be paid for services rendered during the last fiscal year unless such amounts have not been allocated at such time as the registration statement is filed, and (ii) all compensation that would have been paid in cash but for the fact the payment of such compensation was deferred.

2. Paragraph (a) applies to any person who was an executive officer of the registrant at any time during the period specified. However, information need not be given for any portion of the period during which such person was not an executive officer of the registrant, provided a statement to that effect is made.

(b) (1) *Compensation pursuant to plans.* Describe briefly all plans, pursuant to which cash or non-cash compensation was paid or distributed during the last fiscal year, stating such amounts, and all plans pursuant to which cash or non-cash is proposed to be paid or distributed in the future, to the named individuals and group specified in paragraph (a) of this section. Information need not be given with respect to any group life, health, hospitalization, medical reimbursement or relocation plans that do not discriminate, in scope, terms, or operation in favor of officers or directors of the registrant and that are available generally to all salaried employees. Information relating to pension or retirement benefits need not be disclosed if the amounts to be paid are computed on an actuarial basis under any plan which provides for fixed benefits in the event of retirement at a specified age or after a specified number of years of service.

   (2) *Stock option plans.* In addition to providing the information required by paragraph (b)(1) of this section, furnish:

   (i) With respect to stock options granted during the last fiscal year: (A) the title and aggregate amount of securities subject to options; (B) the average per share exercise price; and (C) if such option exercise price was less than 100 percent of the market value of the security on the date of grant, such fact and the market price on such date.

   (ii) With respect to stock options exercised during the last fiscal year, regardless of the year such options were granted, the net value realized upon such exercise, calculated by subtracting the exercise price from the market value.

(c) *Other compensation.* Describe, stating amounts, any other compensation not covered by paragraphs (a) or (b) of this section, such as personal benefits, securities or property, that was paid or distributed during the last fiscal year to the named individuals and group specified in paragraph (a) of this section unless:

   (1) With respect to any named individual, the aggregate amount of such other compensation is the lesser of $25,000 or 10 percent of the compensation reported in the Cash Compensation Table of such person pursuant to paragraph (a) of this section or

   (2) With respect to the group, the aggregate amount of such other compensation is the lesser of $25,000 times the number of persons in the group or 10 percent of the compensation reported in the Cash Compensation Table for the group pursuant to paragraph (a) of this section and a statement to that effect is made.

Instruction: Compensation within paragraph (c) shall be valued on the basis of the registrant's and subsidiaries' aggregate incremental cost.

(d) *Compensation of directors.* Describe briefly, stating amounts, all compensation received by directors of the registrant for all services as a director.

Item 21. Financial Statements.

   (a) General

      (1) The financial statements of the registrant, or the registrant and its predecessors or any businesses to which the registrant is a successor, which are to be filed as part of the registration statement shall be prepared in accordance with generally accepted accounting principles (GAAP) in the United States or in the case of a Canadian registrant, a reconciliation to such U.S. GAAP shall be included in a note or schedule to the financial statements.

      (2) Regulation S-X [17 CFR 210.1-210.12], Form and Content of and Requirements for Financial Statements, shall not apply to the preparation of such financial statements, except that the report and qualifications of the independent accountant shall comply with the requirements of Article 2 of Regulation S-X [17 CFR 210.2], and registrants engaged in oil and gas producing activities shall follow the financial accounting and reporting standards specified in Article 4-10 of Regulation S-X [17 CFR 210.4-10] with respect to such activities. However, to the extent that Article 10 [17 CFR 210.10] (Interim Financial Statements), Article 11-01 [17 CFR 210.11-01] (Pro Forma Presentation Requirements) and Article 11-02 [17 CFR 210.11-02] (Pro Forma Preparation Requirements) offer enhanced guidelines for the preparation, presentation and disclosure of condensed financial statements and pro forma financial information, registrants may wish to consider these items for use in a Form S-18 offering.

      (3) The Commission may, upon the informal written request of the registrant, and where consistent with the protection of investors, permit the omission of one or more of the financial statements herein required or the filing in substitution therefor of appropriate statements of comparable character. The Commission may also by informal written notice require the filing of other financial statements in addition to, or in substitution for, the statements herein required in any case where such statements are necessary or appropriate for adequate presentation of the financial condition of any person whose financial statements are required, or whose statements are otherwise necessary for the protection of investors.

   (b) Consolidated Balance Sheets

      (1) The registrant and its subsidiaries consolidated shall file an audited balance sheet as of the end of the most recent fiscal year, or as of a date within 135 days of the date of filing the registration statement if the registrant (including predecessors) existed for a period less than one fiscal year.

      (2) When the filing date of the registrtation statement falls after 134 days subsequent to the end of the registrant's most recent fiscal year, a balance sheet as of an interim date within 135 days of the filing date also shall be included in the registration statement. Such balance sheet need not be audited and may be in condensed form.

   (c) Consolidated Statements of Income, Changes in Financial Condition and Stockholder's Equity.

      (1) There shall be filed for the registrant and its subsidiaries consolidated statements of income, changes in financial position and stockholders equity for each of the two fiscal years preceding the date of the most recent audited balance sheet being filed (or for such shorter period as the registrant has been in business), and for the interim period, if any, between the end of the most recent fiscal year and the date of the most recent balance sheet being filed. These statements should be audited to the date of the most recent audited balance sheet being filed. Any interim financial statements may be in condensed form.

      (2) If an income statement is filed for an interim period there shall also be filed, except for registrants in the development stage as defined by GAAP, an income statement for a comparable period of the prior year.

      (3) Any unaudited interim financial statements furnished shall reflect all adjustments which are, in the opinion of management, necessary to a fair statement of the results for the interim periods presented. A statement to that effect shall be included. Such adjustments shall include, for example, appropriate estimated provisions for bonus and profit sharing arrangements normally determined or settled at year-end. If all such adjustments are of a normal recurring nature, a statement to that effect shall be made; otherwise, there shall be furnished information describing in appropriate detail the nature and amount of any adjustments other than normal recurring adjustments entering into the determination of the results shown.

Appendix 6.1 *(continued)*

(d) Financial Statements of Businesses Acquired or to be Acquired.

   (1) Financial statements for the periods specified in (3) below should be furnished if any of the following conditions exist:

      (i) Consummation of a significant business combination accounted for as a purchase has occurred or is probable (for purposes of this rule, the term "purchase" encompasses the purchase of an interest in a business accounted for by the equity method); or

      (ii) Consummation of a significant business combination to be accounted for as a pooling of interests is probable.

   (2) A business combination shall be considered significant if a comparison of the most recent annual financial statements of the business acquired or to be acquired and the registrant's most recent annual consolidated financial statements filed at or prior to the date of acquisition indicates that the business would be a significant subsidiary pursuant to the conditions specified in Rule 405 of Regulation C [17 CFR 230.405].

   (3) **(i)** The financial statements shall be furnished for the periods up to the date of acquisition, for those periods for which the registrant is required to furnish financial statements as specified in paragraph (b) and (c)(1).

      (ii) The financial statements covering fiscal years shall be audited.

      (iii) A separate audited balance sheet of the acquired business is not required when the registrant's most recent audited balance sheet filed is for a date after the acquisition was consummated.

      (iv) If none of the conditions in the definitions of significant subsidiary in Rule 405 exceeds 20%, income statements of the acquired business for only the most recent fiscal year and any interim period need be filed.

   (4) If consummation of more than one transaction has occurred or is probable, the tests of significance shall be made using the aggregate impact of the business and the required financial statements may be presented on a combined basis, if appropriate.

   (5) This paragraph (d) shall not apply to a business which is totally held by the registrant prior to consummation of the transaction.

(e) Pro Forma Financial Information.

   (1) Pro forma information shall be furnished if any of the following conditions exist (for purposes of this rule, the term "purchase" encompasses the purchase of an interest in a business accounted for by the equity method):

      (i) During the most recent fiscal year or subsequent interim period for which a balance sheet is required by paragraph (b), a significant business combination accounted for as a purchase has occurred.

      (ii) After the date of the most recent balance sheet filed pursuant to paragraph (b), consummation of a significant business combination to be accounted for by either the purchase method or pooling of interests method of accounting has occurred or is probable.

   (2) The provisions of paragraph (d)(2), (4) and (5) apply to this paragraph (e).

   (3) Pro forma statements shall ordinarily be in columnar form showing condensed historical statements, pro forma adjustments, and the pro forma results and should include the following:

      (i) If the transaction was consummated during the most recent fiscal year or in the subsequent interim period, pro forma statements of income reflecting the combined operations of the entities for the latest fiscal year and interim period, if any; or

      (ii) If consummation of the transaction has occurred or is probable after the date of the most recent balance sheet, a pro forma balance sheet giving effect to the combination as of the date of the most recent balance sheet required by paragraph (b). For a purchase, pro forma statements of income reflecting the combined operations of the entities for the latest fiscal year and interim period, if any, and for a pooling of interests, pro forma statements of income for all periods for which income statements of the registrant are required.

Appendix 6.1 *(continued)*

(f) Age of Financial Statements at Effective Date of Registration Statement.

   (1) If the financial statements are as of a date 135 days or more prior to the date the registration statement is expected to become effected the financial statements shall be updated with a balance sheet as of an interim date within 135 days and with statements of income and changes in financial position for the interim period between the end of the most recent fiscal year and the date of the interim balance sheet. There shall also be filed, except for registrants in the development stage, an income statement for a corresponding period of the preceding fiscal year. Such interim financial statements need not be audited and may be in condensed form.

   (2) When the anticipated effective date of the registration statement falls within 45 days subsequent to the end of the fiscal year, the registration statement need not include financial statements more current than as of the end of the third fiscal quarter of the most recently completed fiscal year: *Provided, however,* That if the audited financial statements for such fiscal year are available they must be included in the registration statement. If the anticipated effective date falls after 45 days subsequent to the end of the fiscal year the registration statement must include audited financial statements for the most recently completed fiscal year.

   (3) When the filing date of the registration statement is near the end of a fiscal year and the audited financial statements for that fiscal year are not included in the registration statement, the registration statement shall be updated with such financial statements if they become available prior to the anticipated effective date.

(g) Special Instructions for Real Estate Operations to be Acquired.

   If, during the period for which income statements are required, the registrant (a) has acquired one or more properties which in the aggregate are significant, or (b) since the date of the latest balance sheet required, has acquired or proposes to acquire one or more properties which in the aggregate are significant, the following shall be furnished with respect to such properties.

   (1) Audited income statements (not including earnings per unit) for the two most recent years, which shall exclude items not comparable to the proposed future operations of the property such as mortgage interest, leasehold rental, depreciation, corporate expenses and Federal and state income taxes: *Provided, however,* That such audited statements need be presented for only the most recent fiscal year if (i) the property is not acquired from a related party; (ii) material factors considered by the registrant in assessing the property are described with specificity in the prospectus with regard to the property, including sources of revenue (including, but not limited to, competition in the rental market, comparative rents, occupancy rates) and expense (including, but not limited to, utility rates, *ad valorem* tax rates, maintenance expenses, capital improvements anticipated); and (iii) the registrant indicates in the prospectus that, after reasonable inquiry, the registrant is not aware of any material factors relating to that specific property other than those discussed in response to paragraph (1)(ii) of this section that would cause the reported financial information not to be necessarily indicative of future operating results.

   (2) If the property is to be operated by the registrant there shall be furnished a statement showing the estimated taxable operating results of the registrant based on the most recent twelve month period including such adjustments as can be factually supported. If the property is to be acquired subject to a net lease the estimated taxable operating results shall be based on the rent to be paid for the first year of the lease. In either case, the estimated amount of cash to be made available by operations shall be shown. There shall be stated in an introductory paragraph the principal assumptions which have been made in preparing the statements of estimated taxable operating results and cash to be made available by operations.

   (3) If appropriate under the circumstances, there shall be given in tabular form for a limited number of years the estimated cash distribution per unit showing the portion thereof reportable as taxable income and the portion representing a return of capital together with an explanation of annual variations, if any. If taxable net income per unit will become greater than the cash available for distribution per unit, that fact and approximate year of occurrence shall be stated, if significant.

(h) Special Instructions for Limited Partnerships.

   (1) In addition to the financial reporting requirements in paragraphs (a) through (g), registrants which are limited partnerships are required also to file the balance sheets of the general partners as described in subparagraphs (2) through (4), below.

   (2) Where a general partner of the limited partnership is a corporation there shall be filed an audited balance sheet of such corporation as of the end of its most recently completed fiscal year. Receivables from the parent or affiliate of the general partner (including notes receivable, but excluding trade receivables), should

Appendix 6.1 *(continued)*

be presented as deductions from the shareholders' equity of the general partner. Where a parent or affiliate of the general partner has committed itself to increase or maintain the general partner's capital then there shall also be filed an audited balance sheet of such parent or affiliate as of the end of its most recently completed fiscal year.

(3) Where a general partner of the limited partnership is a partnership there shall be filed an audited balance sheet of such partnership as of the end of its most recently completed fiscal year.

(4) Where a general partner of the limited partnership is a natural person there shall be filed, as supplemental information, a balance sheet of such natural person as of a recent date. Such balance sheet need not be audited. The assets and liabilities on such balance sheet should be carried at estimated fair market value, with provisions for estimated income taxes on unrealized gains. The net worth of such general partner(s), based on the estimated fair market value of their assets and liabilities, singly or in the aggregate, shall be disclosed in the text of the prospectus.

(i) Special Instructions for Registrants Engaged in Mining Operations.

With respect to companies engaged or to be engaged in the mining business, attention is directed to the instruction to Item 17A concerning the appropriate classification of issuers engaged in the exploratory, development and production stage of mining.

(j) Special Instructions for Companies Engaged in Marketing Computer Software.

(1) Companies shall not capitalize costs of internally developing (other than under a contractual arrangement for which accounting for contracts is appropriate) computer software as a product or process (or a part of a product or process) to be sold, leased, or otherwise marketed to others in financial statements included in documents prepared pursuant to rules adopted pursuant to either the Securities Act of 1933 or the Securities Exchange Act of 1934 and filed with or furnished to the Commission after April 14, 1983, unless they had disclosed the practice of capitalizing software costs in either: (i) audited financial statements issued prior to April 14, 1983; (ii) a report or registration statement filed with the Commission prior to April 14, 1983; or (iii) a document for an offering of securities by the issuer, other than a registration statement, which document was used in such offering prior to April 14, 1983.

(2) Because the term "product" also encompasses services that are sold, leased, or otherwise marketed to others, the prohibition in paragraph (1) of this section applies, for example, to a data processing service bureau or a computer time-sharing company.

(3) A company which, pursuant to paragraph (1) of this section, continues to follow the practice of capitalizing costs of internally developing computer software as a product or process to be sold, leased, or otherwise marketed to others, shall disclose for each period for which an income statement is required to be presented, the net amount of such costs capitalized during the period.

(k) Furnish the information required by Item 304 of Regulation S-K (§239.304 of this chapter), changes in and disagreements with accountants on accounting and financial disclosure.

NOTE: The requirements of this item shall not apply to financial statements which reflect the provisions of a pronouncement adopted after August 4, 1983 by the Financial Accounting Standards Board which provides specific accounting guidance in this area.

Part II — INFORMATION NOT REQUIRED IN PROSPECTUS

Item 22. Indemnification of Directors and Officers.

Furnish the information called for by Item 702 of Regulation S-K [17 CFR 229.702].

Item 23. Other Expenses of Issuance and Distribution.

Furnish the information called for by Item 511 of Regulation S-K [17 CFR 229.511].

Item 24. Recent Sales of Unregistered Securities.

Furnish the information called for by Item 701 of Regulation S-K [17 CFR 229.701].

Appendix 6.1 *(continued)*

Item 25. Exhibits.

Furnish the exhibits as required by Item 601 of Regulation S-K [17 CFR 229.601].

Item 26. Undertakings.

Furnish the undertakings required by Item 512 of Regulation S-K [17 CFR 229.512].

SIGNATURES

Pursuant to the requirements of the Securities Act of 1933, the registrant certifies that it has reasonable grounds to believe that it meets all of the requirements for filing on Form S-18 and has duly caused this registration statement to be signed on its behalf by the undersigned, thereunto duly authorized, in the City of_____, State of _____, on _____, 19_____.

_____
(Registrant)

By _____
(Signature and Title)

Pursuant to the requirements of the Securities Act of 1933, this registration statement has been signed by the following persons in the capacities and on the dates indicated.

_____
(Signature)

_____
(Title)

_____
(Date)

Instructions:

1. The registration statement shall be signed by the registrant, its principal executive officer or officers, its principal financial officer, its controller or principal accounting officer and by at least a majority of the board of directors or persons performing similar functions. If the registrant is a Canadian person, the registration statement shall also be signed by its authorized representative in the United States. Where the registrant is a limited partnership, the registration statement shall be signed by a majority of the board of directors of any corporate general partner signing the registration statement.

2. The name of each person who signs the registration statement shall be typed or printed beneath his signature. Any person who occupies more than one of the specified positions shall indicate each capacity in which he signs the registration statement. Attention is directed to Rule 402 concerning manual signatures and to the exhibit requirements concerning signatures pursuant to powers of attorney.

APPENDIX 6.2
SEC FORM D

Appendix 6.2 *(continued)*

FORM D

UNITED STATES
SECURITIES AND EXCHANGE COMMISSION
Washington, D.C. 20549

FORM D

**NOTICE OF SALE OF SECURITIES
PURSUANT TO REGULATION D,
SECTION 4(6), AND/OR
UNIFORM LIMITED OFFERING EXEMPTION**

SEC USE ONLY	
Prefix	Serial
DATE RECEIVED	

Name of Offering   (☐ check if this is an amendment and name has changed, and indicate change.)

Filing Under (Check box(es) that apply):   ☐ Rule 504   ☐ Rule 505   ☐ Rule 506   ☐ Section 4(6)   ☐ ULOE

Type of Filing: ☐ New Filing   ☐ Amendment

A. BASIC IDENTIFICATION DATA

1. Enter the information requested about the issuer

Name of Issuer   (☐ check if this is an amendment and name has changed, and indicate change.)

Address of Executive Offices (Number and Street, City, State, Zip Code)	Telephone Number (Including Area Code)
Address of Principal Business Operations (Number and Street, City, State, Zip Code) (if different from Executive Offices)	Telephone Number (Including Area Code)

Brief Description of Business

Type of Business Organization
☐ corporation   ☐ limited partnership, already formed   ☐ other (please specify):
☐ business trust   ☐ limited partnership, to be formed

Month   Year

Actual or Estimated Date of Incorporation or Organization: ☐ Actual   ☐ Estimated

Jurisdiction of Incorporation or Organization: (Enter two-letter U.S. Postal Service abbreviation for State: CN for Canada; FN for other foreign jurisdiction)

GENERAL INSTRUCTIONS

Federal:

Who Must File: All issuers making an offering of securities in reliance on an exemption under Regulation D or Section 4(6), 17 CFR 230.501 et seq. or 15 U.S.C. 77d(6).

When To File: A notice must be filed no later than 15 days after the first sale of securities in the offering. A notice is deemed filed with the U.S. Securities and Exchange Commission (SEC) on the earlier of the date it is received by the SEC at the address given below or, if received at that address after the date on which it is due, on the date it was mailed by United States registered or certified mail to that address.

Where to File: U.S. Securities and Exchange Commission, 450 Fifth Street, N.W., Washington, D.C. 20549.

Copies Required: Five (5) copies of this notice must be filed with the SEC, one of which must be manually signed. Any copies not manually signed must be photocopies of the manually signed copy or bear typed or printed signatures.

Information Required: A new filing must contain all information requested. Amendments need only report the name of the issuer and offering, any changes thereto, the information requested in Part C, and any material changes from the information previously supplied in Parts A and B. Part E and the Appendix need not be filed with the SEC.

Filing Fee: There is no federal filing fee.

State:

This notice shall be used to indicate reliance on the Uniform Limited Offering Exemption (ULOE) for sales of securities in those states that have adopted ULOE and that have adopted this form. Issuers relying on ULOE must file a separate notice with the Securities Administrator in each state where sales are to be, or have been made. If a state requires the payment of a fee as a precondition to the claim for the exemption, a fee in the proper amount shall accompany this form. This notice shall be filed in the appropriate states in accordance with state law. The Appendix to the notice constitutes a part of this notice and must be completed.

--- ATTENTION ---
Failure to file notice in the appropriate states will not result in a loss of the federal exemption. Conversely, failure to file the appropriate federal notice will not result in a loss of an available state exemption unless such exemption is predicated on the filing of a federal notice.

SEC 1972 (6-88) 1 of 8

Appendix 6.2 *(continued)*

A. BASIC IDENTIFICATION DATA

2. Enter the information requested for the following:

- Each promoter of the issuer, if the issuer has been organized within the past five years;
- Each beneficial owner having the power to vote or dispose, or direct the vote or disposition of, 10% or more of a class of equity securities of the issuer;
- Each executive officer and director of corporate issuers and of corporate general and managing partners of partnership issuers; and
- Each general and managing partner of partnership issuers.

Check Box(es) that Apply: ☐ Promoter ☐ Beneficial Owner ☐ Executive Officer ☐ Director ☐ General and/or Managing Partner

Full Name (Last name first, if individual)

Business or Residence Address (Number and Street, City, State, Zip Code)

Check Box(es) that Apply: ☐ Promoter ☐ Beneficial Owner ☐ Executive Officer ☐ Director ☐ General and/or Managing Partner

Full Name (Last name first, if individual)

Business or Residence Address (Number and Street, City, State, Zip Code)

Check Box(es) that Apply: ☐ Promoter ☐ Beneficial Owner ☐ Executive Officer ☐ Director ☐ General and/or Managing Partner

Full Name (Last name first, if individual)

Business or Residence Address (Number and Street, City, State, Zip Code)

Check Box(es) that Apply: ☐ Promoter ☐ Beneficial Owner ☐ Executive Officer ☐ Director ☐ General and/or Managing Partner

Full Name (Last name first, if individual)

Business or Residence Address (Number and Street, City, State, Zip Code)

Check Box(es) that Apply: ☐ Promoter ☐ Beneficial Owner ☐ Executive Officer ☐ Director ☐ General and/or Managing Partner

Full Name (Last name first, if individual)

Business or Residence Address (Number and Street, City, State, Zip Code)

Check Box(es) that Apply: ☐ Promoter ☐ Beneficial Owner ☐ Executive Officer ☐ Director ☐ General and/or Managing Partner

Full Name (Last name first, if individual)

Business or Residence Address (Number and Street, City, State, Zip Code)

Check Box(es) that Apply: ☐ Promoter ☐ Beneficial Owner ☐ Executive Officer ☐ Director ☐ General and/or Managing Partner

Full Name (Last name first, if individual)

Business or Residence Address (Number and Street, City, State, Zip Code)

(Use blank sheet, or copy and use additional copies of this sheet, as necessary.)

SEC 1972 (6-88) 2 of 8

Appendix 6.2 *(continued)*

		Yes	No
B. INFORMATION ABOUT OFFERING			

1. Has the issuer sold, or does the issuer intend to sell, to non-accredited investors in this offering? .... ☐ Yes ☐ No

Answer also in Appendix, Column 2, if filing under ULOE.

2. What is the minimum investment that will be accepted from any individual? .... $_____ .

3. Does the offering permit joint ownership of a single unit? .... ☐ Yes ☐ No

4. Enter the information requested for each person who has been or will be paid or given, directly or indirectly, any commission or similar remuneration for solicitation of purchasers in connection with sales of securities in the offering. If a person to be listed is an associated person or agent of a broker or dealer registered with the SEC and/or with a state or states, list the name of the broker or dealer. If more than five (5) persons to be listed are associated persons of such a broker or dealer, you may set forth the information for that broker or dealer only..

Full Name (Last name first, if individual)
_____

Business or Residence Address (Number and Street, City, State, Zip Code)
_____

Name of Associated Broker or Dealer
_____

States in Which Person Listed Has Solicited or Intends to Solicit Purchasers

(Check "All States" or check individual States) .... ☐ All States

[AL]	[AK]	[AZ]	[AR]	[CA]	[CO]	[CT]	[DE]	[DC]	[FL]	[GA]	[HI]	[ID]
[IL]	[IN]	[IA]	[KS]	[KY]	[LA]	[ME]	[MD]	[MA]	[MI]	[MN]	[MS]	[MO]
[MT]	[NE]	[NV]	[NH]	[NJ]	[NM]	[NY]	[NC]	[ND]	[OH]	[OK]	[OR]	[PA]
[RI]	[SC]	[SD]	[TN]	[TX]	[UT]	[VT]	[VA]	[WA]	[WV]	[WI]	[WY]	[PR]

Full Name (Last name first, if individual)
_____

Business or Residence Address (Number and Street, City, State, Zip Code)
_____

Name of Associated Broker or Dealer
_____

States in Which Person Listed Has Solicited or Intends to Solicit Purchasers

(Check "All States" or check individual States) .... ☐ All States

[AL]	[AK]	[AZ]	[AR]	[CA]	[CO]	[CT]	[DE]	[DC]	[FL]	[GA]	[HI]	[ID]
[IL]	[IN]	[IA]	[KS]	[KY]	[LA]	[ME]	[MD]	[MA]	[MI]	[MN]	[MS]	[MO]
[MT]	[NE]	[NV]	[NH]	[NJ]	[NM]	[NY]	[NC]	[ND]	[OH]	[OK]	[OR]	[PA]
[RI]	[SC]	[SD]	[TN]	[TX]	[UT]	[VT]	[VA]	[WA]	[WV]	[WI]	[WY]	[PR]

Full Name (Last name first, if individual)
_____

Business or Residence Address (Number and Street, City, State, Zip Code)
_____

Name of Associated Broker or Dealer
_____

States in Which Person Listed Has Solicited or Intends to Solicit Purchasers

(Check "All States" or check individual States) .... ☐ All States

[AL]	[AK]	[AZ]	[AR]	[CA]	[CO]	[CT]	[DE]	[DC]	[FL]	[GA]	[HI]	[ID]
[IL]	[IN]	[IA]	[KS]	[KY]	[LA]	[ME]	[MD]	[MA]	[MI]	[MN]	[MS]	[MO]
[MT]	[NE]	[NV]	[NH]	[NJ]	[NM]	[NY]	[NC]	[ND]	[OH]	[OK]	[OR]	[PA]
[RI]	[SC]	[SD]	[TN]	[TX]	[UT]	[VT]	[VA]	[WA]	[WV]	[WI]	[WY]	[PR]

(Use blank sheet, or copy and use additional copies of this sheet, as necessary.)

SEC 1972 (6-88) 3 of 8

Appendix 6.2 *(continued)*

C. OFFERING PRICE, NUMBER OF INVESTORS, EXPENSES AND USE OF PROCEEDS

1. Enter the aggregate offering price of securities included in this offering and the total amount already sold. Enter "0" if answer is "none" or "zero." If the transaction is an exchange offering, check this box ☐ and indicate in the columns below the amounts of the securities offered for exchange and already exchanged.

Type of Security	Aggregate Offering Price	Amount Already Sold
Debt	$_____	$_____
Equity	$_____	$_____
☐ Common ☐ Preferred		
Convertible Securities (including warrants)	$_____	$_____
Partnership Interests	$_____	$_____
Other (Specify _____)	$_____	$_____
Total	$_____	$_____

Answer also in Appendix, Column 3, if filing under ULOE.

2. Enter the number of accredited and non-accredited investors who have purchased securities in this offering and the aggregate dollar amounts of their purchases. For offerings under Rule 504, indicate the number of persons who have purchased securities and the aggregate dollar amount of their purchases on the total lines. Enter "0" if answer is "none" or "zero."

	Number Investors	Aggregate Dollar Amount of Purchases
Accredited Investors	_____	$_____
Non-accredited Investors......................................	_____	$_____
Total (for filings under Rule 504 only)	_____	$_____

Answer also in Appendix, Column 4, if filing under ULOE.

3. If this filing is for an offering under Rule 504 or 505, enter the information requested for all securities sold by the issuer, to date, in offerings of the types indicated, in the twelve (12) months prior to the first sale of securities in this offering. Classify securities by type listed in Part C - Question 1.

Type of offering	Type of Security	Dollar Amount Sold
Rule 505	_____	$_____
Regulation A	_____	$_____
Rule 504	_____	$_____
Total	_____	$_____

4. a. Furnish a statement of all expenses in connection with the issuance and distribution of the securities in this offering. Exclude amounts relating solely to organization expenses of the issuer. The information may be given as subject to future contingencies. If the amount of an expenditure is not known, furnish an estimate and check the box to the left of the estimate.

Transfer Agent's Fees	☐	$_____
Printing and Engraving Costs	☐	$_____
Legal Fees	☐	$_____
Accounting Fees	☐	$_____
Engineering Fees	☐	$_____
Sales Commissions (specify finders' fees separately)............	☐	$_____
Other Expenses (identify) _____	☐	$_____
Total...	☐	$_____

SEC 1972 (6-88) 4 of 8

Appendix 6.2 *(continued)*

b. Enter the difference between the aggregate offering price given in response to Part C - Question 1 and total expenses furnished in response to Part C - Question 4.a. This difference is the "adjusted gross proceeds to the issuer." .... $_____

5. Indicate below the amount of the adjusted gross proceeds to the issuer used or proposed to be used for each of the purposes shown. If the amount for any purpose is not known, furnish an estimate and check the box to the left of the estimate. The total of the payments listed must equal the adjusted gross proceeds to the issuer set forth in response to Part C - Question 4.b above.

	Payments to Officers, Directors, & Affiliates	Payments To Others
Salaries and fees	☐ $_____	☐ $_____
Purchase of real estate	☐ $_____	☐ $_____
Purchase, rental or leasing and installation of machinery and equipment	☐ $_____	☐ $_____
Construction or leasing of plant buildings and facilities	☐ $_____	☐ $_____
Acquisition of other businesses (including the value of securities involved in this offering that may be used in exchange for the assets or securities of another issuer pursuant to a merger)	☐ $_____	☐ $_____
Repayment of indebtedness	☐ $_____	☐ $_____
Working capital	☐ $_____	☐ $_____
Other (specify): _____	☐ $_____	☐ $_____
_____	☐ $_____	☐ $_____
Column Totals	☐ $_____	☐ $_____
Total Payments Listed (column totals added)	☐ $_____	

The issuer has duly caused this notice to be signed by the undersigned duly authorized person. If this notice is filed under Rule 505, the following signature constitutes an undertaking by the issuer to furnish to the U.S. Securities and Exchange Commission, upon written request of its staff, the information furnished by the issuer to any non-accredited investor pursuant to paragraph (b)(2) of Rule 502.

Issuer (Print or Type)	Signature	Date
Name of Signer (Print or Type)	Title of Signer (Print or Type)	

—ATTENTION—
Intentional misstatements or omissions of fact constitute federal criminal violations. (See 18 U.S.C. 1001.)

SEC 1972 (6-88) 5 of 8

Appendix 6.2 *(continued)*

E. STATE SIGNATURE

1. Is any party described in 17 CFR 230.252(c), (d), (e) or (f) presently subject to any of the disqualification provisions of such rule? . . . .   Yes ☐ No ☐

See Appendix, Column 5, for state response.

2. The undersigned issuer hereby undertakes to furnish to any state administrator of any state in which this notice is filed, a notice on Form D (17 CFR 239.500) at such times as required by state law.

3. The undersigned issuer hereby undertakes to furnish to the state administrators, upon written request, information furnished by the issuer to offerees.

4. The undersigned issuer represents that the issuer is familiar with the conditions that must be satisfied to be entitled to the Uniform limited Offering Exemption (ULOE) of the state in which this notice is filed and understands that the issuer claiming the availability of this exemption has the burden of establishing that these conditions have been satisfied.

The issuer has read this notification and knows the contents to be true and has duly caused this notice to be signed on its behalf by the undersigned duly authorized person.

Issuer (Print or Type)	Signature	Date
Name (Print or Type)	Title (Print or Type)	

Instruction:
Print the name and title of the signing representative under his signature for the state portion of this form. One copy of every notice on Form D must be manually signed. Any copies not manually signed must be photocopies of the manually signed copy or bear typed or printed signatures.

SEC 1972 (6-88) 6 of 8

Appendix 6.2 *(continued)*

	APPENDIX								
1	**2**		**3**	**4**				**5**	
	Intend to sell to non-accredited investors in State (Part B-Item 1)		Type of security and aggregate offering price offered in state (Part C-Item1)	Type of investor and amount purchased in State (Part C-Item 2)				Disqualification under State ULOE (if yes, attach explanation of waiver granted) (Part E-Item1)	
				Number of Accredited Investors	Amount	Number of Non-Accredited Investors	Amount		
State	**Yes**	**No**						**Yes**	**No**
AL									
AK									
AZ									
AR									
CA									
CO									
CT									
DE									
DC									
FL									
GA									
HI									
ID									
IL									
IN									
IA									
KS									
KY									
LA									
ME									
MD									
MA									
MI									
MN									
MS									
MO									

SEC 1972 (6-88) 7 of 8

208

Appendix 6.2 *(continued)*

1	2 Intend to sell to non-accredited investors in State (Part B-Item 1)		3 Type of security and aggregate offering price offered in state (Part C-Item1)	4 Type of investor and amount purchased in State (Part C-Item 2)				5 Disqualification under State ULOE (if yes, attach explanation of waiver granted) (Part E-Item1)	
State	**Yes**	**No**		**Number of Accredited Investors**	**Amount**	**Number of Non-Accredited Investors**	**Amount**	**Yes**	**No**
MT									
NE									
NV									
NH									
NJ									
NM									
NY									
NC									
ND									
OH									
OK									
OR									
PA									
RI									
SC									
SD									
TN									
TX									
UT									
VT									
VA									
WA									
WV									
WI									
WY									
PR									

☆U.S. Government Printing Office: 1988—202-408/85204

SEC 1972 (6-88) 8 of 8

209

APPENDIX 6.3
INVESTOR QUESTIONNAIRE

Applecore, Incorporated
(A New York Corporation)
Direct Placement of Common Shares

INVESTOR QUESTIONNAIRE

ALL INFORMATION HEREIN WILL BE TREATED CONFIDENTIALLY

Applecore, Incorporated

_____

Suite 200
New York, N.Y. 100____

Ladies and Gentlemen:

The information contained herein is being furnished to you in order for you to determine whether the undersigned's Subscription Agreement to purchase common stock (the "shares") representing ownership in Applecore Incorporated, a New York corporation (the "Corporation"), may be accepted by you in light of the requirements of Section 4(2) of the Securities Act of 1933 (the "Act"), and Rule 506 of Regulation D promulgated thereunder ("Rule 506"). I understand that (a) you will rely on the information contained herein for purposes of determining that the shares offered hereby are exempt from registration pursuant to Section 4(2) of the Act and Rule 506 promulgated thereunder, (b) the shares will not be registered under the Act in reliance upon the exemption from registration afforded by Section 4(2) of the Act explained in Rule 506, and (c) this Questionnaire is not an offer of shares to the undersigned.

THE UNDERSIGNED HEREBY GIVES EXPRESS WRITTEN CONSENT TO THE CORPORATION, ITS EXECUTIVE OFFICERS, OR THEIR AFFILIATES TO REQUEST ADDITIONAL INFORMATION, OBTAIN CONSUMER CREDIT REPORTS ON THE UNDERSIGNED OR THEIR BUSINESS, AND TO CONTACT THE BANKS, BROKERS, AND PROVIDERS OF SERVICES LISTED IN THIS INVESTMENT QUESTIONNAIRE TO VERIFY AND/OR CLARIFY THE INFORMATION CONTAINED HEREIN.

NOTE, if you will be utilizing the services of a Purchaser Representative in connection with this investment, please be sure that the Purchaser Representative completes the attached "Purchaser Representative Questionnaire."

Please print or type your answers. If the answer to any question is "No" or "Not Applicable," please so state. Please provide information for all subscribers, using separate questionnaires if necessary.

Appendix 6.3 *(continued)*

ALL QUESTIONS MUST BE ANSWERED

1. Name: _____ Age: _____

    U.S. Citizen: _____ Yes _____ No Tax Exempt Entity: _____ Yes _____ No

    Social Security Number: _____

    Date of Birth _____/_____/_____ Marital Status: _____

2. Permanent residence address (other than Post Office Box), and telephone number:

    _____

    _____

    _____

    _____

3. (a) Name of current business, business address, and telephone number:

    _____

    _____

    _____

    _____

    (b) Type of current business position held, responsibilities involved in position, and number of years employed in position:

    _____

    _____

    _____

    _____

4. Position(s) held during past five (5) years, responsibilities involved, and number of years employed or if retired, position held in previous business, responsibilities involved in position, and number of years employed in position:

    _____

    _____

    _____

    _____

5. Send correspondence to: Home: _____   Office: _____

    Other: _____

Appendix 6.3 *(continued)*

6. List any accountant, lawyer, or other person who is familiar with your personal finances who may be contacted to provide financial information and his or her relationship to you. State whether he or she should receive copies of correspondence sent to you, if any:

Name: _____

Address: _____

_____

_____

Telephone: ( ) _____

Copies Sent: _____ Yes _____ No

Name: _____

Address: _____

_____

_____

Telephone: ( ) _____

Copies Sent: _____ Yes _____ No

7. Bank Information: **Account Numbers:**

(a) Bank: _____ Checking: _____

Telephone: _____ Savings: _____

Address: _____ Other: _____

_____

Person Familiar with your Account: _____

(b) Bank: _____ Checking: _____

Telephone: _____ Savings: _____

Address: _____ Other: _____

_____

Person Familiar with your Account: _____

It is understood and agreed that verification of reference(s) can be conducted by, or on behalf, of the Corporation or its Affiliates. If written authorization is required, I will supply such information ahead of time to my bank. (If the following credit references may be verified in any other name than that supplied in Item 1 above, please supply for each applicable credit reference the name(s) reported on that account):

Name(s) reported on account: _____

8. Business or professional education and the degrees received are as follows:

School	Degree	Year Received
_____	_____	_____
_____	_____	_____

9. Please provide the following information regarding actual or projected income:

	Gross Income (exclusive of spouse's)	Gross Income of Spouse	Taxable Income (exclusive of this investment)	Highest Tax Rate at Which Federal Income Taxes Were or Are Anticipated to be paid
1988	_____	_____	_____	_____

Current Year

1989	_____	_____	_____	_____

Projected Income

1990	_____	_____	_____	_____
1991	_____	_____	_____	_____

10. My federal income tax return is filed on the following basis (check one):

   (1) married individual filing joint return _____,

   (2) head of household _____,

   (3) unmarried individual _____, or

   (4) married individual filing separate return _____ .

11. Please provide the approximate percentage of the current income of you and your spouse by source:

	Undersigned		Spouse	
Salary	_____	%	_____	%
Bonus & Commissions	_____	%	_____	%
Dividends and Interest	_____	%	_____	%
Real Estate Income	_____	%	_____	%
Other Income	_____	%	_____	%
TOTAL	_____	100%	_____	100%

Appendix 6.3 *(continued)*

12. Please provide the following information in the Balance Sheet immediately following this page. (PLEASE NOTE: IF THE INVESTOR IS A PARTNERSHIP, PROVIDE FIGURES FOR BOTH THE PARTNERSHIP AND EACH GENERAL PARTNER; IF A CORPORATION, ATTACH THREE-YEAR CERTIFIED OR AUDITED FINANCIAL STATEMENTS; IF A TRUST, THE BALANCE SHEET MUST BE FOR THE TRUST [IF THE TRUST IS A REVOCABLE TRUST, YOU MUST ALSO PROVIDE A BALANCE SHEET FOR THE GRANTOR].)

Appendix 6.3 *(continued)*

BALANCE SHEET AS OF MONTH _____ DAY _____ YEAR _____

ASSETS		LIABILITIES	
Cash & Cash Equivalents	$ _____	Notes Payable to Banks—Secured	$ _____
Market Value U.S. Government Bonds	_____	Notes Payable to Banks—Unsecured	_____
Market Value Listed Municipal Bonds	_____	Margin Account Balance	_____
Market Value Listed Corporate Bonds	_____	Notes Payable to Others	_____
Market Value Listed Commercial Stocks	_____	Account/Bills Payable	_____
Nonmarketable Securities (itemized below if in excess of $50,000)	_____	Unpaid Income Taxes	_____
		Mortgage Payable	
Accounts & Notes Receivable		Home	_____
From Relatives & Friends	_____	Other	_____
From others	_____		
Pension & Profit-sharing Vested (___ % liquid)	_____		
Investment in Own Company	_____	Other Debts—(Itemize)	_____

	Cost	Market		
Investment in Real Estate:				
Home	_____	_____		
Second Home	_____	_____		
Undeveloped	_____	_____		
Developed	_____	_____		
Other	_____	_____		
Auto & Other Vehicles		_____		
Home Furnishings		_____		
Personal Property		_____		
Cash Value Life Insurance		_____	Total Liabilities	_____
Other Assets (itemize if in excess of $50,000)		_____	Net Worth	_____
Total Assets		$ _____	Total Liabilities & Net Worth	$ _____

Appendix 6.3 (continued)

13. Are you purchasing Shares in the Corporation for your own account?
_____ Yes _____ No.   If no, for whom and for what purpose? _____
_____
_____

14. Do any significant contingent liabilities exist (including actual or threatened litigation, contested taxes, guarantees of obligations or others) for which you may be obligated, such as by your being an endorser, guarantor, surety, indemnitor, or otherwise?
_____ Yes _____ No.   If yes, please provide complete details: _____
_____
_____
_____

15. Have you or any corporation or business association of which you were or are an executive officer or principal stockholder ever been subject to a bankruptcy, reorganization, debt restructuring, lawsuits for collection, garnishment of wages, or attachments of other assets or earnings?
_____ Yes _____ No.   If yes, please provide complete details: _____
_____
_____
_____

16. Are you involved in any litigation that if an adverse decision occurred would adversely affect your financial condition?
_____ Yes _____ No.   If yes, please provide complete details: _____
_____
_____
_____

17. Have you been refused a loan or a letter of credit or a surety bond that supported your payments under any debt obligations within the last five (5) years?
_____ Yes _____ No.   If yes, please provide complete details: _____
_____
_____
_____

18. List your partnership investments (public offering or private placement) and any nonpartnership real estate investments to date (if more than five, list five largest only):

Name of Investment	Type of Investment (e.g., oil and gas, real estate)	Amount of Investment (initial plus deferred)	Remaining Obligation	Date of Investment
_____	_____	_____	_____	_____
_____	_____	_____	_____	_____
_____	_____	_____	_____	_____
_____	_____	_____	_____	_____
_____	_____	_____	_____	_____
_____	_____	_____	_____	_____

19. Describe any other substantial experience in business or financial matters that enable you to evaluate the merits and risks of this investment: _____
    _____
    _____
    _____
    _____

20. Method of Investment Qualification:

    Under federal and certain state securities laws and applicable regulations, you may acquire Shares either as an Accredited Investor or a Qualified Nonaccredited Investor. Shares may be sold to an unlimited number of Accredited Investors without registration under federal and certain state securities laws; however, the shares may be sold, in general, only to 35 Qualified Nonaccredited Investors.

    An individual will qualify as an Accredited Investor if he or she meets any one of the following requirements. Please indicate which, if any, of the following requirements you meet:

    (A) I am a natural person and had an individual income (without including any income of my spouse) in excess of $200,000 in each of the two most recent years and reasonably expect an income in excess of $200,000 in the current year. For these purposes, "income" means my individual adjusted gross income for federal income tax purposes, plus (i) any deduction for long term capital gains, (ii) any deduction for depletion, (iii) any exclusion for interest, and (iv) any losses allocated to me with respect to the Unit(s).

    _____ Yes   _____ No

Appendix 6.3 *(continued)*

(B) I am a natural person and have an individual net worth (total assets, including home, home furnishings, and automobiles less total liabilities) at the time of purchase (or joint net worth with spouse) in excess of $1 million.

_____ Yes   _____ No

(C) I am purchasing shares with an aggregate purchase price of $450,000, and the aggregate amount of my investment is no more than 20% of my net worth or joint net worth with my spouse.

_____ Yes   _____ No

(D) I am an entity in which all of the equity owners meet the standards set forth in either of the preceding subparagraphs (A) or (B).

_____ Yes   _____ No

An individual will qualify as a Qualified Nonaccredited Investor if he or she meets the following requirement:

(A) I have a net worth (i.e., total assets in excess of total liabilities), **exclusive** of home, home furnishings, and automobiles, of at least $250,000 per _____shares subscribed for.

_____ Yes   _____ No

(B) I am a partnership not formed for the purpose of investing in shares in which one or more of the general partners meets the standard set forth in the preceding subparagraph (A).

_____ Yes   _____ No

21. Method of Investment Evaluation:

Each prospective Investor is required to retain the services of an advisor when such prospective Investor does not have sufficient knowledge and experience in finance and business matters to be capable of evaluating the merits and risks of acquiring Shares. Please indicate below if you have such knowledge and experience, or alternatively, require the services of an advisor:

(A) I have such knowledge and experience in financial matters that I am capable of evaluating the merits and risks of an investment in the shares and will not require the services of a Purchaser Representative. I offer as evidence of such knowledge and experience in these matters the information contained in this Investor Questionnaire.

_____ Yes   _____ No

Appendix 6.3 *(continued)*

(B) I have retained the services of a Purchaser Representative(s). I acknowledge the following named person(s) to be my Purchaser Representative(s) in connection with evaluating the merits and risks of an investment in shares.

_____ Yes   _____ No

_____

_____

The above-named Purchaser Representative(s) has furnished me with a completed Purchaser Representative Questionnaire, a copy of which I reviewed prior to signing this Questionnaire and which I am delivering to you herewith. I and the above-named Purchaser Representative(s) together have such knowledge and experience in financial and business matters that we are capable of evaluating the merits and risks of an investment in the shares.

_____ Yes   _____ No

IF YOU HAVE CHECKED "YES" UNDER METHOD B, THIS INVESTMENT QUESTIONNAIRE **MUST** BE ACCOMPANIED BY ONE COMPLETED AND SIGNED COPY OF THE PURCHASER REPRESENTATIVE QUESTIONNAIRE.

I understand the Corporation will rely upon the accuracy and completeness of my responses to the foregoing questions, and I represent and warrant to the Corporation as follows:

1. The answers to the above questions are complete and correct and may be relied upon by the Corporation in determining whether the offering in which I propose to participate is exempt from registration under the Securities Act of 1933, pursuant to Section 4(2) and Rule 506 promulgated thereunder;

2. I will immediately notify the Corporation of any material change in any statement made herein occurring prior to the closing of any purchase by me of the Shares;

3. I am a person who is able to bear the economic risk of an investment in the shares of the size contemplated. In making this statement, consideration has been given as to whether I can afford to hold the investment for an indefinite period of time and whether I can afford a complete loss of my investment. I offer as evidence of my ability to bear the economic risk the information contained in this Investor Questionnaire; and

4. The purchase of the shares will be solely for my account (except as otherwise set forth in Item 13 above), and not for the account of any other person or with a view toward transfer, resale, assignment, fractionalization, or distribution thereof.

Appendix 6.3 *(continued)*

IN WITNESS WHEREOF, I have executed this Investor Questionnaire this _____ day
of _____ 19 _____ and declare that it is truthful and correct.

(Check One)

_____ Individually (1)   X _____

                                                     Signature of Prospective Investor

_____ Joint Tenants with Right of Survivorship

                                                     _____

                                                     PRINT Prospective Investor Name

_____ Tenants in Common   _____

                                                     Title, if applicable

_____ In Partnership (2)

_____ As Custodian or agent for

         _____ (3)   X _____

                                                     Signature of Prospective Investor

_____ Corporation (4)

_____ As Agent (5)   PRINT Co-Investor Name

_____ Power of Attorney (6)   _____

                                                     Title, if applicable

(1) For unmarried individuals, please provide a signed Investor Questionnaire for **each** individual.

(2) If a partnership, please include a copy of partnership agreement and certificate authorizing investment.

(3) If a custodian, trustee, or agent, please include trust, agency, or other agreement and certificate authorizing investment.

(4) If a corporation, please include articles of incorporation, bylaws, certified corporate resolution or other document authorizing investment, certificate of incumbency of officers, and certified or audited financial statements for the preceding three (3) fiscal years.

(5) Please provide a letter from the prospective Investor stating that the agency relationship is in full force and effect as of the date of the subscription documents and will continue to be in full force and effect.

Appendix 6.3 *(continued)*

(6) Please provide a copy of the Power of Attorney dated prior to the date on which the subscription documents were signed, stating that the Power of Attorney is coupled with an interest, is irrevocable, and survives the Investor's death or disability, and binds the Investor's heirs, administrators, successors, and assigns.

State of _____)

_____) ss

County of _____)

Sworn to Before Me this _____ day of _____ , 19 _____.

_____
Notary Public

The undersigned Account Representative hereby certifies that he or she has reasonable grounds to believe the above Investor is a person who is able to bear the economic risk of an investment in the Shares and that the above information has been properly completed.

X_____
Signature of Account Representative

_____
PRINT Account Representative Name

_____
Firm Name

_____
Office Address

_____

_____
Office Telephone Number

APPENDIX 6.4
PURCHASER REPRESENTATIVE QUESTIONNAIRE

(A) The individual (if any) designated as your Purchaser Representative must complete all questions on the Purchaser Representative Questionnaire. The Purchaser Representative's signature is required.

(B) Investor Signature/Acknowledgement is also required on the letter on page 224.

APPLECORE, INCORPORATED
(a New York Corporation)
PURCHASER REPRESENTATIVE QUESTIONNAIRE
Direct Placement of Common Shares

Applecore, Incorporated
_____ Place
Suite 200
New York, N.Y. 100__

Ladies and Gentlemen:

The information contained herein is being furnished to you in order for you to determine whether a sale of common shares (the "Shares") in Applecore, Incorporated, a New York corporation (the "Corporation"), may be made to the following prospective Investor:

_____ (Insert name of Prospective Investor)

in light of the requirements of Section 4(2) of the Securities Act of 1933 (the "Act") and Regulation D promulgated by the Securities and Exchange Commission ("Regulation D"). The undersigned understands that (a) you will rely on the information set forth herein for purposes of such determination, (b) the Shares will not be registered under the Act in reliance upon the exemption from registration afforded by Section 4(2) of the Act and Rule 506, and (c) this Questionnaire is not an offer to sell the Shares or any other securities to the undersigned Purchaser Representative.

I note that you have provided the above-named Prospective Investor a Confidential Memorandum dated October _____, 19__, prepared by the Corporation in connection with the placement of the Shares (the "Confidential Memorandum"). It should be noted by you that nothing herein shall be construed as a representation by me that I have attempted to verify the information set forth in the Confidential Memorandum; RATHER, TO THE CONTRARY, THE SCOPE OF MY ENGAGEMENT BY, AND MY DISCUSSIONS WITH, THE ABOVE PROSPECTIVE INVESTOR HAVE BEEN LIMITED TO A DETERMINATION OF THE SUITABILITY OF AN INVESTMENT IN THE SHARES BY THE ABOVE-NAMED PROSPECTIVE INVESTOR IN LIGHT OF SUCH INVESTOR'S CURRENT INVESTMENT CIRCUMSTANCES AS SUCH CIRCUMSTANCES HAVE BEEN PRESENTED TO ME. FOR THIS PURPOSE I HAVE ASSUMED, BUT DO NOT IN ANY WAY REPRESENT OR WARRANT, EITHER TO YOU OR TO THE ABOVE-NAMED PROSPECTIVE INVESTOR, THAT THE INFORMATION SET FORTH IN THE CONFIDENTIAL MEMORANDUM IS ACCURATE AND COMPLETE IN ALL MATERIAL RESPECTS. EACH AND EVERY STATEMENT MADE BY ME IN THE FOLLOWING PARAGRAPHS IS QUALIFIED BY REFERENCE TO THE FOREGOING.

With the above in mind, I herewith furnish you with the following information:

1. (i) I have reviewed the Confidential Memorandum describing the offering; (ii) the Corporation has made available to me all documents relating to an investment in the Corporation that I have requested and has provided answers to all of my

questions concerning the offering; (iii) I have discussed the Confidential Memorandum with the above-named Prospective Investor with a view to determining whether an investment in the Shares by such Prospective Investor is appropriate in light of such Investor's financial circumstances, as such circumstances have been disclosed to me by such Prospective Investor; and (iv) I have advised the offeree whom I represent as to the merits and risks of an investment in the Corporation. In evaluating the suitability of an investment in the Corporation for such offeree, I have not relied upon any representation or other information, whether oral or written, other than as set forth in the Confidential Memorandum or as contained in any documents or answers to questions so furnished to me by the Corporation.

2. I have such knowledge and experience in financial and business matters as to be capable of evaluating, alone, or together with other Purchaser Representatives of the Prospective Investor, the merits and risks of an investment in the Corporation. I offer as evidence thereof the following additional information (e.g., investment experience, business experience, profession, education):

_____

_____

_____

_____

3. I am not "affiliated" with and am not "compensated" by the Corporation or any affiliate or selling agent of the Corporation, directly or indirectly (see "Note" below).

There is no material relationship between me or my affiliates and the Corporation or its affiliates that now exists or is mutually understood to be contemplated or that has existed at any time during the previous two years.

(State "No exceptions," or set forth exceptions and give details. Please note that any exceptions must not cause you to be "affiliated" with or "compensated" by the Corporation or an affiliate of the Corporation as defined by the "Note" below).

_____

_____

_____

_____

_____

If any exceptions exist and are described above, please confirm that such exceptions were disclosed to the above-named Investor in writing prior to the date hereof by attaching hereto a copy of such disclosure statement.

I agree to notify you promptly of any changes to the information described in this Questionnaire that may occur prior to the completion of the transaction.

Very truly yours,

X _____
Signature of Purchaser Representative

Appendix 6.4 *(continued)*

_____
Print Purchaser Representative Name

_____
Street Address

_____
City and State

Dated: _____

_____
Telephone

State of _____)
)SS
County of _____)

On this _____ day of _____, 19 ____, before me personally
appeared _____, known to me as the
individual(s) described in and who executed the foregoing instrument, and who duly
acknowledged to me having executed the same

_____
Notary Public

My commission expires:

NOTE:

The relationships that will render a person "affiliated" include (1) a present or
intended relationship of employment, either as an employee, employer, independent
contractor, or principal, (2) any relationship within the definition of the term affiliate set
forth below, or as an officer, director or general partner of an affiliate and (3) the
beneficial ownership by the Purchaser Representative of securities of the Corporation
or its affiliates or selling agent, except that the ownership of 1% or less of such securities shall not render a Purchaser Representative affiliated.

"Affiliate" of the Corporation shall mean a person controlling, controlled by, or
under common control with the Corporation. A person controls another person within
the meaning of this definition through the possession, direct or indirect, of the power to
direct or cause the direction of the management, policies, or actions of such other
person.

Appendix 6.4 *(continued)*

_____, 19 _____

_____
Investor

_____
Address

Dear Sir/Madam:

You have asked me to act as your Purchaser Representative in connection with the offering to you by Applecore, Incorporated, a New York corporation (the "Corporation") of common shares in the Corporation. Prior to such appointment, I am required to disclose to you any material relationship between the Corporation and its affiliates, and me that now exists or is contemplated or that has existed at any time during the last two years.

I have no other relationship to the Corporation or its affiliates that is material to this offering.

Very truly yours

X _____
Purchaser Representative

Received and acknowledged:
By:
X _____
Signature of Investor

Date: _____

APPENDIX 6.5
PRIVATE PLACEMENT MEMORANDUM
(Excerpt)

CONFIDENTIAL PRIVATE PLACEMENT MEMORANDUM

This Memorandum Does Not Constitute an Offer to Anyone Other Than:

Name of Offeree   Offeree Number
Dated: October 27, 19____

APPLECORE, INCORPORATED
(A New York Corporation)

15,000 shares of Common Stock of $100.00 par value

This confidential private placement memorandum (the "Memorandum") relates to the private placement (the "Offering") to a limited number of qualified investors of fifteen thousand (15,000) shares of common stock (the "Shares") at $100 per share, in Applecore, Incorporated (the "Corporation"), a New York Corporation. The Corporation will become part of and own an interest in the joint venture, _____ Associates, a Maryland General Partnership (the "Joint Venture"). The members of the Joint Venture shall be the Corporation, and _____. The Joint Venture will acquire certain real property, erect site improvements, and construct and sell 100 single-family homes on a site located in _____, Maryland (See "THE PROPERTY").

	Price to Investors	Sales Commissions	Proceeds to Corporation
Per 500 Shares	$ 50,000	$ 5,000 (10%)	$ 45,000 (90%)
Total	$1,500,000	$150,000 (10%)	$1,350,000 (90%)

THE SHARES HAVE NOT BEEN REGISTERED WITH, APPROVED, OR DISAPPROVED BY THE SECURITIES AND EXCHANGE COMMISSION NOR BY THE SECURITIES REGULATORY AUTHORITY OF ANY STATE. NO SUCH COMMISSION OR AUTHORITY HAS PASSED UPON OR ENDORSED THE MERITS OF THIS OFFERING OR THE ACCURACY OR ADEQUACY OF THIS PRIVATE PLACEMENT MEMORANDUM, NOR IS IT EXPECTED OR INTENDED THAT IT WILL. ANY REPRESENTATION TO THE CONTRARY IS A CRIMINAL OFFENSE.

ANY SUPPLEMENTS AND/OR STICKERS WHICH UPDATE THIS MEMORANDUM ARE CONTAINED INSIDE THE BACK COVER.

Trading Company, Inc.
_____

Street
New York, N.Y. 100__
Distributor

A total of $1,500,000 in common stock is being offered with a minimum purchase of 500 shares per subscriber. In no event, however, will subscriptions be accepted from more than thirty-five (35) investors who are not "Accredited Investors," as that term is defined in Rule 501 of Regulation D by the United States Securities and Exchange Commission (the "Commission"), promulgated under Section 4(2) of the Securities Act of 1933, as amended (the "Act").

The Offering will terminate on or before December 31, 19__, subject to extension at the discretion of the Corporation until April 30, 19__ (such date, as it may so be extended, the "Offering Date"). Unless all Units have been subscribed for and accepted by the Offering Date, all subscriptions will be cancelled, and all subscription payments will be returned with interest and without deduction; provided, however, that the Corporation may effect a partial closing of the Offering ("Partial Closing") after at least 12,000 shares have been subscribed for and accepted and continue to offer the shares at any time prior to the Offering Termination Date, as extended.

The shares are being offered for sale by the Corporation on a "best efforts," "all or none" basis through _____ Company, Inc., _____, Suite 200, New York, N.Y. 100__, (See "PLAN OF DISTRIBUTION"). The proceeds of the offering will be received and held in trust for the benefit of the investors and will be retained in trust after closing to be used only for the purposes set forth in this Memorandum. Funds will be held in a special segregated trust account with: National _____ Bank, ___ Main Street, New York, N.Y. 100__.

This Memorandum is submitted in connection with the private placement of the shares and may not be reproduced or used for any other purpose. Recipients of this Memorandum not purchasing shares must return this Memorandum to the Corporation. Any distribution of this Memorandum other than by the Corporation, in whole or in part, or the divulgence of any of its contents, is totally unauthorized.

THE SECURITIES OFFERED HEREBY HAVE NOT BEEN REGISTERED UNDER THE SECURITIES ACT OF 1933, AS AMENDED, AND MAY NOT BE SOLD, TRANS-FERRED, OR OTHERWISE DISPOSED OF BY AN INVESTOR WITHOUT AN EFFEC-TIVE REGISTRATION STATEMENT OR AN OPINION OF COUNSEL FOR THE COR-PORATION THAT AN EXEMPTION FROM REGISTRATION IS AVAILABLE.

THIS INVESTMENT INVOLVES SUBSTANTIAL RISKS. IT IS SUITABLE ONLY FOR THOSE PERSONS WHO CAN MEET MINIMUM STANDARDS OF INCOME AND NET WORTH (SEE "SUITABILITY STANDARDS - WHO MAY INVEST"). THE SHARES ARE NOT READILY TRANSFERABLE AND SHOULD ONLY BE PURCHASED FOR LONG-TERM INVESTMENT (SEE "RESTRICTIONS ON TRANSFER"). ACCORDINGLY, EACH INVESTOR MUST DEMONSTRATE THAT HE HAS THE ABILITY TO EVALUATE THIS OFFERING OR THAT HE HAS RETAINED THE SERVICES OF PURCHASER REPRESEN-TATIVES WHO HAVE SUFFICIENT KNOWLEDGE AND EXPERTISE TO EVALUATE

Appendix 6.5 *(continued)*

THIS INVESTMENT. ADDITIONAL CONSIDERATIONS FOR THE INVESTORS IN-
CLUDE TAX RISKS (SEE "RISK FACTORS").

NO OFFERING LITERATURE OR ADVERTISING IN ANY FORM SHALL BE EM-
PLOYED IN THE OFFERING OF THESE SECURITIES EXCEPT TO THE EXTENT INDI-
CATED IN THE SECTION ENTITLED "PROMOTIONAL AND SALES LITERATURE." NO
PERSON HAS BEEN AUTHORIZED TO MAKE ANY REPRESENTATION OTHER THAN
THOSE CONTAINED IN THIS MEMORANDUM OR THE EXHIBITS HERETO, AND, IF
MADE, SUCH REPRESENTATION MUST NOT BE RELIED UPON.

THE STATEMENTS SET FORTH IN THIS MEMORANDUM AS TO THE TERMS OF
OTHER AGREEMENTS OR DOCUMENTS ARE NOT NECESSARILY COMPLETE;
HOWEVER, COPIES OF ALL DOCUMENTS NOT ANNEXED HERETO MAY BE OB-
TAINED FROM THE CORPORATION.

PROSPECTIVE INVESTORS ARE NOT TO CONSTRUE THE CONTENTS OF THIS
MEMORANDUM AS LEGAL, BUSINESS, OR TAX ADVICE. EACH INVESTOR
SHOULD CONSULT HIS OR HER PERSONAL COUNSEL, ACCOUNTANT, AND
OTHER ADVISERS AS TO LEGAL, TAX, ECONOMIC, AND RELATED MATTERS
CONCERNING THE INVESTMENT DESCRIBED HEREIN AND ITS SUITABILITY FOR
HIM OR HER (SEE "TAX CONSEQUENCES").

TO THE BEST OF THE CORPORATION'S KNOWLEDGE, THIS MEMORANDUM
DOES NOT CONTAIN AN UNTRUE STATEMENT OF A MATERIAL FACT, OR OMIT
TO STATE A MATERIAL FACT NECESSARY TO MAKE THE STATEMENTS MADE, IN
LIGHT OF THE CIRCUMSTANCES UNDER WHICH THEY WERE MADE, NOT MIS-
LEADING. IT CONTAINS A FAIR SUMMARY OF THE DOCUMENTS PURPORTED TO
BE SUMMARIZED HEREIN.

NO RULINGS HAVE BEEN SOUGHT FROM THE INTERNAL REVENUE SERVICE
WITH RESPECT TO ANY OF THE MATTERS DESCRIBED IN THE MEMORANDUM. IN
ADDITION, OTHER INTERNAL REVENUE SERVICE AUDIT ADJUSTMENTS MAY
AFFECT BOTH THE TIMING AND THE AMOUNT OF THE TAX BENEFITS AVAILABLE
(SEE "RISK FACTORS").

THE FINANCIAL PROJECTIONS CONTAINED IN THIS MEMORANDUM HAVE BEEN
PREPARED BY THE CORPORATION ON THE BASIS OF ASSUMPTIONS AND HY-
POTHESES STATED THEREIN. FUTURE OPERATING RESULTS ARE IMPOSSIBLE TO
PREDICT, AND NO REPRESENTATION OF ANY KIND IS MADE RESPECTING THE
FUTURE ACCURACY OR COMPLETENESS OF THE PROJECTIONS.

DURING THIS OFFERING AND PRIOR TO THE SALE OF ANY SHARES, THE CORPO-
RATION SHALL MAKE AVAILABLE TO EACH INVESTOR OR HIS AGENT THE OP-
PORTUNITY TO ASK QUESTIONS OF AND RECEIVE ANSWERS FROM ANY PERSON
AUTHORIZED TO ACT ON BEHALF OF THE CORPORATION CONCERNING ANY
ASPECT OF THE INVESTMENT. THE CORPORATION SHALL UPON REASONABLE
REQUEST, PROVIDE SUCH ADDITIONAL INFORMATION AS MAY BE NECESSARY
TO VERIFY THE ACCURACY OF THE INFORMATION CONTAINED IN THIS MEMO-
RANDUM, TO THE EXTENT THE CORPORATION POSSESSES SUCH INFORMATION
OR CAN ACQUIRE IT WITHOUT UNREASONABLE EFFORT OR EXPENSE (SEE
"ADDITIONAL INFORMATION").

SALES OF THESE SECURITIES CAN BE CONSUMMATED ONLY BY THE CORPORA-
TION'S ACCEPTANCE OF OFFERS TO PURCHASE SUCH SECURITIES THAT ARE

Appendix 6.5 *(continued)*

Appendix 6.5 *(continued)*

TABLE OF CONTENTS

Appendix 6.5 *(continued)*

Appendix 6.5 *(continued)*

EXHIBITS:

    A.   **Financial Forecast**
    B.   **Joint Venture Agreement of _____ Associates**
    C.   **Marketing and Feasibility Study by _____ & Company, Ltd.**
    D.   **Agreement**
    E.   **Form of Opinion of _____ & _____**
    F.   **Prior Performance of the Corporation and its Affiliates (Chart form)**
    G.   **Subscription Documents:**
        G.1.   **Instructions to Subscribers**
        G.2.   **State Securities Notice**
        G.3.   **Subscription Agreement Including Power of Attorney**
        G.4.   **Counterpart Signature Pages**
        G.5.   **Purchaser Questionnaire**
        G.6.   **Purchaser Representative Questionnaire**

Additional Information: A prospective investor may obtain for his or her review any of the documents referred to in this Memorandum by contacting _____, _____, Suite 200, New York, N.Y. 100__ during normal business hours. Any prospective investor may ask questions and receive information from the Corporation concerning the terms of this Offering. The Corporation will also provide any additional information necessary to verify the accuracy of the information contained in the Memorandum, to the extent that the Corporation possesses such information or can acquire it without unreasonable expense.

Appendix 6.5 *(continued)*

SUITABILITY STANDARDS—WHO MAY INVEST

General

Investment in the Shares involves a high degree of risk and is suitable only for persons of substantial financial means who have substantial financial resources and who have no need for liquidity in their investments.

The Shares offered hereby are suitable only for those investors whose business or investment experience, either alone or together with an experienced investment advisor ("Purchaser Representative" as defined below) (who must be neither affiliated with nor compensated by the Corporation or any placing brokers), makes them capable of evaluating the merits and risks of their prospective investment in the Corporation and who can bear the economic risk of their investment for an indefinite period of time.

The Corporation intends to conduct the Offering without registration under the Securities Act of 1933 (the "Act") pursuant to exemptions provided by Section 4(2) of the Act and Regulation D promulgated by the Securities and Exchange Commission. Shares may be sold to persons who are "Accredited Investors," as that term is defined in Regulation D and "excluded purchasers" for purposes of certain state exemptions. This is necessary because of certain restrictions on the number of purchasers who are not Accredited Investors and excluded purchasers. The availability of these exemptions depends, among other things, on the financial condition and the nature of the purchasers, the manner of the Offering, and the number of purchasers. In order to satisfy the requirements of Regulation D, the Shares may be sold to any number of Accredited Investors and excluded purchasers under state laws. Up to 35 Qualified Nonaccredited Investors who are not both Accredited Investors and excluded purchasers may be accepted as investors.

Shares will be sold to a person or entity only if the Corporation has reasonable grounds to believe, and shall believe, immediately prior to sale, and after making reasonable inquiry, either (a) that such person or entity has the knowledge and experience in financial and business matters necessary to enable the investor to evaluate the merits and risks of this investment, or (b) that a prospective investor and such investor's "Purchaser Representative" (as that term is defined in Rule 501 promulgated under Section 4(2) of the Act) together, have such knowledge and experience in financial and business matters that they are capable of evaluating the merits and risks of this investment. In addition, shares will be sold only to a purchaser who makes a written representation that he is the sole and true party in interest and is not purchasing for the benefit of any other person or entity, or that he is purchasing for another person or entity meeting all of the conditions set forth herein.

Shares will be sold only to Accredited Investors or to a maximum of thirty-five (35) Qualified Nonaccredited Investors who represent that they either have a net worth of at least $250,000 (exclusive of home, home furnishings, and automobiles); or that their marginal federal income tax bracket is at least 28%, and their net worth (exclusive of home, home furnishings, and automobiles) is not less than $150,000.

Appendix 6.5 *(continued)*

Accredited Investors

An Accredited Investor is an investor who (a) together with his or her spouse has a net worth (that is, total assets in excess of total liabilities) in excess of $1,000,000, or (b) individually (without his or her spouse) had an annual income in excess of $200,000 in each of the last two years and reasonably expects an income in excess of $200,000 in the current year or joint income with his or her spouse in excess of $300,000 in each of those years and who has reasonable expectations of reaching the same income level, or (c) any entity in which all of the equity owners are Accredited Investors.

Each prospective investor must represent that:

(a) He or she is either an Accredited Investor or a Qualified Nonaccredited Investor;

(b) The investor must acquire the shares for investment, and not with a view of resale or distribution;

(c) The investor must be able to bear the economic risk of losing his/her entire investment;

(d) The investor's overall financial commitment to investments that are not readily marketable must not be disproportionate to his/her net worth, and his/her investment in the shares must not cause his/her overall commitment to become excessive;

(e) The investor must have adequate means of providing for his/her current needs and personal contingencies and have no need for liquidity in his/her investment in the shares; and

(f) The investor (and his/her Purchaser Representative, if he/she uses one) must have sufficient knowledge and experience in financial and business matters to be capable of evaluating the merits and risks of this investment.

Each investor will be required to (a) represent in writing that he/she meets the foregoing requirements and (b) make such other representations contained in the Subscription Documents. The suitability standards referred to above represent minimum suitability requirements for prospective investors. The satisfaction of these standards by a prospective investor does not mean necessarily that the shares are a suitable investment for that investor.

Investment Considerations

Each prospective investor should undertake an independent investigation with his/her own financial, legal, and tax advisors regarding the desirability, practicality, and risk of an investment in the Corporation. The desirability of an investment in the Corporation depends upon a number of factors. These include but are not limited to:

(a) The ability of the Joint Venture to successfully obtain financing, complete the site improvements, and build the 100 homes (See "RISK FACTORS");

(b) The desirability to the investor of a long-term investment that has virtually no likelihood of cash distributions prior to the sale of one or more of the homes to be built by the Joint Venture (See "RISK FACTORS");

(c) The income-tax consequences resulting from an investment in the Corporation (See "RISK FACTORS - Tax Aspects" and "TAX CONSEQUENCES");

(d) The Joint Venture's ability to sell or otherwise dispose of the homes (See "RISK FACTORS").

APPENDIX 6.6
PPM EXCERPT
SUMMARY OF THE OFFERING

This summary of certain provisions of the Memorandum is intended only for quick reference, is not intended to be complete, and is qualified in its entirety by reference to the full text of the Memorandum. Prospective investors should read the Memorandum in its entirety.

General

The Corporation has been formed pursuant to the New York Business Corporation Law. The Corporation has been organized to acquire an interest in the profits and losses of the Joint Venture known as _____ Associates. The Joint Venture was formed to acquire a certain parcel of land consisting of approximately 39-plus acres; erect site improvements; and build, market, and sell the approximately one hundred (100) single-family homes in a project located in _____ County, Maryland to be known as _____. The address of the Corporation is _____, Suite 200, New York, N.Y. 100____.

Terms of the Offering

A total of 15,000 shares of common stock is being offered at a price of $100 per share, with a minimum purchase of 500 shares per subscriber. In no event will subscriptions be accepted from more than thirty-five (35) investors who are not Accredited Investors as that term is defined by Regulation D, Rule 501, promulgated under Section 4(2) of the Securities Act of 1933, as amended (See **"SUITABILITY STANDARDS—WHO MAY INVEST"**). The shares will be offered on a "best efforts" basis by the Corporation.

Termination of the Offering

The Offering will terminate on or before December 31, 19__, subject to extension at the discretion of the Corporation until April 30, 19__. Unless all shares have been subscribed for and accepted by the Offering Date, all subscriptions will be cancelled, and all subscription payments will be returned with interest and without deduction.

Costs of the Offering

The Corporation shall bear all organizational costs, which include legal and accounting fees, costs of complying with state regulatory laws, administrative, and other miscellaneous expenses. Each investor shall bear his or her personal expenses incurred in connection with the acquisition of the shares.

The Property

The Joint Venture intends to acquire a parcel of land consisting of approximately thirty-nine (39) acres located in _____ County, Maryland for improvement into 100 single-family lots in a subdivision to be known as _____. The site is located approximately _____. The Joint Venture shall erect all site improvements upon the Property and plans to build the 100 homes on the lots.

Appendix 6.6 *(continued)*

Three types of homes are planned for the Property, ranging from approximately 1,850 to 2,200 square feet, with initial selling prices anticipated to be from $175,000 to $195,000. The homes will all be of Victorian styling, and each will have a basement. A two and one-half (2-1/2) acre lake is within the boundaries of the project and directly adjoins 18 of the planned homesites (See **"THE PROPERTY"**).

Acquisition of the Property

The Joint Venture intends to purchase the Property pursuant to an Agreement of Sale that has been entered into by the Joint Venture. _____, one of the Joint Venturers, is currently the owner of the Property and has entered into the Agreement of Sale to sell the Property to the Joint Venture. The purchase price of the Property to the Joint Venture is $3,412,100. An additional premium in the amount of $20,000 per lot for each of the 18 lakefront lots will be paid to _____ contingent upon such lots commanding a premium upon sale. _____ shall receive up to $20,000 of any such premium, with the balance of any such premium from the sale of the lakefront lots in excess of $20,000 inuring to the benefit of the Joint Venture. The premium is payable only upon sale and settlement of a lakefront lot, provided that a premium is obtained. It is anticipated that _____ is realizing a substantial gain in its sale of the Property to the Joint Venture. _____ 's basis in the Property is not known to the Corporation.

Conditions Precedent to Closing

Closing of the Agreement of Sale is subject to a number of conditions. If these conditions are not satisfied in a timely manner, the Sales Agreement may not close within the time period contemplated by the Financial Forecast or at all (See **"RISK FACTORS - Financial Forecast"**).

No Additional Capital Contributions

The investors will not be required to contribute any additional capital to the Corporation in excess of the purchase price for their shares (See **"TERMS OF THE OFFERING"**).

Subscription Procedures

In order to subscribe for shares, each investor shall complete the attached subscription documents and deliver to the Corporation as follows:

(a) Read, complete, date, sign, and have notarized two copies of the Subscription Agreement, which incorporates a Power of Attorney.

(b) Read, complete, date, sign, and have notarized two copies of the Purchaser Questionnaire.

(c) Read and sign two copies of the securities notice for the purchaser's state of residence.

(d) If you choose or are required to utilize a Purchaser Representative, you and your Purchaser Representative must read, complete, date, and sign the Purchaser Representative Questionnaire.

(e) If you are subscribing for a corporation, partnership, trust, or other entity, read, complete, date, and sign the Investor Questionnaire.

Appendix 6.6 *(continued)*

Source of Funds

Upon completion of the Offering, the funds available to the Corporation will be $1,500,000. The uses of the proceeds are discussed in the **"USES OF PROCEEDS"** section of this Memorandum (See **"USES OF PROCEEDS"**).

Associated Professionals

Counsel:

_____ & _____
____ _____ Street, N.W.____
Washington, DC 200____
(202) 785-0000

Independent Accountant:

_____ , _____ & _____
1000 _____ Avenue
New York, New York 100____
(212) 832-0000

Marketing Consultant:

_____ & Company, Ltd.
_____ Street, Suite 200
Alexandria, VA 223____
(703) 360-000

Risk Factors

The purchase of shares involves a high degree of risk. Investment in the shares also involves certain tax risks and restrictions on the transferability of shares.

APPENDIX 6.7
PPM EXCERPT
RESTRICTIONS ON SHARE TRANSFERS

RESTRICTIONS UPON TRANSFER AND OTHER INVESTMENT CONSIDERATIONS

Each Investor should undertake an independent investigation with his or her own advisors regarding the desirability and practicality of an investment in the Corporation. In addition to other aspects of the Corporation and important considerations mentioned elsewhere in this Memorandum, the following aspects of an investment in the Corporation dealing with restrictions on the transferability of the shares should be considered.

Restrictions Imposed by Securities Laws

Investors should be fully aware of the long-term nature of their investment. A purchaser of shares must bear the economic risk of the investment for an indefinite period of time because the shares have not been registered under the Act and therefore may not be sold unless they are subsequently registered under the Act or unless an exemption from registration is available. The availability of each such exemption is dependent, in part, upon the investment intent of each investor, and an exemption from registration would be unavailable if any purchaser were purchasing shares with a view to their redistribution.

Each person acquiring shares will be required to represent that he or she is purchasing them for his or her own account for investment purposes and not with a view to resale or distribution, and to agree not to sell any shares without registration under applicable federal and state securities laws unless there are available exemptions thereunder (See **"SUITABILITY STANDARDS—WHO MAY INVEST"**). In addition, the Corporation may require that before an Investor's interest is transferred, the transferor, at his or her own expense, deliver to the Corporation a legal opinion, in form and substance satisfactory to it and to its counsel, to the effect that the transfer will not violate federal or state securities laws. In order for the transferor to obtain such an opinion, either the shares must be registered under such laws or an exemption from registration must exist. Interests in the Corporation will not be registered under such laws. Additionally, the Corporation may not be obligated to make information required pursuant to Rule 144 under the Act public in order to permit resale of the shares without registration under the Act.

Absence of Market for Shares

Although it may be possible under certain circumstances to dispose of an investment in the Corporation, no market currently exists for the shares, and it is not anticipated that a market will exist at any time in the future.

A legend will be placed on the share certificates stating that the shares have not been registered under the Act and referring to the restrictions on transfer and sale of the shares. In addition, a notation will be made on the records of the Corporation that the sale and transfer of the shares is restricted (See **"RISK FACTORS—No Market for Shares"**).

Index